Color

My

Horse

Bev Pettersen

Cover art design by Vivi Designs
Editor: Patricia Thomas

DEDICATION

To my daughter, Brenna, with gratitude and love.

Also available from

Bev Pettersen and Westerhall Books

Jockeys and Jewels

Fillies and Females

Thoroughbreds and Trailer Trash

Riding For Redemption

ACKNOWLEDGMENTS

Thanks for your staunch support, interest and enthusiasm—Barb Snarby, Becky Mason, Patricia Thomas, Virginia Janes, Anne MacFarlane, Chelsea Thornton, Julianne MacLean, Judith James, Pamela Callow, Donna Alward, Lauren Tutty and Cathy McDonald. You ladies are simply wonderful.

CHAPTER ONE

The track's scenic infield was usually deserted, but today the police cars and body bag had drawn a hushed crowd. Mark sucked in an achy breath and stared over the heads of all the solemn onlookers.

"Who'd they pull from the pond?" Mark's assistant, Dino, asked in a voice a shade too loud. "Heard old Lefty didn't show up for work."

No one answered. Attention was riveted on the grim-faced officials clustered around a pitiful corpse. A police officer with a long stick waded into the murky water and snagged a dripping hat. Lefty's hat.

Mark blew out a ragged sigh. Lefty: gruff, single and a confirmed alcoholic. Tragic, but at least it wasn't a child who had drowned. The Belmont track had two infield ponds, and the backstretch kids sometimes climbed over the rail, lured by the quacking ducks.

He dragged a regretful hand over his jaw then tilted his head, signaling to Dino. Nothing they could do to help, and gawking seemed disrespectful and downright rude. He trudged away from the ring of watchers and followed the flattened path back to the barns. Later the dirt would be harrowed, groomed for fragile Thoroughbred legs, but it was difficult to worry about horses when a man was dead.

"Heard Boone's filly was impressive this morning," Dino called, his voice muffled by the thud of his boots as he rushed to catch up.

Mark gave a wry nod, amazed his race assistant could be so upbeat. Nothing ever bothered Dino. "That's right," Mark said. "Horse ran great. Rider said Belle's never felt better."

"Things are picking up now that you're training for Old Man Boone." Dino flashed his irreverent grin. "But somehow I can't see you kissing ass to keep him."

Mark shrugged, still unable to banish the image of Lefty's limp body, although Boone was certainly a more optimistic topic. His mood lightened a notch as he considered Boone's two talented horses. The filly, Belle, was good but the second horse, Ambling Assets, was better, and it seemed Mark finally trained a horse good enough to compete in the Breeders' Cup.

Success was so close he could taste it.

A truck engine roared. He jerked sideways as a blue Ford whipped past, crunching gravel, going too fast. Dust clogged his nose as the vehicle cut along the squat row of barns, leaving a spiraling trail of gray.

"Damn. Doc Walker's truck," Dino said.

Mark's phone beeped. He waited a taut moment then pulled his cell out, his gaze locked in the direction of the speeding vet.

"Better come quick, boss," Carlos said, his voice thick with a heavy accent and barely concealed panic. "Boone's filly is colicing. I already called the doc."

Mark snapped the phone shut, running even as he jammed it back into his pocket. "Colic. Belle," he said over his shoulder.

His stalls were in barn forty-eight, usually a five-minute walk, but he charged through the cloying dust left by Doc's truck and was there in less than a minute. A knot of people gathered in the shedrow but they stepped back, forming a glum-faced passageway.

Mark groaned when he spotted the beautiful filly thrashing in the straw. The signs of shock were obvious: increased respiration, darkened eyes, trembling muscles. "Gotta get up, baby," he said, joining Carlos at her head. "Hurry up with the Banamine, Doc!"

Sweat streaked Belle's neck, and her eyes rolled with pain as they urged her to her feet. The vet injected a shot of pain reliever and pushed a tube up her left nostril so oil could be pumped into her stomach. She was too distressed to argue. Her sleek body trembled, wracked with belly pain.

"Carlos, grab a blanket. Dino, hook up the trailer." Mark heard the snap in his words and tried to calm his voice around Belle but could scarcely control his dismay. Only an hour ago, the filly had radiated health. She'd worked four furlongs and been prancing when her groom led her away to be bathed and cooled.

Trish. His eyes narrowed as he scanned the circle of anxious faces for Belle's groom. "Where the hell is Trish?"

"Don't know, boss." Carlos dipped his head, avoiding Mark's gaze as he scuffed his worn boot in the dirt. "Don't think the filly was cooled out after her work."

Mark's mouth clamped. He'd suspected it had been a mistake to hire Trish, despite her impressive credentials. She was too young, too selfish, too concerned with her own agenda. And admittedly, he'd been swayed by a pretty face.

Belle groaned, a helpless visceral sound. It ripped at his gut, and he shoved aside his regret. He'd deal with Trish later. Right now the stricken horse needed him.

"She might make it without surgery," Doc said. "Let's get her to the clinic and see if she responds to the laxative. But you'll need to sign some permission forms, just in case."

Just in case. Christ. Sometimes a horse came back after colic surgery, but often they were never as good. And sometimes they never left the clinic.

He swiped his damp forehead as Dino eased the truck and trailer to the entrance and dropped the ramp with a thud. Belle twisted, biting at her stomach, but Mark tugged her forward. She gamely tried to follow, but her trembling legs splayed.

"Push her on, Dino," Mark said, hating to see her pain. Some colics were unavoidable, but not this one. For some reason Trish had neglected to cool out the filly after her gallop—utter negligence—and his compassion for the filly churned along with his growing anger.

He tied Belle in the trailer and pressed a kiss against her wet neck. "Come back to me, baby," he whispered. But his voice hardened when he turned to Dino. "She might need emergency surgery. I'll meet you at the clinic once I find out when she ate."

He stalked past several barns, searching for Trish, using the walk to cool his anger. Maybe she had an excuse—maybe she was hurt or upset about Lefty. Understandable. Best to stay open-minded. Give her a chance. Ah, there she was, and she looked fine. He blew out a sigh of relief then jerked to such an abrupt stop his heels trenched the dirt.

She posed outside the track kitchen, flashing white teeth and flirtatious eyes, flanked by three reporters. A white panel van with red WFAN lettering perched on the edge of the rutted grass, and thick snakelike cables coiled around her feet.

"Yes, I knew Lefty well," she said, her melodious voice carrying through the still air. "Last night was my turn for barn watch. He rode his bike across the infield, probably on the way to the liquor store. I was the last one to see him alive." Her voice tapered to a sigh, and she gave her eyes an exaggerated swipe.

Not a bad performance, Mark thought, crossing his arms. Almost as good as when she'd pleaded for a groom's job. Sounded like she and Lefty were the best of friends when in reality Trish considered hot walkers beneath her. However, the media was hooked.

"So you believe alcohol contributed to his death? There was no foul play?" A man with a red Yankees cap shoved a shiny microphone closer to her face.

"Well, drugs and liquor are a huge problem. Some of the trainers ignore it—" she broke off, as though sensing Mark's hard stare. "I have to hurry and cool out a horse, but we can talk later. Just drop by barn forty-eight. Don't forget my last name. C-h-a-n-d-l-e-r."

She sashayed over to Mark while two reporters openly ogled her ass. "Hi, boss," she said, and her satisfied smile hit him like a sucker punch. "I'm going to be on television today. Even more press was here earlier. Not just the usual *Thoroughbred Times* or *Racing Form* reporters either. This is a big New York station."

Mark's jaws clenched so tightly they hurt. Unbelievable. She'd neglected her job, abandoned a dependent horse and pumped Lefty's accident—for a media interview. He couldn't speak.

"If we hurry, we can watch the news at your place. Where your 'no sex' rule doesn't apply. Just make someone cool out Belle for me." She trailed a suggestive finger down his arm and gave a pretty pout, oblivious to his turmoil.

A muscle ticked in his jaw as he fought his self-loathing. Twice he'd taken Trish home. Simple pleasure, no commitment, but Belle had paid a huge price for his weakness.

Trish's voice trilled on, her fingers tightening over his forearm. "This is so exciting. Lefty never had this much attention when he was alive. He's probably digging it." Mark jerked away from her clinging hand, unable to hide his aversion, and her smile turned to a pout. "What's eating you?"

"Lefty's dead. He's not digging it." The words ground out between gritted teeth. "And Belle just coliced. Did you walk her at all? Did she eat anything?"

"All you ever think about are horses." She brushed her hair over her shoulder with a disdainful sniff. "I'm going now to walk the filly. Maybe later, I'll go home with you. But maybe not."

She still didn't get it. Expected to get by with a wiggle and a smile, but he was finished thinking with his dick. "You're not going anywhere near Belle," he said wearily. "She's fighting for her life. And you're fired. I'll give you three months' pay. Dino will have your check ready by the end of the day."

"You're firing me? Me?" She tapped her shapely chest in disbelief. "I can get a job with almost any of the top trainers."

"Good. Go get one." He spun away, disgusted with her yet more disgusted with himself. She'd been a mistake—one he wouldn't repeat.

Frivolous girls always upset the dynamics of a race stable. They'd certainly messed up his father's. Best to stick to his usual hiring policy. From now on, the only type of female allowed in his shedrow would be fat, forty and flatulent.

Tears blurred Jessica's vision as she absorbed the numbing headline. *Olympic Hopeful Engaged to Team Trainer.* A cry choked in her throat and the paper slid from her stiff fingers. Anton, her ex-boyfriend, and Cindy, her best friend—engaged! She hadn't even received a courtesy call.

Last year she'd been the team darling. Last year she'd been the woman on Anton's arm. Last year a knee injury had knocked her off the ski team. Her friends and sponsors had dumped her so quickly, her head spun. And now this.

People were pricks.

She leaned forward, automatically rubbing the swelling that ridged her right knee. The best doctors her grandfather could find hadn't helped. Sure, she could walk, even ski, but never again would she race.

A dog barked an amiable greeting. She glanced through the window as Casey, the caretaker's black Lab, crossed the manicured lawn to greet a sleek Audi. Finally Gramps was home from one of his countless business trips. Maybe he'd join her when she took Casey for a walk. The dog was eleven, fat and arthritic; she could keep pace with him. Later, if she had enough energy, she'd dust off her ski trophies.

Damn. She gave her head a weary shake. Whiners had always irritated her, and it seemed she was turning into one. She reached down and retrieved the newspaper, hating how she'd let news of Anton push her into another tailspin.

Minutes later, her grandfather strolled into the library, carrying his briefcase along with a hint of expensive cologne. "Good evening, Jessica. The office said you didn't come by again today. Have you made any decision yet?"

The words were mild, but his tone carried a definite bite. He'd always pushed her to join the huge Boone enterprise and with her mother no longer alive to run interference, that pressure had escalated. He had a ruthless streak that was often daunting and never approved of anything she did. Still, it was time to take back control of her life even though he wouldn't like her direction.

"I've been looking at the employment section," she said, placing the paper on the table. "And apartments." Disapproval darkened her grandfather's face, but she took a resolute breath and forged on. "I appreciate your job offer and letting me live here until I finished my degree, but I really wouldn't be happy working at Boone."

Her grandfather raised a palm. "Now be reasonable. There's no need to leave. But it *is* time to stop playing on a mountain. Time to forget that life. Forget those friends. Move on."

Her chest twisted at his casual dismissal of years of hard work, but she kept her voice level. "All my so-called friends are training in Europe," she said. "And I *have* moved on."

His briefcase thumped on the floor, and he picked up the newspaper, evading her hasty attempt to grab it. "So I see," he said as he scanned the black glasses and moustaches she'd drawn on Anton's and Cindy's beaming faces. He tossed the paper back on the table, his expression inscrutable. "It's lonely since your mom died, so naturally I prefer you live with me on the estate. *And* that you work at Boone. But maybe you have another plan? An idea for a business…something that could support you?"

He was a wily negotiator accustomed to control, and his caustic tone filled her with despair. She hardly had enough energy to function, let alone fight Gramps. It seemed over the past year, her customary grit had fizzled. The only time she felt alive was when she was outside with Casey. He was so loving, so non-judgmental, so faithful.

"But I do have a plan," she said. "I intend to start a dog daycare." He looked blank, and her words rushed out. "That's a place where people take their dogs so they're not cooped up all day. I'd brush them, walk them, play with them. You know I'm happiest when I'm outside. Casey keeps me sane."

Her grandfather's mouth tightened to a thin line. He sank into a leather armchair and smoothed an imaginary crease from his tailored gray pants. "It's clear you haven't thought seriously about a real career. I told your mother all that skiing was frivolous. At least she did one thing useful and helped me entertain." He frowned so deeply his bushy eyebrows touched. "But letting you live in Europe—"

"Please, Gramps." Jessica hated her grandfather's disparaging tone and rushed to deflect the inevitable criticism of her mother. "I don't want to work for Boone. And if Mom were alive, she'd encourage me to start my own business. Don't you see, the dog idea is perfect. Perfect for me."

He snorted. "I can't picture you scooping poop. Or living on a pauper's income."

"Money isn't everything," she said. "And I've never been extravagant. Or lazy."

His piercing gaze made her squirm, and she averted her gaze. Lately, she had been sleeping a lot. Couldn't seem to shake her odd lethargy. "I never used to be lazy," she choked, struggling with her own doubts.

"You don't know anything about looking after a bunch of animals. What makes you think you can run a kennel?"

"Of course I can run a kennel." She grabbed a framed camp photo off the mantle, waving it with renewed vigor. "I know plenty about animals. Remember these ponies? I fed them hay and cleaned their stalls. Every day. And working outside is way better than being cooped up in an office."

She squared her shoulders and tried to look confident, aware her grandfather would pounce at any hint of weakness. "My business courses said no career can be successful unless you really love it. I just need a little startup money. And if I can't borrow from you," she gave a little shrug, "I'll go to my friend's bank."

His eyes narrowed. For a long moment, neither of them spoke. She slipped a hand behind her back and crossed her fingers, trying to hide her desperation. She didn't have a friend at any bank, didn't have any other options, only knew she had to escape her grandfather's relentless control.

He waited another full minute, staring at her over steepled fingers, but she held his gaze.

"Here's the deal then," he finally said, his voice thoughtful. "You'll work at Belmont racetrack. No credit cards, no money except what you can earn. If you last until the end of the fall meet, I'll finance your dog kennel. If you quit or are fired, you'll live here and work at Boone. Agreed?"

"Agreed." She triumphantly thumped the picture of her and a rather nasty gray pony back on the shelf, scrambling to remember everything she knew about Belmont Park.

The venerable New York track was in Queens, about a two-hour drive. Gramps had become interested in racing ten years ago when she'd been sixteen and immersed in the ski circuit. She'd accompanied him once to the races, and the dinner had been delicious, the hats elegant and the attentive men chatty and helpful. She frowned, trying to remember the horse barns, but their table had been high in the clubhouse, behind a spotless sheet of glass.

Didn't matter. She'd see the animals soon enough, and at least she'd be working outside. The job shouldn't be too difficult. All her old magazines had said horses were much easier to handle than ponies.

She pumped her grandfather's hand to cement the deal, ignoring her twinge of unease at his smug smile.

Mark pulled out the desk drawer and flipped through his owner listings. Edward T. Boone. Time to call the man. He hated giving owners bad news, but at least Belle's prognosis was good, and maybe Boone wouldn't want many details. Incompetence was something Mark didn't tolerate, but he couldn't lie. It was a relief

Trish was gone and his female staff were now all steady women—older, committed women.

Boone's voice, curt and brusque, answered the phone on the second ring. Mark took a deep breath and squared his shoulders. Owners paid the bills; they deserved the unvarnished truth.

"Good morning, Edward. Your filly, Belle, had a bout of colic," Mark said. "We sent her to the clinic, but she's okay. Didn't need surgery. We just received the final clear. They'll watch her for a few days." He squeezed his eyes shut, waiting for Boone to ask the cause.

"What's the bottom line?" Boone asked.

"Bottom line?" Mark cracked open his eyelids. "Your horse is fine, but she'll miss the stakes race next week." Regret thickened his words. Belle had been training perfectly, almost as well as Boone's colt, and would have been a key contender.

"But I have the company box reserved." Boone's voice hardened with impatience. "Clients flying in to watch. She has to run."

"Sorry. She can't."

Mark sensed the scowl on Boone's patrician face, could feel his displeasure radiating through the phone, but remained silent. He'd only met Boone eleven months ago, and it was clear the man craved control. However, Belle's health was Mark's first priority, and he refused to run a horse that wasn't ready, no matter how many people Boone had invited for dinner. Unfortunately a trainer also had to please his owners, and Boone's silence was ominous.

"You don't want clients watching a poor race. Seeing a subpar result," Mark added, sensing that angle might sway Boone much more than Belle's welfare.

"Definitely not." Boone gave a disgruntled sigh. "Okay. Maybe she shouldn't run. But I do need a favor."

"Sure." Mark swallowed, trying to ignore the distaste souring his mouth. The man hadn't even asked the cause of Belle's colic. To Boone, it was always the bottom line, and the hell with the horse. Owners could be strange and ruthless people. Shaking his head, Mark propped his boots on the corner of his desk and tucked the phone against his shoulder, already thinking of Belle and the best feeding program for colic recovery.

"My granddaughter needs a job," Boone said. "Needs to see what grunt work is all about. She won't last a week on the backstretch but should learn plenty. And the experience will straighten her out. Force her into a real career."

A real career. Mark's hand tightened around the phone at the man's blatant condescension, but his voice remained level. "And you want me to do the straightening?"

"Yes," Boone said. "She'll be safe with you, and she's experienced with horses. Had lessons at summer camp."

Mark jerked forward so abruptly his boots slammed the floor. A greenie! Just what his barn needed. "Not a good idea. The backside is a different world. Hard, physical," he paused as an image of the body bag crossed his mind. "Even dangerous."

"Oh, I don't expect her to last longer than a week. Don't want her to." But Boone's chuckle lacked humor, and Mark understood why the man was reputed to be a cutthroat negotiator. "I just want her eyes opened. Want her to see the opportunities she's passing up. She'll quit and be working for me long before Breeders' Cup rolls around."

The wily bastard. Just the mention of Breeders' Cup made Mark's stomach kick. Finally he trained a horse fast enough to compete—Boone's colt, Ambling Assets, was his big hope. Good enough to run. Good enough to win.

But owners could move their horses to different trainers at any time, and Boone's reference to Breeders' Cup wasn't an accident. It was a threat. A girl for a horse. A no-brainer.

Mark paused but knew what his decision was long before he spoke. "Sure," he said. "Send her by Monday morning."

CHAPTER TWO

The security guard refused to let her through the formidable chain link gate. Jessica gestured at her departing cab, but the driver roared away in a backwash of dust and gas fumes.

She sighed and peered through the mesh, studying the activity around the rows of buildings beyond the guardhouse. Several horses circled on contraptions resembling merry-go-rounds, and figures bustled between barns. However, no one bothered to look her way. The backside was much different from the public side. It was foreign, unfriendly and dauntingly big.

She plunked her leather bag on the ground, reached in her pocket and pulled out the creased paper with her grandfather's brief instructions: Mark Russell, barn forty-eight. The numbers on these barns were in the twenties. There must be another entrance.

She gave the guard a scornful eye roll before turning away to follow the walkway edging the outer wall. Too high to climb and even if she managed, the six strands of spiked wire along the top looked effective. These people were anal about security.

Her right knee throbbed after five minutes of walking but she trudged beside the wall, ignoring the honks of passing traffic, determined to find another gate. Gramps wanted her to fail, expected her to, but there was no way she'd be coerced into joining Boone. Barn work would be a cinch compared to working for her grandfather. She wouldn't let him control her life like he had her parents. She tightened her grip on the bag and continued walking, her steps as forceful as her thoughts.

A wiry man on an ancient bike vanished into a service entrance, and she squared her shoulders and followed. Maybe they weren't as vigilant at this gate. But the slit-eyed guard glanced up from his inspection of a car's trunk, dashing her hopes with his gesture to stop.

She didn't have a phone number for this Russell fellow. Probably a deliberate oversight by her grandfather, hoping she might give up and slink home. Gramps was sneaky mean about getting his own way.

A man wearing a dark cowboy hat strolled past with an easy smile and an officious pass clipped to his jeans. He nodded at both the guard and Jessica as he sauntered through the gate. She slotted his type instantly—relaxed, friendly and receptive to women. "There you are!" she called, dashing forward. "A bit late." Pouting, she placed her hand on his elbow. "I've been waiting forever."

He hesitated but only for a second. "So sorry, darling." With a mischievous grin, he looped his arm around her waist and tugged her close. "She's with me, Jake," he called as he escorted her past the guard and onto the grounds.

"Thank you," she said after walking a safe distance. "You can let go of me now."

His hand had already drifted along her hip, but he immediately lowered his arm and winked. "Shucks. I knew this was too good to last. Who you looking for, sweetheart?"

"Mark Russell."

"Dammit, he always gets the gorgeous brunettes." He grinned, his eyes sweeping her with such blatant appreciation, she smiled back. "I'm Dino, Mark's assistant." He sobered as his gaze drifted to her bulky bag. "But I'm sorry to say he won't hire you."

"Bet he will."

"You're on." He stuck out his hand. "Beer and pizza. Loser buys."

Dino was clearly a ladies' man, but his easy charm was a salve to her soul. And he'd just made a sucker bet. She shook his hand without an ounce of guilt. Her grandfather had insisted she turn over all her credit cards so a free dinner would come in handy.

"It's a bet," she said. "Where's Mark?"

Dino gestured over his shoulder. "He's that big ugly guy watching us from the shedrow. The one who's scowling."

She adjusted her sunglasses and stared in the direction of Dino's grin. The hard-muscled man framed in the doorway wasn't scowling, but he didn't look very welcoming either. And he definitely wasn't ugly. His faded shirt and chinos fit his body flawlessly. She gulped and tried not to stare.

It wasn't his powerful body or rugged face that was so compelling, but his distinct air of confidence. His very stillness as he watched made her fingers tighten around the handle of her bag. He didn't look...easy.

She tossed her bag over her shoulder and sauntered toward him, hiding behind a composure she didn't feel. "Hello, I'm Jessica Boone. Here to work."

Only his gaze moved, his deep blue eyes studying her with calm objectivity. "Good morning," he finally said.

His voice was slow and deep and sexy, and she stared at his chiseled mouth, trying to pin down his accent. He extended his hand and she automatically shook it, still absorbing his slight drawl, then realized her fingers clung much too long and dropped her arm in embarrassment.

He glanced over her head, apparently used to clinging females. "Thanks for showing her the way, Dino."

"You're hiring her?" Dino's eyes widened. "But what about the Three-F rule?"

"Temporarily suspended," Mark said with a humorless smile she didn't understand. "Come with me, Jessica."

Dino looked stunned and she shot him a teasing wink before following Mark into the barn, into the primal smell of leather, liniment and horses. She breathed through her mouth, needing a moment to adjust. Not exactly a distasteful smell, just overwhelmingly strong. Horses loomed everywhere, presenting an orderly row of heads as they stretched over stall guards.

Mark stopped so abruptly she almost bumped into him. He gestured into an airless room where a narrow cot occupied a third of the rough planked floor. "These are your sleeping quarters. The girl before you did some night watch and rubbed three." His gaze flickered over her spotless boots and crisp jeans. "We'll see how this works out. You might be better walking hots."

He seemed to be speaking a different language, but she kept her mouth shut and tried to hide her jerk of dismay. Sleeping quarters was a euphemism. Her bedroom was just a stall converted from horse use to human, and she didn't want to look too closely at the dark splotches staining the floor.

"Accommodations okay?" He reached over her head and lazily brushed a cobweb off the ceiling. They both watched as the transparent threads drifted through the air and landed on the middle of the cot.

"Perfect." She forced brightness into her voice hoping he didn't hear its quaver.

He gave a bland smile and stepped from the room. "Carlos," he called, and a grim-faced man appeared like a well-trained butler. "This is Jessica. Have another groom, maybe Maria, show her around. See if she can do Trish's job, but you'll probably have to shuffle horses. Maybe put her on hots."

Someone groaned and muttered 'newbie', and heat rushed to her face. Even the horses stared with fresh disdain.

Carlos gestured, and a dark-haired woman in a frayed jacket stepped forward. Carlos spoke in Spanish, a rapid fire of words that exposed a chipped front tooth, then turned and rushed after Mark.

"Come on, kid," Maria said. "There's one horse left to walk. Buddy, stall eight." She passed Jessica a leather lead with a chain and clip on one end.

Jessica cautiously approached the imposing horse. Buddy had a jagged white stripe down the center of his black face and held his head so high she could barely attach the lead to his leather halter.

The woman shook her head and pushed forward. "I see you don't know anything. You never want a horse to get loose so always run the chain through the left ring, over the nose, then on the right. The colts get the chain under the lip. Then you walk the horse until he's cool. Be careful they don't bite. *Comprendo?*"

Jessica gulped, noting that half of Maria's right index finger was missing. "Where should I walk?" she asked humbly.

"The tow ring." Maria pointed at the sand oval between the barns, where a stocky woman in a shapeless shirt led a gray horse.

"Let's go, Buddy," Jessica said. The horse just stared, ears pricked, eyes bright with interest. She tugged on the lead, but he refused to move. "Please," she said, and Buddy lowered his head and followed.

Her confidence returned as the big animal followed her around the oval. It seemed easy work, and the September sun was pleasantly warm. Her knee ached a bit from the deep sawdust, but it wasn't a hard job walking the obliging horse, and she relaxed enough to check out her surroundings.

Mark's barn was neat and orderly with the initials MR on the side. Not much color though. The brown and white on the saddle pads was boringly bland, although freshly washed bandages draped the wall, providing accents of blue and green. A man in faded jeans dumped manure in a concrete pit behind the barn.

Someone raked the aisle while a short rider in a dented helmet and fringed chaps cleaned leather. Similar activities took place in the adjoining barns, and her worries eased. This didn't seem very hard.

"Eight weeks of this. It'll be a cinch," she murmured, reaching back and feeling Buddy's chest. She didn't know a horse's normal respiration rate but was an expert on cooling down human athletes and guessed animals involved the same general principles. Already she could see from Buddy's flanks that his breathing had steadied.

Maria motioned her toward an assortment of wash sponges. "You have to hold him for his bath. Since Trish left, Buddy doesn't have a groom, so I've been stuck with the extra work." She gave a long-suffering sigh, but Jessica sensed Maria was really a helpful soul.

"Thanks for showing me around," Jessica said. "Buddy's a nice horse." She scratched him on the shoulder while Maria sloshed soapy water over his chest, saturating the air with the smell of sweat, horsehair and lavender.

"Yeah, he's a dream compared to the others." Maria's eyes narrowed in speculation. "Boss is sure starting you out easy."

"Boss is Mark?" Jessica asked as she helped rinse the dripping suds from Buddy's back.

"Of course. I thought you knew him?"

"Just met him this morning," Jessica said, "but I'm broke and really need the job."

Maria's round face filled with empathy. "Yeah, he's one of the best-paying trainers around, but he doesn't tolerate mistakes. Strange he'd hire someone so green."

"You can tell I'm green?"

Maria smiled as she rescued Buddy's lead shank from the muddy ground. "Everyone can tell. And dangling equipment is dangerous. Boss will skin your ass if he sees that." She sobered, and worry lines fanned her eyes as she checked over her shoulder. "I think, for job security, you better come with me to the kitchen for a chat."

Ten minutes later, they were seated in the track kitchen, a dining area vastly different from the elegant clubhouse Jessica remembered. It was merely a clapboard hut stuffed with linoleum tables and air thick with kitchen grease. But the shouts to Maria were warm and welcoming, and the cafeteria line efficient.

Jessica took a cautious bite of the fried egg sandwich Maria recommended. For years, her breakfast had consisted of a protein smoothie, but eggs seemed the popular backside fare and anything that gave her more time with Maria was worth forcing down.

"Listen up, kid." Maria propped her elbows on the table and leaned closer. "There's a strict pecking order here, from lowly hot walkers to grooms, exercise riders and jockeys. Way at the top are trainers. Obey them like they're God. We're lucky because Mark is one of the decent ones, and he's getting better runners every month. He's good to his horses and won't expect you to sleep with him. In fact, sex and alcohol are prohibited in his barn."

Jessica coughed, almost choking on her food.

"Don't worry," Maria said. "Plenty of girls are fighting to be Trish's replacement."

"Who's Trish?" Jessica wiped her mouth and took another bite of the egg sandwich. It really was delicious, much better than her tedious shakes.

Maria snorted. "The reigning backstretch beauty. Sucks up to all the trainers, only works for the top stables, a real snob."

Jessica shrugged and glanced around the bustling room, more interested in the people she could see. "So the little people with whips stuck in their pockets are exercise riders?"

"Yeah. All they do is ride. Some are working toward their jockey licenses, but most are too tall or too heavy."

"What about the owners? Where do they fit?"

Maria sniffed. "The trainer deals with them. The fancy owners don't come around unless it's to meet for dinner. They only think of their horse on race day."

Jessica hid a finger of guilt. Obviously her grandfather fell in that category. They hadn't visited the backside on her last visit, and she hadn't thought about where the horses went before and after the race. She did remember the trainer though, a creaky, white-haired man who thumped his cane and swore at the jockey. Mark was vastly different from that man—so calm, so muscled, so…hunky.

Heat swept her face, and she shoved aside improper thoughts of her new boss. "Thanks for giving me the scoop. So what do we do after breakfast?"

"No races or yard sales today, so we nap."

"Nap?" Jessica smiled. "I believe I'm going to like it here."

Mark leaned over his desk as he flipped through the Keeneland auction catalogue. Several yearlings drew his interest, well-bred but not fashionable enough to attract big bidders from the Middle East. Still, they'd be pricey, and unfortunately only one of his owners had expressed any interest in the sale: Edward T. Boone.

Boone and his baggage. Mark sighed, sipping his coffee as he considered the leggy granddaughter. Clearly she knew nothing about horses, and her striking looks were an obvious liability. Even the disciplined Carlos had been sneaking peeks, and accidents always happened when staff was distracted.

Fortunately Maria was looking after Jessica and explaining the rules. Maybe they could keep the girl busy scrubbing buckets and coiling hoses. His main concern was that she didn't impact the horses. They were sensitive athletes and needed a calm, orderly environment.

A shrill squeal sliced the air. *What the hell?*

He jerked to his feet, painfully ramming the top of his knee against the edge of the desk. Clearly a horse was in trouble. Please, not Assets, he prayed, thinking about Boone's other horse.

He charged down the shedrow, breaking his own rule about not running in the barn. Assets stared down the aisle, healthy, happy and merely curious about the racket coming from Trish's old tack room, the sleeping quarters now occupied by Boone's granddaughter.

Mark shoved the door open and burst in.

Jessica teetered on the cot, legs tangled in blankets, her face twisted with revulsion.

"Mouse!" She gestured at the far corner.

He jerked to a stop, his breath escaping in a relieved whoosh.

"Mouse," he repeated, distracted by the way she jumped on shapely legs, making the bed protest in a cacophony of squeaks. She'd limped earlier, but there was no sign of that now, although her right knee was definitely swollen. His gaze lifted, leg analysis forgotten as bouncing breasts grabbed his attention. Damn, she was built. His irritation faded as he admired the enticing view.

"Well, can you catch it?" she asked.

He gave a guilty jerk, jamming his attention back to her face. Her expression was so desperate that his appreciation of her stunning body flipped to concern. Concern he quickly crushed.

She was an inconvenient presence at a very inconvenient time. After watching her lead Buddy, it was obvious she was useless. He dragged a hand through his hair, hating how Boone had forced him into such an awkward position. A Breeders' Cup season, and he was forced to baby-sit a newbie. "There are always lots of mice around," he said, trying to keep the impatience from his voice. "Difficult to control. It's more important to keep them out of the horses' feed. Just shake your boots in the morning, and you won't squash them."

"Yuck!" She shuddered, staring at the floor with renewed suspicion. "So they mainly come out at night?"

"Or when it's quiet, and they think the room is empty." He crossed his arms. "Look, Jessica, it's clear you don't belong here. Why don't we call your grandfather and arrange for a drive home? Tomorrow I'll take you on a tour of the backside, explain how it all works and anything else you want to know."

"No, I'm fine. I'm just not used to mice beneath my bed. That's all." She clamped her mouth, and the staunch set of her chin surprised him. "I'll be fine. You'll see."

Her voice was stubborn but also oddly desperate. Had her grandfather kicked her out? Surely she had better places to go than the backside of Belmont Park. She was staring at him though, and there was no mistaking the plea in those beautiful brown eyes. A deer in the headlights look he simply couldn't resist.

He scooped her fancy jeans off the floor and tossed them to her with a resigned sigh. "Get dressed and meet me in my office. We'll figure out something you can do."

He stopped in front of Assets' stall to check the colt. Two minutes later, Jessica bounded behind him.

"Quiet. Always move slow. Never scare the horses." He thought he did a good job hiding his frustration. "This is Ambling Assets. Heard of him?"

"Don't think so." She spoke cautiously, as though it were some kind of test.

"He's my big horse." A definite understatement. The two-year-old had won several Grade 1 races and was an early favorite for the Breeders' Cup Juvenile.

"He doesn't seem that big." She edged closer. "Buddy is taller."

"Big horse is just an expression. Careful, he bites. Your grandfather owns this guy."

"Ah." She dodged the colt's playful nip. "And you have to please my grandfather?"

"Exactly."

"So I'm kind of your boss." She gave him such a teasing smile, he grinned back.

"Guess it just means we're stuck with one another for a bit," he said. But his smile lingered as he studied her intelligent face. It shouldn't be too disastrous to have her around for a week. Boone expected she'd only last a couple days. At least she'd put on a bra, although her breasts still strained against her tight shirt.

He'd have to review the dress code. It was hard on the guys staring at jiggling breasts all day, and owners' wives didn't like it much either. She clearly had a top notch set—

Something grabbed his hand, and Assets' teeth pinched his skin. Obviously not only his staff were distracted. His smile flattened, and he wheeled away.

She followed him into his office, ballsy as an agent, wandering around and checking out his wall pictures while he rummaged through the drawers for her backside pass. He finally found it in the middle drawer behind his cache of peppermints.

"Here are your credentials," he said. "You'll have to stop by the office and have your picture taken. Officially you're a groom, but I only want you handling Buddy. Dino or I will help with the poultice and wraps. If you have any other questions, ask Maria. Stay out of everyone's way, and don't get kicked."

"Does this mean I get a raise?" she asked as she clipped the laminated pass on the pocket of her jeans. "Now that I've been promoted from hot walker to groom?"

"A raise?" He lifted an eyebrow. Couldn't remember any of his staff ever asking for a raise.

"Well, yes, since I'm taking over Trish's job. Her job as a groom, I mean," she added, so quickly he wondered what the hell Maria had said.

She was breathing fast now, maybe wasn't quite as cocky as she appeared. And she definitely knew how to stick out her lower lip. It was thicker on the bottom. Pink. Ripe. *Jesus.*

He grabbed a rubber bucket and slammed a rectal thermometer on the desk. "Naturally if you want to do a bit more—assume some of Trish's other duties—that'll be fine. Maybe I can consider a raise. Ten horses. By the way, Trish always used gloves."

She backed up a step, her nose wrinkling as she absorbed the implications of the thermometer, the tail clip, the brown-crusted string. "Actually," she said, "let's forget the raise for now. And maybe it's best if I only groom Buddy."

He nodded gravely. "Good call." But he was smiling as she fled the office, and it was another full minute before he turned his attention back to the Keeneland sale catalogue.

CHAPTER THREE

Jessica forced herself from the cocoon of blankets and tried to shake off her bleariness, a definite result of sleep deprivation. Mice had scurried beneath the cot all night, and the prospect of a furry body joining her beneath the covers had been too horrifying to allow any sleep.

But it was four a.m., and already voices leaked from the aisle. Horses nickered, buckets rattled and a challenging day loomed. She'd already decided that instead of napping later she would find a store and buy some much-needed mousetraps.

Mark was wrong. There was absolutely no reason to tolerate mice, and she'd never be able to sleep with rodents rustling three feet from her head. At least he'd made her a groom and not a hot walker; she didn't want to be at the bottom of any organization, no matter how temporary her position.

She tugged on her jeans, wincing at the stab of pain in her knee. It had ballooned up during the night even though her grandfather's doctor had drained the fluid only two days earlier. A warm bath always helped, but the rusty showers across the road didn't have tubs.

Yawning, she limped into the aisle. The lights were on, but it was black outside and the air crisp. Figures drifted from the shadows, exchanging a series of grunts and terse greetings.

No one paid her any attention, so she wandered down to Buddy's stall. It was filthy. So was the horse. Straw clung to his mane and tail, and manure stains streaked his belly.

"Morning," Maria called, gesturing at a giant whiteboard. "Better get to work. Buddy is scheduled to go out with the second set."

Riders with boots, helmets and safety vests gathered around the board, reading out names and making comments.

"Boss put me on Jed today. Man, I hate that horse," someone said.

Jessica scanned the aisle but didn't see Mark. It seemed everything happened fast in the morning so she rushed across the road to the bathroom, washed her face and tied her hair in a ponytail. She cast a longing look at the shower but hurried back.

Already five horses were saddled and in the aisle where grooms legged riders onto their backs. She checked the board. Except for her, each groom cared for three horses, five exercise riders worked the sets, and five hot walkers cooled out the horses when they returned to the barn. It appeared grooms cleaned the stalls while the horses were ridden. It was also clear she'd been assigned much less than any other worker. She squelched her spike of guilt. At least she was up and working long before the trainer.

"Hurry up, kid," Maria said as she brushed past with a loaded wheelbarrow. "Tie Buddy to the wall and get him ready. Boss will have your skinny ass if you mess up his schedule."

"He's not here yet," Jessica said as she picked up Buddy's grooming kit.

"Of course he's here," Maria said. "He's checking the track."

Damn. Mark was here, and her horse was the dirtiest one in the barn. Jessica rushed into the stall and rubbed furiously at Buddy's manure stains, even using some of her herbal hair conditioner to tame his knotted tail. Buddy stood obligingly, flicking his ears as though mystified by her panic. The gelding's serenity amused her. According to Maria, grooms were supposed to calm the horses, not the other way around.

"You're a good boy, Buddy," she whispered. He pressed his velvety muzzle into her hand, tickling her fingers with his whiskers. He needed a shave, she decided, remembering that Assets' ears and muzzle had been neatly trimmed. Obviously 'big horses' received special attention, and she frowned with a mother's indignation. Assets was a cocky brat who pushed and nipped, while Buddy was a sweet, undemanding horse who only wanted to please.

She rushed to the tack room, resolving to be the best groom Buddy ever had. Besides, it would be good experience for her dog business.

Buddy's tack, soft, clean and freshly oiled, hung beneath his nameplate. The saddle was tiny, and she carried it gingerly down the aisle, amazed riders would dare gallop in something so flimsy.

"Make sure it's tight," Maria warned. "A slipping saddle can kill."

"Could you check it for me?" Jessica asked, trying to keep the alarm from her voice. "Just to make sure? It's been a while since...well, since I saddled a racehorse."

"I'll check it." Mark's deep voice sounded behind her.

Relieved, she glanced over her shoulder to where he sat on a muscular gray horse. She'd known skiers who were hurt because of poorly adjusted equipment, and she didn't want to be responsible for any wrecks.

Mark stepped off his horse and passed the reins to Maria. "Good grooming job," he said as he entered the stall. "I noticed Buddy was dirty this morning."

She flushed with pleasure, suddenly glad she hadn't wasted time with a shower.

"Saddle pad needs to be shoved above the withers. Girth tightened another two holes." He adjusted the tack with expert hands. "Buddy doesn't need wraps but when he comes back, check his legs. He's your responsibility. You can walk over to the gap now and watch him work."

She nodded, deciding she'd ask someone else what and where the gap was. She didn't want to risk shattering Mark's patience. Besides, his virile presence seemed to suck away all her oxygen. He was standing so close she could feel his heat, smell a whiff of aftershave, something nice and piney and...appealing.

He strode from the stall, remounted his patient gray, and the second set of horses followed him from the shedrow.

"Quit daydreaming and get Buddy in the aisle," the last exercise rider called, impatiently snapping his whip against his boot.

"May I follow you to the gap?" she whispered as she boosted him into the saddle, copying the method the other grooms used.

The rider, a young man called Slim, was amazingly light with muscle-corded arms, and he laughed once he was on Buddy's back. "Just follow any horse, greenie. We're all going to the gap."

He spoke much too loud, and she winced as Mark's amused chuckle drifted down the aisle.

She trailed the string of horses past endless rows of barns but didn't gawk around, too fascinated by the animals' sheer beauty. All the horses looked majestic, even mysterious as they walked through the mist, but Buddy looked much the best. The rising sun painted a glint on his coat, and every strand of his thick tail gleamed. He glanced back twice, as though checking if she were following, but that could have been her imagination. Mark definitely didn't look back.

Clearly her boss was well-respected; people called out greetings as he led his line of horses. The amiable joshing reminded her of ski events. Odd, she hadn't thought about skiing in almost twenty-four hours. Hadn't thought about Anton and Cindy's engagement. Horse work was certainly a consuming affair.

The eager horses outstripped her awkward walk, and she had no idea how much further the gap was. When a golf cart slowed and offered a lift, she accepted with a grateful smile.

"Heading to the gap?" the silver-haired driver asked.

"Sure am," she said. "Going to watch my horse work."

She was quite certain she had the lingo right but noticed his gaze flickered over her credentials. He didn't speak again, only whipped the golf cart up to the rail just as Buddy walked onto the track. Mark twisted in the saddle, one hand on his horse's rump, face expressionless as she stepped from the cart.

She gave him a breezy smile before leaning over the rail to concentrate on the five horses from her barn. *Her barn.* The notion filled her with a heady sense of belonging. Not one day, and already she was bursting with information. The gap was self-explanatory and merely an opening in the rail where the horses walked from the backside onto the track.

Every horse on the property seemed to be exercising. Some riders were standing, some trotting, others galloping. They looked like monkeys hunched over the horses' necks; it was rather incredible they didn't tumble into the dirt.

For a moment she lost sight of Buddy, but suddenly he was visible again, trotting toward her through the thinning mist, his breath mingling with the primal thud of hooves. It was sheer magic. She gripped the rail, drinking in the sights, the sounds, the smell, savoring the moment like a snapshot.

Buddy trotted past and when Slim nodded a greeting, she puffed up, feeling like she'd just received the secret handshake. Her gaze slid back to Mark. He was watching his five horses, although with all the traffic it was probably hard to keep a visual. On the mountain, skiers wore bright jackets and helmets but at the track, most of the horses looked identical. Mark's brown saddle pads were simply too nondescript to stand out.

She crossed her arms. Tomorrow she'd braid bright ribbons along Buddy's mane so he'd be easier to spot.

Mark stiffened and abruptly galloped off, without any obvious signal to his aggressive horse. He pulled alongside Buddy. The two riders spoke for a moment before turning and heading toward the gap. Slim grinned, Buddy looked frustrated and Mark looked pissed.

"Did you bring a shank, Jessica?"

She wheeled at Dino's abrupt question and shook her head. Dino stood five feet to her left, a stopwatch and clipboard in one hand and wearing a serious expression instead of his usual grin.

"You should always have a shank, towel and hoof pick," he added, "and judging from Mark's face you're going to need it."

"I didn't know," she sputtered. "He told me to go the gap. He didn't say pack a bag."

"He shouldn't have to," Dino said as he jotted something on his clipboard.

Jessica sighed. Mark did look annoyed—rather unfortunate as the morning had been going so well. The nice man in the golf cart had a tangle of equipment in his basket; maybe he had an extra shank. She walked up to him, flashing her most charming smile.

"Do you have a lead shank I could borrow?" she asked. "I seem to have misplaced mine, maybe dropped it when I was getting into your cart."

He lowered his binoculars in surprise. "A shank? Yeah, sure. Just return it to barn thirty-nine."

She accepted it with grateful thanks and was back at the gap by the time Mark arrived with Buddy.

"Did this horse have all his shoes when you cleaned his feet?" Mark asked.

Her hands tightened around the leather line. She hadn't cleaned Buddy's feet. But now she remembered her camp lessons and how important it was—the most important part of grooming. She studiously linked the chain through Buddy's bit, the way other grooms had done with their horses, and managed to avoid Mark's hard stare.

"The shoes were good and tight this morning," she said.

"He probably lost the shoe on the walk over," Slim said quickly. "I felt him take a funny step."

Mark blew out a sigh. "Take Buddy back and walk the shedrow. He's hopping out of his skin." But he gave Jessica a long look before trotting off.

"You owe me one, greenie. But it works for me." Slim shrugged off her grateful smile. "Stop this old guy so I can grab a coffee before the next set. I'm a little hung over today." He gave Buddy a quick pat before swinging to the ground and hurrying off.

"I'm sorry, fellow," she whispered as she led Buddy away. "I'm just learning how to take care of you."

Her arms and knee throbbed by the time she wrestled Buddy back to the barn. The gelding had been primed to run and was unwilling to accept the day was over. Several times he balked as though positive they were going the wrong way, and she was relieved to see one of Mark's hot walkers, a rather large woman, returning a cooled-out horse to a waiting groom.

"This guy is supposed to walk the shedrow," Jessica said, reaching out to pass her Buddy's lead.

"Well, I'm not doing it." The woman raised a hammy elbow and barged past. "I'm already walking an extra horse this week because *somebody* can only handle Buddy."

"Well, somebody's cranky," Jessica said under her breath, feeling a tad cranky herself. After all, she'd risen at four with no shower, no coffee, no breakfast.

Buddy gave her shoulder an impatient nudge, so she turned back to the horse. He was a sweet fellow, and she really didn't mind walking him around the shedrow. But as she passed the row of stalls, she noticed every single one bristled with fresh straw. Every stall but Buddy's.

"Stick him on the hot walker, kid," Maria called, pointing at the mechanical arms that guided the horses in small circles. "Then you can clean his stall before boss gets back."

Jessica nodded and turned Buddy toward the far corner. She'd seen horses walking on the contraption yesterday, and it seemed a clever, labor-saving device. There was a nasty brown horse already tied to the walker who squealed and kicked when they approached. However, Buddy didn't seem at all concerned about the horse's poor manners so she clipped him on the opposite side and stepped back to watch the action. The brown horse stopped kicking, and both animals strolled around by themselves, seemingly best of friends. Perfect.

She grabbed a wheelbarrow and rushed to Buddy's stall, guessing she had about twenty minutes before Mark returned. Plenty of time to pass inspection. But Buddy was a messy horse, not pooping in one corner but spreading it around as though undecided which part of the stall was best.

Clink. Her pitchfork hit the tip of a horseshoe protruding from the straw. She stepped back and scanned the aisle. No one was looking, so she hid the shoe in the soiled straw and rushed the laden wheelbarrow to the manure pile.

She finished by shaking out three bales of straw then stood back and admired the comfortable stall. Buddy would surely sleep well tonight; in fact, it looked more inviting than her dark room.

Maria sniffed as she shuffled past lugging two buckets of soapy water. "Boss will go broke if you waste that much straw every day. Now grab your horse and lead him around the shedrow. Boss doesn't like us to use the hot walker much."

Boss, boss, boss. It was apparent Maria was intimidated by Mark, and Jessica was beginning to feel she couldn't do anything right, no matter how hard she tried. However, she shrugged off the criticism and hurried to get Buddy. He nickered when she approached, and the welcoming sound put a bounce back in her step—she was glad his stall was full of fresh straw.

A set of horses, hot and sweaty, returned from the track. She plastered on an innocent smile and led Buddy past Mark.

He didn't smile back, just stared at her with astute blue eyes. "Now what have you been up to while I was gone?" he asked as he stepped down from his gray.

"I cleaned Buddy's stall. And walked him. And he has lots of fresh straw. Fresh water too," she said. "Guess my work is finished."

"That part of your work might be finished," he drawled, "but the aisle needs cleaning. Plus the farrier is coming in half an hour. So stick around. You'll have to hold your horse for him."

Her shoulders slumped, but she grabbed a rake and helped tidy the shedrow. She'd been looking forward to a shower, breakfast and nap. It was amazing one horse could be so much work.

Maria shrugged in sympathy. "You won't have time to join us for lunch, but there's still time to check out the dorm yard sale."

A yard sale. Jessica had never been to one before, but her hope sparked at the possibility of finding a mousetrap. She simply couldn't sleep in a mice-infested room. Despite Mark's casual acceptance of rodents, something needed to be done. She checked her watch then happily followed Maria.

After twenty minutes of checking an assortment of items spread on mismatched tables, she hadn't found any mousetraps but had discovered several balls of purple yarn. Now her attention leaped to a rickety bike propped against a red milk carton.

She straddled the bike and checked the pedals, imagining how much time it would save walking to the kitchen. "How much?" she asked, glancing at the brown-eyed boy who seemed to be in charge.

"For you, lady, special price. Thirty dollars. All profits to Anna House."

Maria elbowed her way forward and squeezed the front tire. "Not a bad deal, kid. But he'll take twenty."

"*Si.*" The boy flashed an amused smile. "I'll take twenty."

The bike was old and dented, but Jessica loved it. It even had a front basket and a cheeky bell. The purchase left her with a meager fifteen dollars in her pocket, but she happily waved to Maria and headed back to the shedrow, head bent and legs pumping.

The wind whipped her face and she felt gloriously alive, free to let her imagination run. Soon she was careening down a mountain again, with perfect snow, cheering crowds and honking horns. It took a second to realize the honking behind her was real. She jammed on the brakes, skidding to a spectacular stop on the gravel, her adrenaline still pumping.

A security guard in a crisp uniform stepped from a Jeep. "Speed limit is fifteen miles per hour, miss."

"You must be kidding. I was just trying out my new bike."

"It doesn't look new." He waved a thick ticket book. "And horses don't like bikes that go faster than them."

It took her five minutes to convince him to forego a fine, but her relief fizzled when she rounded the corner and saw the farrier's truck had already arrived. She leaned her bike against the wall and cautiously entered the barn. Her boss was holding Buddy in the aisle while a stocky man in a leather apron studied the gelding's left hoof.

Mark glanced up, his expression inscrutable. "Glad you finally showed up. We were just discussing his shoes. If it rains, we'll go with a raised toe. But if it's nice, the inner rims might be best. What do you think?"

She glanced at the bewildering array of shoes, remembering her coach's headaches when faced with wax choices and volatile weather conditions. "I think I'm late," she said humbly, "and I'm truly sorry. I could hold Buddy while you ponder the weather, but maybe it would be best if I went to the kitchen and bought you a coffee?"

"I do appreciate a coffee while I'm pondering." He smiled then, a slow, deep grin that made her pulse kick, and she felt like she was back on her bike again.

She pedaled to the kitchen but couldn't resist stopping to chat with Maria. By the time she returned to the barn, Buddy was back in his stall and Mark stood in front of the shedrow, studying the looming clouds. She braked to a stop, balancing the coffee in her left hand, quite proud of her riding prowess.

"Borrowed a bike?" His gaze drifted over the bike as he accepted the warm cup.

"Bought it," she said.

His mouth thinned, and a tiny wrinkle appeared between his eyes. "I see." He snapped the plastic tab off his lid. "Does that mean you intend to work here a lot longer than a week?"

"Of course," she said. "What made you think it was only a week?"

His dismay was so obvious, her throat tightened. Clearly, he didn't want her around either, and he'd obviously been duped by her grandfather. She bent down and pretended to adjust the chain, fighting her sense of worthlessness.

"Need help with that?" he asked.

"It's okay," she murmured, keeping her head averted so Mark wouldn't see her face. "The chain's just a bit loose."

He stepped closer, reached down and traced the deep scratches on the bike's frame. "This must be old Lefty's," he said.

"Yes." She glanced up, surprised by the obvious regret in his voice. "Lefty's name is carved all over it."

"Guess it's good someone's using it," Mark said. "Come on inside. I'll teach you how to wrap Buddy. You might as well learn to bandage since you'll be here a bit longer than I expected."

He softened his words with one of his gorgeous smiles, and suddenly she didn't feel quite so unwanted. She propped the bike against the wall and eagerly followed him. "Where did Lefty go?"

Mark glanced back and shrugged, but his eyes shadowed. "Police say he drowned."

She jerked to a stop. "You mean that was the guy in the infield? The one Maria and her friends spoke about. The guy they found just before I came?"

"That's right."

"Oh." Her voice squeaked and she rubbed her arms, trying to ward off the sudden chill. However, she couldn't stop the goose bumps shivering down her spine and found it undeniably creepy she now rode a dead man's bike.

CHAPTER FOUR

Mark drummed his fingers on the steering wheel, frowning at the line of glowing brake lights while he waited his turn to inch through the track gate.

"Morning, sir. Sorry for the delay." The guard leaned over his window. "New security procedures. Gotta check your trunk."

Mark stifled his groan, pulled the lever to open the trunk and checked the dashboard clock again. Four thirty seven a.m. Already seven minutes late. He'd scheduled Assets for an early-morning work, trying to avoid the press. The colt had two more works before Breeders' Cup. Afterwards Assets would have some time off, and hopefully next spring Mark would have his first Derby contender. Holy shit, who would have believed it—the Kentucky Derby.

His fingers clamped the wheel as he tried to rein in his thoughts. Horses were fragile and unpredictable. Planning too far ahead always invited heartache. Best to take one race at a time... Still, things were looking damn good.

The guard jotted on his clipboard, nodded, and Mark eased his vehicle onto the grounds. The arrival of Middle East owners added complications, but at least the increased security kept everyone's horses safe.

"Did they all eat up?" he asked Dino as he strolled into the barn, only twelve minutes behind schedule.

"Feed tubs clean as a whistle. Assets is ready to go and climbing the walls."

"Let's get him ready," Mark said. "The less attention, the better."

His exercise riders called out perfunctory greetings, but Mark's focus remained on the colt as the groom brushed and saddled the horse. This was a critical workout, one of the fast gallops scheduled to help a horse peak. Assets would be working four furlongs today, and his performance would prove whether or not he was ready to compete in next month's Breeders' Cup.

Mark checked the board, remembering he'd scheduled one other work—Buddy, the cheap claiming horse who'd left the track yesterday because of his missing shoe. Buddy and Jessica. He blew out a sigh as he glanced down the aisle, hoping she had her horse ready. It was damn difficult dealing with the granddaughter of his most influential owner.

"Here's your horse," Dino said as he led up Ghost, Mark's stable pony.

Mark swung into the saddle, eager to make up for lost time. "I'm going to pony Assets over now. Get him started while it's still dark. You can bring over the rest of the set."

The work was perfect, a trainer's dream. Assets had galloped aggressively, scorching around the track and leaving no doubt he was primed for a big race.

"What'd you get him in?" Mark asked the clocker.

"A shade over forty-seven," the gray-haired man called back.

Four furlongs in forty-seven seconds. Excellent. Mark smiled as he checked his own stopwatch and headed to the gap. He'd call Boone tonight and report Assets was ready for the world stage. The colt's work should be a bullet, the fastest work of the day.

Someone hooted, and Mark stopped thinking of bullets as chuckles erupted along the rail. Mist still blanketed the track, but Dino's cowboy hat was discernible as he escorted four shapes onto the track.

More guffaws.

"What's up, Mark!" Someone chuckled. "Getting ready for a parade?"

Hooves thudded as Mark's string of horses emerged from the mist. He finally saw them, saw Buddy and understood why everyone snickered. Goddammit! Garish purple plaits adorned the horse's mane and tail. Buddy looked like a circus horse, and he felt like a fool.

He clamped his jaw, trying to blank his expression, trying to pretend he wasn't just as shocked.

"I feel like an idiot up here, boss," Slim said as he tugged his helmet over his forehead and guided Buddy further from the railbirds. "And this horse stinks like flowers."

Mark scowled and looked at Dino. "Couldn't you have stopped her?"

But Dino was leaning on the rail, laughing, and even the unflappable Ghost snorted. Meanwhile Jessica stood at the gap, beaming like a proud parent, oblivious to the furor.

"Get the work in," Mark said to Slim. "Then get Buddy off the track while it's still dark."

"It's getting light, and photographers are already here." Slim's scowl deepened. "This is damn embarrassing. I don't want to ride this horse anymore."

"You'll ride as assigned," Mark snapped. He straightened in the saddle, trying to concentrate, trying to control his frustration. For ten years he'd struggled to establish his fledgling stable, and now that girl was making him look like his father—an undisciplined failure who'd let women lead him around by the dick. And it wasn't just him who felt like an idiot.

The poor rider. The poor horse.

His gaze narrowed on Buddy. Despite the silly braids, the gelding strutted around the track, pushing at the bit and looking like a stakes winner as Slim warmed him up. Mark had never seen the horse so on the muscle.

When Slim moved Buddy to the quarter pole and loosened the reins, Buddy sizzled around the track, galloping out another furlong before Slim could pull him up. Christ, the horse actually looked good.

Mark shot Dino a glance.

"Unbelievable." Dino shook his head. "I never thought that horse could run a lick."

They watched silently as Slim turned Buddy and trotted back to Mark. "Maybe the braids aren't so bad," Slim said, looking slightly bemused.

Mark squeezed his eyes shut. When he opened them, Buddy still strutted like a hero, and railbirds still buzzed about the purple-braided horse.

"Nice work," someone said.

Mark nodded, hiding his shock, then turned Ghost and followed the set off the track. A photographer stepped forward, pushed past Assets and snapped a picture of Buddy. Maybe the braids were okay, he told himself. Anything that lessened attention on Assets had to be a good thing. He felt Jessica's gaze but couldn't look at her, only wheeled Ghost and rode back onto the track.

It was ten a.m. when his last set finished. He stopped Ghost in front of the shedrow and stared down at Dino.

"What happened out there?" Dino's forehead wrinkled.

"Well, we got the bullet," Mark said, patting Ghost and dismounting from his hard-working horse.

"Not surprising," Dino said. "Assets ran well, and not many older horses worked four furlongs today."

"One older horse did." Mark shook his head at the unsettling development. "Buddy had the fastest work," he added.

Dino's eyes widened. His mouth opened but no words came out, and Mark was reassured that his capable assistant was just as stunned. The usual chatter sounded from the shedrow, but the two men only stared.

"Maybe Buddy liked those funny braids," Dino finally said. "*She* slept in his stall last night too. Worried about mice in her room. Guess any male would be energized after sleeping with someone like that."

Mark flipped his stirrup over the horn and tugged on the cinch. "I planned to call Buddy's owners and suggest they retire the old fellow. Horse deserves to go out while he's still sound."

"Kind of screws up that call, doesn't it," Dino said.

"Kind of does." Mark passed his reins to Dino. "Get Carlos to look after Ghost. Doc is dropping by to scope Assets. I'll have him pull blood from Buddy too. Something's damn weird."

He leaned against the wall of his shedrow, watching as horses were walked, aisles raked and bandages hung to dry. The same daily activity, the same order. But somehow his stable didn't feel orderly; it felt off kilter.

A Ford truck pulled up. Doc Walker hopped out, dropped his tailgate and assembled his tray of needles. "Never saw so much security." He tilted his watch, frowning at the time. "Heard there's a high alert because of that Saudi sheikh who just arrived."

"Not Saudi. The sheikh's from Dubai," Mark said as he approached the tailgate.

"Whatever." Doc shrugged. "He's causing a stir. Apparently he has ten bodyguards. I saw some of them at the quarantine barn. Tough-looking men."

"Got two horses to scope and want some blood pulled from an old claimer," Mark said, disinterested in the sheikh and his level of security. He glanced up the road, aware the media were wandering around, digging for stories. A vet's truck parked in front of his shedrow could cause rumors and worse, scare owners.

"Whoa, that's a sight." Doc shielded his eyes as he studied Buddy's purple braids.

"Horse loves them though." Mark crossed his arms over his chest. "He had a bullet work today."

"I'm talking about the girl leading him," Doc said.

Mark's mouth tightened as he reluctantly studied Jessica. She was bathing Buddy, but there was more water on her than the horse. Enough to plaster her shirt to her chest and mold her pants to those endlessly long legs. When she reached up to rub Buddy's back, her sleek curves twisted, her breasts—

Damn. Already his jeans tightened. He pivoted, impatient with his reaction, but it was obvious he and Doc weren't the only ones distracted. Even Squeaky, his best hot walker, was sneaking peeks as he led Assets around the tow ring. The discipline of his shedrow was crumbling, and Mark didn't like it. Not one bit.

A white limo sped past and gravel ricocheted against Doc's truck in a staccato of noise that made Doc curse. Assets jerked sideways, twisting on his haunches. His lunge ripped the shank free from his preoccupied handler and the colt stilled, then wheeled and bolted down the road.

Fuck! Assets was loose. Mark leaped around the truck, knowing he'd be too late. But Jessica, with an athleticism that shocked him, dove sideways and grabbed the whipping line, snagging it with her fingers.

She hit the gravel, bouncing like a rag doll as the horse swerved to the left. The colt tilted his nose, fighting her weight, but she wrapped both hands around the lead, slowing him enough so Mark could intercept.

He grabbed Assets' halter and yanked the spooked animal in a circle. His breath escaped in a hiss of relief as he glanced back. "You okay?"

She raised her head, slowly. His gut twisted at the bloody abrasions streaking her face. Squeaky rushed up, apologetic and red-faced, and Mark shoved the lead in his hands and rushed to Jessica's side.

"Thank you," he said simply as he smoothed a tangle of hair off her forehead. "Can you move your arms?"

"I'm fine. Nothing hurts too much. Sorry I let go of Buddy." They both glanced at the barn, then looked at each other and grinned. Buddy lingered only ten feet away, gobbling grass by the vet's truck, not a bit perturbed by his sudden freedom.

"Let's see your hands." Mark helped her up and inspected her scrapes, trying not to wince at the mangled skin. He shot a quick glance at her face, surprised she was so tough. Not a hint of a tear.

"Ouch. That looks sore," Doc Walker said as he shuffled up. "Take some aspirin and soak in a warm tub of Epsom salts."

"A shower will have to do." She glanced ruefully over her shoulder at the tiny bathrooms, so bloodied, so brave—and she'd just saved his ass.

"You can clean up at my place," Mark heard himself say.

Mark drove Jessica to his house in Garden City, a twenty-minute drive from Belmont Park. She followed him down the hall, past his room crammed with exercise equipment and into the bathroom, squealing with delight when she spotted his Jacuzzi.

She can't be hurt too badly, he told himself. But when he reached into the cabinet for the Epsom salts, he brushed her shoulder. She winced, and his guilt deepened. It was unbelievable she had the grit to hang on to a thousand-pound colt, but she'd definitely earned his gratitude. And respect.

"Soak as long as you want," he said. "I'll bring you a beer."

Her lips curved in a teasing smile. "Maria said we weren't allowed to drink on the job."

"It's okay when you're employee of the week." He lingered by the door, still puzzled by her heroics. "That was really brave. Was it because Assets belongs to your grandfather?"

"Actually I didn't know what horse it was," she admitted. "I'm just delighted it earned me a bath."

She smiled, still utterly beautiful even after being bounced over gravel. The cuts probably weren't too deep, although her chin had clearly taken the brunt of the gravel. Some pebbles were embedded.

"Hold still." He stepped forward and cupped her face. Reached in his pocket and pulled out his jackknife.

Her eyes widened and she tried to jerk away, but he smiled and opened the tweezers. "I'll be gentle," he said, and carefully extracted the tiny pebbles.

She didn't squeak, didn't twitch. He stared down, still cupping her upturned face. She had beautiful brown eyes fringed with dark lashes and even devoid of makeup, her skin was velvety soft, lips slightly parted—

Shit. He dropped his hand. "Enjoy your bath." He quickly backed away and retreated to the kitchen.

When he returned with a chilled Corona, jets pounded along with the sound of muted singing. He paused. Had never had a woman in his Jacuzzi who he hadn't undressed first, and he wasn't at all sure of the etiquette. She was probably submerged in bubbles anyway. Images rifled through his head, and the thought of foam clinging to her dripping body made his knock much crisper than intended.

No answer.

He rapped again, inched the door open and thrust the beer around the corner. The singing stopped. Water sloshed. Warm drops splashed his fingers as she accepted the cold bottle.

"Thank you, boss," she called, pushing the door shut. "I'm really enjoying this. Sure hope another horse escapes tomorrow."

He returned to the den, smiling but slightly disappointed he hadn't caught a peek. He pulled out his phone, took a fortifying sip of beer and began his calls. This was the part of the job he liked least, but owners expected regular updates. Ironically, the cheapest horses usually had the most demanding owners while a few, such as Boone, didn't like to be bothered with any details. Of course, rich owners were hard to find and harder to keep.

Boone had a reputation for flipping trainers when he thought a horse wasn't performing well, but at least he didn't call every day with ridiculous suggestions. In fact, sometimes he didn't call for weeks. Mark tilted his beer and took another contemplative swallow. Boone might be immersed in some demanding business project, but it was odd the man hadn't showed more interest in

Jessica's progress. She certainly had a lot more backbone than Mark had expected.

Unease pricked him as he thought of Boone's naked granddaughter washing away the dirt and blood in his tub. Fortunately she hadn't been badly hurt, but he'd have to keep closer tabs on her. He hadn't realized mice had scared her out of the tack room and into Buddy's stall.

Good thing it was a horse she was sleeping with. Her grandfather definitely wouldn't approve of relations within the track community. Boone viewed backstretch workers as third-class citizens, definitely not good enough for a high-society heiress.

And Buddy. That horse surprised him almost as much as Jessica. The gelding was a nine-year-old who competed in the lowest claiming ranks. Hell, he hadn't won a race in two years, but something had injected him with renewed vigor.

Mark dragged a hand over his jaw. Women and horses. They fooled you every time.

He was finishing the last of his calls when Jessica padded down the hall. He twisted, relieved the scrapes on her face were superficial and she was restored to normal. Actually better than normal.

His breath thickened, and he lowered the phone from his ear. Forgot to check if she was limping. Forgot he was talking to Buddy's irritating owner. For that moment, he could only think of sex. Hard, hot sex with Jessica spread-eagled beneath him.

He didn't understand why he was so aroused. Yeah, she was gorgeous, but he'd had plenty of good-looking women. Maybe it was her hair—that glorious caramel color that reminded him of his first horse. She usually kept it in a ponytail, but now it tumbled over her shoulders, and errant tendrils corkscrewed around her face.

Or maybe it was the way her shirt scooped over those beautiful breasts. Or possibly it was because she'd been naked in his tub, and an image had been planted in his horny brain.

Didn't matter but as she paused in the hall outside his bedroom, for one wild, crazy, hopeful moment he prayed she'd make a right turn and climb into his bed. His mouth dried, his gaze hung on her lips. She stiffened.

"Let's go for dinner after Buddy's race." The voice on the phone tugged at him.

He pressed the phone back to his ear, unable to make up an excuse while his mind was so absorbed with sexual possibilities. "Dinner on Friday's good," he muttered, still eyeing Jessica. "Yeah, the track is absolutely safe. No foul play. The man drowned."

He flipped the phone shut, watching as Jessica flushed and retreated toward the front entrance. Couldn't drag his eyes off the way her hips moved—subtle, slinky, sexy. It would be stupid to bring her here again. Best to drive her back now, even though they had another full hour before feeding and he'd originally planned to buy her supper.

But Jesus, she was hot. She was gutsy. She was Boone's granddaughter.

He slapped the papers in his briefcase and jerked to his feet, resolving to finish his calls when his brain was working better. He'd already agreed to have dinner with Buddy's owners—a couple he usually avoided—and his fragile business couldn't afford any more mindless mistakes.

CHAPTER FIVE

The next morning, Jessica gingerly groomed Buddy, trying not to jolt her throbbing shoulder. She'd managed to clean his stall too, even though Mark had said someone else would do it. Her scrapes were also healing although compared to previous ski wrecks, her 'snag and drag,' as Maria dubbed it, had been relatively benign.

However, her status had skyrocketed, and other grooms and hot walkers now included her in their ribald teasing. If a little pain resulted in Mark's goodwill—and therefore the barn's acceptance—she was more than happy to be dragged behind the occasional runaway horse.

"Hey, kid. Will you teach me how to do those fancy braids?" Maria asked, watching as Jessica wrapped Buddy's legs. "By the way, who taught you to wrap?"

"Mark," Jessica said, standing back to admire her bandaging job. She'd chosen a royal purple today and was delighted with how the richness contrasted with Buddy's inky coat.

"Damn good job, considering last week you didn't know how to lead a horse. I think Buddy perks up around you. I hope some of his energy rubs off on Missy this afternoon. You coming over to watch her race?"

"Yes. Mark wants Dino to show me everything a groom does so I can help with Buddy in the paddock tomorrow."

A laugh bubbled behind them, and they both wheeled as a tiny blonde strutted down the aisle.

"Mark Russell around?" the lady asked a passing groom who jabbed a thumb over his shoulder.

Jessica forgot about her bandages and peered over the door. She'd never seen anyone so tiny yet so perfectly proportioned.

She also recognized an athlete when she saw one, and this lady exuded confidence and grace.

"Is that an exercise rider?" she whispered, eying the whip jutting from the blonde's back pocket.

"Jockey," Maria said. "Apprentice jock. Emma Rae MacDonald. Tacks one hundred and four pounds."

Jessica studied Emma Rae with open envy. The riders who galloped every morning were always cocky, but this lady was far more self-assured and looked like someone who knew exactly what she wanted.

"Good morning, Mark," Emma Rae called. "Saw the bullet your Buddy horse had yesterday. Wanted to remind you I still have my bug."

Mark gave an enigmatic smile. His arms were crossed, but he didn't walk away.

"What on earth is she talking about?" Jessica whispered, edging to the side of the stall so she could better hear the conversation.

"Emma Rae wants to ride Buddy because he had the fastest work yesterday," Maria said. "That's called a bullet. Apprentices get a five-pound weight allowance. That's a bug, and you'd understand why if you ever bothered to study a race program."

Jessica didn't understand why Maria was so irritated. Racetrack slang was confusing, and her brain was already stuffed with new terms. But when Mark nodded and he and Emma Rae headed down the aisle, smiling like conspirators, she felt rather irritated too.

"Mark's a sucker for a pretty face. He can't say no," Maria said. "Bet he gives her the ride."

"She sure is tiny." Jessica gave a mournful sigh and glanced down at her own size nine feet. If Mark preferred tiny, she had no hope, no hope at all.

Fifteen minutes later, Mark reappeared in front of Buddy's stall with the smiling jockey strutting at his side.

"Wow, what a nicely turned out horse." Emma Rae smiled at Jessica. "Are you his groom? You've done a fantastic job."

Jessica's chest swelled from a rare compliment, and she decided Emma Rae was undoubtedly an excellent jockey.

"Think your guy would like a girl on him?" Emma Rae added.

Jessica glanced at Mark then realized the jockey was talking about Buddy. Her cheeks flamed. "Where's his regular rider?" she asked, fumbling with Buddy's hay net.

"Out with a broken leg," Mark said. "Come to my office, Emma Rae. You too, Jessica, once you finish up."

She grabbed Buddy's late morning grain, diligently measured his twelve different herbs, vitamins and minerals, topped up his water bucket and raked the aisle. By the time she rushed to Mark's office, Emma Rae had gone and Mark jotted notations on a huge wall sheet.

"Just a sec," he said. She watched as he wrote an S by Buddy. She guessed G was for the horses that galloped, J for jogged, W for worked but the S by Buddy worried her.

"S isn't sick, Jessica," he said, studying her expression. "It just means he walked the shedrow."

"I knew that."

The smile he gave her was both amused and perceptive so she shut up. He knew when she was trying a little too hard, yet always seemed to combine the right amount of encouragement along with his ironclad rules. He made her want to work harder. It was strange Maria and some of the other women were intimidated by him. He would have made a great coach, although in a sense that's what he already was—a coach to horses and people.

"How are your hands today?" he asked.

She started to shrug off his question, but the idea of another hot bath in his luxurious Jacuzzi was rather appealing. "Really sore. Could do with some more soaking in Epsom salts."

"Lots of buckets around for that." He continued to insert dates and times on his training sheet. "I'm wondering if you're healthy enough to lead Buddy over for paddock work later."

She had no idea what paddock work was but certainly didn't want anyone else to lead Buddy. "Sure," she said. "I can wear gloves."

His approving nod more than compensated for the lack of a bath invite. He really had the most amazing smile, and she liked how his jaw softened as he scooped a huge hairball off his chair.

"Here." He shoved the gray pile of fur into her bewildered hands. "He's neutered, seven months old and already a good hunter. There's a bag of cat food in the feed room. He'll keep your mice away."

She yanked her gaze off Mark's mouth and glanced down. The kitten had a splash of white on his nose, dark stripes on his tail and snuggled into her arms as though completely confident of her care. The little guy probably didn't realize she knew nothing about cats, that she'd never had a pet of her own. Boarding schools, summer camps and later the ski circuit had made animals impossible.

She stared at the purring kitten—silent, terrified, ecstatic. "He's all mine? R-really?" Her voice quavered. "What's his name?"

"Whatever you want. He's your cat."

The kitten lifted his paw and placed it on her chest. A lump balled in her throat. Wow! This was definitely the nicest, most thoughtful present she'd ever received. Ever.

"Th-thank you." She tried to work out the proper words, but her emotions were too shaky, and her eyes itched—and damn, she was going to cry. She looked at Mark, saw his gentle smile and jerked her head back down. Cradling the precious bundle, she turned and fled before he spotted the telltale sheen of her tears.

Buddy pranced beside Jessica, ears pricked and elegant neck bowed. He was definitely the most beautiful horse on the track, but now he also looked the wildest. She'd put his halter over the race bridle, just as she'd been told, but he chomped at the bit. She even saw white flecks of saliva.

"This visit will help him be calmer tomorrow?" She glanced dubiously at Mark, who rode beside her on Ghost.

"Not calmer, just ready. Every horse is different. Buddy is a smart fellow, and he likes to see the paddock before his race. I school some horses so they can't anticipate when they're running. With Buddy, it's best if he knows. You're the groom," Mark added, "and Buddy trusts you. If you're going to lead him over for his race tomorrow, you need to know what he's like when he's revved. Think you can handle him?"

She nodded, somewhat reassured. Buddy looked rank, prancing and pushing at the bit, but he wasn't uncontrollable. He didn't drag her around like some of Maria's animals. Maybe that was why Mark hired so many big women, so they could better anchor excited horses.

They followed the rim of the oval, veering onto a walkway that looped past green grass and stately horse statues. Colorful trees already dropped leaves and the huge paddock was empty, its loneliness punctuated by rattling trash cans as workers prepared for the afternoon crowd.

"That's the saddling enclosure. Buddy's drawn the five hole." Mark pointed to a wall of open stalls. "Watch the paddock procedure this afternoon so you'll know what to do tomorrow."

"Will you be around today?" she asked, instantly regretting the question, afraid she sounded like an infatuated teenager. "In case I have questions," she added quickly.

"I've got two horses running so I'll be busy with owners. But Dino will be here."

"My God, Russell!" A man's harsh voice erupted behind them, shattering the tranquility. "You're sure scraping the barrel running that nag."

Mark's smile flattened, and he turned to face the sneering man. Jessica recognized the golf cart man but not his hostility. He'd been very nice the other day when she'd borrowed the lead line—*aw, crap.* She averted her head, remembering she'd forgotten to return it.

"This horse can beat anything you have," Mark said, his voice curiously flat, his lips scarcely moving.

The man blew out a derisive snort, and Jessica felt his gaze settle on the back of her neck.

"Times must be tough when your groom has to beg for my equipment." His laugh was ugly.

Jessica edged around Buddy who had relaxed and now soaked up the autumn sun, resting a hind foot and happily oblivious to the slurs.

"Jessica?" Mark's voice had a dangerous edge. "Did you borrow anything from this man?"

"Just the leadie thing." She peeked around Buddy's shoulder. "I planned to return it this afternoon."

Mark leaned across Ghost's neck, whipped the shank off Buddy and tossed it over the rail. "Take this one," he snapped.

"I see you're scraping the barrel for grooms too," the man said as he grabbed the shank. "Making the same mistakes your father did. And obviously for the same reasons." He snickered and walked away, but the nasty sound left a stain over the paddock.

Jessica scraped her toe in the dirt, not daring to look up. She didn't understand the comment about Mark's father, but it was true she wasn't much of a groom. Sure, she was getting better, but it was a slow process.

"Guess I'll just walk Buddy around," she said miserably, hating that she'd embarrassed Mark in front of that sour old man. "Maybe lead him in that little room below the number four."

"It's called a slot, or hole, or stall," Mark said. "The leadie thing is called a shank or a lead. And I'm sorry about what happened. His problem is with me. I hate it when he takes it out on my people."

Relief jerked her head up. Mark was scowling at the man's back but he wasn't mad—at least not with her. Warmth spread through her chest. She squared her shoulders; the idea of being one of Mark's people, a member of his team, instilled her with a sense of belonging.

"I want to beat that asshole tomorrow," Mark said. "Maybe if Buddy's feeling really, really good..." But his expression turned rueful as he looked at the horse. Buddy seemed to be snoozing now. Both eyelids drooped, and his slack bottom lip hung like a Clydesdale's.

Jessica jigged the bridle, trying to prod Buddy awake. "Maybe he's dreaming of his race strategy," she said hopefully.

"Generally the jockey tells the horse what to do," Mark said.

"Of course," she said quickly. "I know that." But his understanding wink made her giggle and even Buddy jerked awake, throwing his head up and looking around as though wondering what he'd missed.

They both laughed then, so spontaneously the white-haired man stopped and turned, raking them both with his malevolent glare.

CHAPTER SIX

Maria fiddled with Missy's bridle, wiping imaginary specks of dirt and adjusting and re-adjusting each buckle. Jessica had never seen her friend so frazzled.

"Wait until Buddy races tomorrow," Maria said, gnawing at her lower lip. "You'll understand then. I just pray I can lead Missy back after her race."

Jessica swelled with indignation. "I'm sure Mark will let you lead her back. Why wouldn't he? You're her groom."

"Oh, kid. You're so green, it cuts me up. It really does." But Maria didn't say anything more, just wiped her shiny brow and continued to recheck every stitch of tack.

The barn speakers crackled, warning runners of the next race.

"Okay, Maria," Dino called. "Take the filly to the assembly barn. Mark will meet you in the paddock." He sighed. "Jessica, put down the killer kitten and come with me."

Jessica gave Kato one last pat and shut him in her tack room. The cat had a naughty habit of attacking humans, but Mark was a powerful protector, and no one dared complain about his gift. And Mark was right. Kato's presence cleared her room of mice.

She shoved *The Racing Form* in her hip pocket and rushed after Dino. She'd spent hours poring over the information in *The Form*, asking questions until all but the most tolerant had lost patience. But now she understood the glut of information, the cryptic abbreviations, and felt betting would be tremendous fun.

They followed the line of horses being led over by their grooms. The animals radiated vitality, prancing and eager to strut their stuff, but the handlers looked apprehensive. Several carried buckets, and almost all of them had rags stuck in their back pocket for last-minute nose wipes.

"Some of the grooms look worried," she said.

Dino shrugged and adjusted his cowboy hat. "This is a claiming race. Grooms develop the closest bond, and they know there's a chance they won't lead their horse home. Any trainer can claim them."

Jessica jerked to a stop. "So that's what Maria meant. That's horrible! Why do they even have races like that?"

"It's an easy way to keep races fair. If a horse wins at that level, trainers risk losing them. Or else they can choose to move them up in class and compete against better horses." Dino glanced at her, his eyes narrowing. "You can't fall in love at the track, Jessica."

"I know. Horses are business. Mark says that too." But her voice wobbled. "What kind of race does Buddy run in?"

"Claiming. But no worries. He hasn't won in a while, and he's nine years old. There are much better claims in his race. Mark is pushing the owners to retire him."

She blew out a breath, her concern about Buddy easing as they approached the busy paddock, so different from the serene spot she'd visited earlier that morning. Now the air buzzed. A smiling lady with high cheekbones and ruby lipstick conducted an interview, and a man rushed past with a huge camera perched on his shoulder. Spectators clumped around the rail as horses gathered in the walking ring for the first race.

The excitement made her own breath quicken and she pressed closer, eager to see the runners. She'd already chosen a consistent bay as the likely winner, but doubt filled her when she spotted the horse. He was too nervous, neck frothy with sweat, and his handler seemed unnecessarily rough. She skimmed her fingers along the program and found her second pick, number four. That horse was a beautiful chestnut with a wide forehead and a businesslike attitude.

"How do you bet?" she asked Dino, deciding to put her paltry money on number four, the horse with the good attitude.

"You're supposed to be watching what the grooms do so you can look after Buddy tomorrow."

"I already know," she said. "Lead him over from the barn, walk him around until the valet brings the saddle and then hold him for Mark to saddle. Keep him calm, and make sure he knows he's special."

Dino chuckled. "I've never heard it simplified quite like that, but I suppose you're right. Who you betting?"

"The four horse."

Dino's smile flattened as he glanced at his program. "Not a bad choice, but I can't back that sonofabitch." The distaste in his normally carefree voice was startling.

Jessica flipped open *The Racing Form* and noted the horse's connections: Paul G. Radcliff was listed as the trainer. She glanced across the rail, studying the knot of people gathered around the four horse. "Is Radcliff the older guy in the nice Hugo Boss suit?" she asked, unable to hide her own aversion.

"Don't know if his suit is all that nice, but yeah, he's the bossy prick with the white hair."

"I met him this morning when I was with Mark and Buddy." She didn't want to admit she'd borrowed a lead shank from the man. "I don't think Mark likes him much either," she added, hoping Dino would keep talking.

"He definitely doesn't," Dino said. "We all raced in Texas when Mark's dad was alive. Charlie liked the women. Not entirely his fault—he couldn't keep them away with a stick. But Radcliff's wife was one of Charlie's buckle bunnies, and Radcliff retaliated by claiming Charlie's horses.

"Mark hated seeing his father with all the women," Dino added, shaking his head. "Left Texas when his mom died. Couldn't escape Radcliff though. That man has stables all over the country. Unfortunately, he also holds a grudge."

Jessica sighed, regretting how her ignorance had placed Mark in a tough position. At the time, it hadn't seemed such a big deal to borrow the lead shank. If only she'd known. If only she'd returned it. Yet Mark had been annoyed at Radcliff; he hadn't even given her a lecture. No wonder his people were so loyal.

She sighed and turned away, not wanting to brood about Radcliff any longer. She was learning. She'd do better. A bearded man slouched in the corner and stared at her with a face so expressionless, so devoid of emotion it made her skin crawl. He jerked his gaze away, but the boy beside him kept staring until the man grabbed the kid's shoulder.

The bearded guy was a stranger, but she definitely remembered the child from last week's yard sale. Same black T-shirt and dirty jeans, same pinched expression. He'd stood at the end of the tables and stared at Lefty's bike. Her bike now.

"Who is that guy?" she asked.

The man yanked the boy's shoulder, and they edged back into the flowing crowd.

"Can't see," Dino said, following her stare. "Maybe one of the Mexican Mafia. There's a large Latin American group on the backside."

"But they don't do anything really bad, do they?" She rubbed her arms, inexplicably chilled.

Dino chuckled, his attention back on the horses. "They don't just write graffiti. Stay away from them, and you'll be fine. Mark's barn is known to be clean. No one should bother you."

"Riders up!" a thick-jowled man in a red jacket yelled, and trainers legged the jockeys into their saddles.

"If you're going to bet, do it now," Dino said as the horses filed under the tunnel to the track. "I'm meeting Mark by the finish line."

"I'm not betting this race." She turned away from the rail and the spot where she'd last seen the spooky man. No way was she putting her precious money on Radcliff's horse. Besides, she hadn't seen Mark for hours, and the prospect of watching the race with him was way more appealing than waiting in a long betting line. "I thought Mark was hanging out with owners today?" she asked.

"He is, but he's free the first race and wants to see how the horses handle the track. The inside seems cuppy. Not good, because Maria's filly runs best on the rail. Racing is tough," Dino added. "Even if you're a top trainer like Mark, with a twenty percent win rate, it still means you lose eighty percent of your races. But owners and bettors expect a win every time you send a horse to the gate. Come on."

He weaved through the throng with Jessica sticking to his heels. She spotted Mark by the finish line, and her steps slowed as her throat turned dry. He looked gorgeous, dressed in a sports jacket and tie, strikingly handsome even in the crowd. She smoothed her own shirt, feeling at a disadvantage, although earlier today she'd considered clean jeans and loose hair the ultimate fashion statement.

Mark barely looked at her. "How's Maria and the filly?" he asked, his gaze pinned on the parading horses.

"Fine." Both Dino and Jessica spoke at the same time, their voices rushed.

Mark wheeled, eyes narrowing. "Okay, what do I need to know?"

Jessica pretended an interest in her program; Dino began an animated conversation with the man on his right. Mark's warm fingers covered her hand, forcing her to look up. "What's wrong with Missy?" he asked.

He looked so worried, she impulsively squeezed his hand. "The horse is fine," she said. "But Maria wanted to learn to braid and we got a little carried away, matching colors with the owners' pretty silks. Dino was annoyed when he saw the braids, but it was too late to take them out."

Mark groaned, but it seemed more in resignation than anger. At least, she hoped. His warm hand lingered over hers, and the resultant tingle made her brain stall. He scanned a box in the clubhouse where two ladies with pink scarves gave exuberant waves.

"Their colors are pink, purple and white," Mark said, waving back. "Does that mean...?"

Jessica nodded, somewhat abashed. The braids had looked a little bright, even to her, and Mark preferred woodsy colors. However, Maria had been so excited.

Luckily Mark released her hand so her head didn't feel quite so wooly, although her fingers still tingled and her chest was kicking like it did before a ski race.

"I can't believe Maria went along with you," Mark said. "The owners will love it though. Hell, maybe the filly will too." He dragged a hand through his hair and looked at the track. "Did you bet anything?"

"No. But I think the four horse will win."

"Radcliff's horse? Christ, I hope not," he said as the horses entered the gate.

The crowd hushed. Someone jostled her, trying to squeeze into the prime spot by the rail, but Mark's arm quickly circled her hip, defending their space. He smelled so good, an enticing mix of spice and leather. She fought a crazy impulse to snuggle into his chest.

"They're in," he said. He'd lowered his arm, but his warm breath feathered her hair. "The one horse has early speed. If she doesn't get the lead, it means the rail is slow."

Good grief. She was intensely attracted to this man, yet he was immune to her. She stood silently beside him while he rattled on, explaining stuff about fractions, surface and the track bias.

"They're off!" the announcer yelled. The crowd roared as the horses exploded from the gate, but she was slightly numb. How could he ignore her? Men never ignored her. She'd even freed her ponytail. She automatically cheered with the crowd as the horses galloped down the backstretch and her hip grazed his thigh. He immediately eased away.

She pretended to watch the race but was too conscious of Mark's hard body only inches away. He hadn't moved *really* far away though, and it seemed as though his heat radiated like a wave. Curious, she edged closer, deliberately brushing his leg. When the horses rounded the turn, she leaned sideways to graze her breast over his forearm. She heard the sharp intake of his breath, but he didn't move again. In fact, his big body turned very still. *Ah, ha.* Now he wasn't ignoring her.

The crowd cheered at something the horses were doing, and she added another jump and wiggle. Nothing too obvious—

His arms jerked out, trapping her wrists. Her heart slammed against her ribs. He smelled like pure male now, hot, aroused and angry. "I don't play games, Jessica," he said.

She stilled, trying to decide if she should answer or pretend she didn't know what the hell he was talking about. The horses swept around the track, but she was oblivious to the jumbled mass of horses, the cheering spectators. Was conscious only of the virile body pinning her against the rail.

A charging chestnut passed Radcliff's four horse in deep stretch to win the race by a length.

"You lose," Mark said. He dropped his arms and left her alone at the rail.

Mark waited near slot six as the horses for the second race were led into the saddling enclosure. He didn't see Maria or My Silent Miss but when the crowd chuckled, he guessed they'd arrived.

Flexing his knuckles, he turned, reluctant to look. Stared down the walkway. Goddammit.

Nothing was silent about Missy today. Gaudy braids of pink and purple highlighted the filly's mane and tail. She wasn't usually an aggressive horse, but now her head was bent to her chest, pulling at the bit as she pranced beside Maria.

He kept his face impassive and prayed Radcliff wasn't around to witness this debacle.

"Oh my, she's beautiful! Thank you for the wonderful turnout."

A hand tugged at his sleeve, and he looked into the glowing face of one of Missy's two owners. The New Jersey ladies made the drive to Belmont every time their horse ran and always appreciated Missy's efforts, no matter where she finished. Sometimes they were almost too appreciative. Both ladies were single, eager to enjoy life. When they went for dinner, he was careful never to go alone.

"You like the braids?" He couldn't keep the disbelief from his voice.

"Love them. So do the fans. Look at the little girl in the flowered shirt taking pictures. It makes the day extra special."

Mark stopped fisting his hands. A couple of trainers pointed and shook their heads but hell, if the owners liked it, and Jessica and Maria had fun doing it, he wasn't inclined to make them stop. He even smiled as he signaled Maria to lead the filly in for saddling.

"What do you think of her turnout?" Maria asked with shy pride.

"Not my favorite colors, but the owners like it." He softened his words with another smile. Maria was one of his best grooms but for some reason was shy around him. Quite the opposite of Jessica who didn't give a rat's ass about anyone and certainly wasn't shy. She must have felt his reaction when she'd rubbed against him, reducing him to a horny asshole in seconds. He'd hated it.

He saddled Missy, automatically following the pre-race routine, but his thoughts swerved back to Jessica. She was smart, fun, beautiful and brave. Also an owner's granddaughter. He wasn't going there. Didn't need that kind of trouble.

He tightened the girth too abruptly. The filly leaped forward, knocking him with her shoulder. Maria expertly brought her under control and backed her up.

Jessica and Dino watched from the public side of the enclosure and he shot them a dark glower simply for being there. Dino looked puzzled, but Jessica flashed a saucy smile that made his thoughts careen.

Man, she was screwing up his day. He wasn't ready for this race, didn't know what his jockey instructions would be—stay on the rail, or go wide. He hadn't been able to analyze the race or the way the ground played, not with her hot body rubbing against him. Strange, because he usually had plenty of control, didn't think of sex at the track. Didn't want to be like his father—

"Should I lead her around now, boss?" Maria stared, her forehead creased in confusion.

Mark nodded and searched for his rider as the jockeys filed into the paddock.

Steve, a seasoned veteran, looked disconcerted when he saw the pink braids but quickly rallied. "Usually I'm prettier than the horse," he said with a grin, twirling his stick in the air. He shook hands with the owners and turned to Mark.

"You rode the first race," Mark said. "What's the rail like?"

"Sticky. Best to go wide if the filly will take me."

"Do it. She's got some air and should be running at the end. Good luck."

At the call for 'riders up' he legged Steve into the saddle. Maria led the filly into the tunnel. And that was it. Up to Missy and Steve now.

He smiled at his beaming owners, enjoying their excitement. Hopefully Missy would run well. She was moody and could throw a clunker but when she was on her game, she was brave enough. One just never knew what Missy would do. It was much easier to train colts and geldings. Fillies, like women, were forever frustrating.

He escorted the owners up the steps to his box, where they had a perfect view of the finish line. Good view of his staff too. Jessica's hair was blowing and her blond streaks shone. She gestured with her hands when she talked. Something she said made Dino laugh. Mark wondered what it was—she always made him laugh too. He jerked his head away.

"Is Maria ever going to join us?" the younger of the two owners asked.

"She likes to watch from the rail," he said, glancing back to where Maria stood beside Dino and Jessica. A skinny boy in a black T-shirt squeezed in beside Jessica, then abruptly turned and bolted. Jessica wheeled with indignation.

Mark watched from his vantage point as the kid scooted through the crowd and joined a man at the edge of the grandstand—a stranger, possibly of Middle East descent. At least the kid wasn't hooked up with Manuel who was ostentatiously a trainer but in reality controlled the drug traffic that too often derailed the lives of many workers.

If the kid were a pickpocket, he wouldn't have filched much from Jessica. Just that morning she'd triumphantly delivered him a list of ten horses and their morning temperatures. He'd felt sick realizing she'd been handling rambunctious colts and snapped at her when she'd asked for a raise. But, Christ, he didn't want her to get hurt. It was a mystery why Boone's granddaughter was so broke—why she was working so hard—but her presence in his shedrow definitely added spice. Not that he wanted spice.

No fucking way.

He tightened his mouth and turned his attention to Missy, guiltily aware he hadn't watched her warm-up. At least the owners were unaware of his distraction. Their binoculars were fixed on the horses circling behind the gate. Missy usually loaded well, but Mark blew out a relieved sigh when she walked in and the gate crew slammed the door shut.

The crowd hushed. The horses were loaded.

"They're off!" the announcer yelled as jets of color burst across the track.

The filly broke hard and was near the front, but her speed was limited and three horses stormed past. She galloped fourth down the backstretch, a distinctive splash of pink and purple, with the jockey's silks matching her braids.

They covered the first quarter in just over twenty-three seconds. She seemed to be running easy, but coming into the turn a blue-blinkered horse loomed on her outside. The front runner weakened, and the crowd groaned as two horses burst past the favorite.

"Not yet, Steve," Mark muttered, but the filly surged forward, propelled by the onslaught of horses. At the top of the stretch, she'd already seized the lead.

Mark's two owners jumped up and down, ecstatic to see their horse in front. They pumped his arm, spilling their drinks, screaming encouragement. Mark muzzled his concern—it was way too early.

The filly charged down the stretch, three lengths in front, her colors vivid against the dirt. Mark's fists clenched, hoping she'd hang on for the win but knowing the fractions were too fast, the stretch too long.

The horse on the sticky rail floundered and was no longer a threat, but a small gray closed like a missile on the outside. Steve smacked Missy twice but the filly was exhausted. The gray swept by, full of run. Missy staggered across the line in a photo for second with a hard-charging bay.

"What a fun race!" The owner clinging to his arm squealed. "I think she came second. What do you think, Mark?"

"I think the bay got it," he said watching the tote board with a sinking sensation. "Are you ladies dropping by the barn?"

"Definitely, and we'd like to take you and Maria out for dinner. A win is marvelous, but a second is good too."

"How about a third?" he asked wryly as numbers flashed across the tote board. What shitty luck. The filly had lost second by a nose. "I want to talk to the jockey," he added. "Be right back."

He joined the knot of trainers and grooms waiting on the track and studied Missy as the jockey trotted her back. This was always his most anxious moment, waiting to see if his horse returned from the race healthy.

"Sorry, Mark. I couldn't hold her once she saw daylight," Steve said, his voice uneven as he tried to regain his breath. "I'd sure like to ride her again though."

"Sure," he replied, helping Maria control the dancing filly. "We'll work her in company. Teach her to relax a little more."

Steve nodded, his teeth white through his dirty face. He vaulted off, unbuckled the saddle and headed to the scales.

"I'll need you tonight, Maria," Mark warned, giving the gutsy filly a pat. "The owners want to have a quick dinner. Nothing to worry about, real casual."

Her glum nod made him smile. She hated spending time with owners, avoiding them like a plague.

Mark glanced at Dino and Jessica who lingered at the rail.

"It was a whisker for second," Dino said mournfully. "Eight thousand bucks down the toilet. Guess it's pizza again tonight."

Jessica just grinned. She was a quick learner but there was much she didn't know. Probably thought they raced for fun. Her work stint was a lark, something to appease her grandfather. But to the stable, placings were critical. Worker bonuses were calculated on percentage of the purse, and everyone benefited. Or not.

He'd known the filly was in tough, but it had been so close. Disappointment churned in his gut: for Maria, for the dedicated owners, for all his employees. Tomorrow he only had two horses running, and one was Buddy—Buddy, who hadn't managed to win in two years. It could be a lean week and Breeders' Cup, with its lucrative purses was still a month away.

Curbing his frustration, he studied Jessica's face. At least she'd enjoyed seeing Missy run; her skin still glowed from an adrenaline high and her vitality was contagious. Suddenly, he didn't feel quite so disappointed.

"Our newbie hit the trifecta," Dino said. "She might not know much about horses, but she sure knows how to bet."

A trifecta! So that explained her excitement. Mark twisted, checking the board. Unbelievable. Somehow she'd picked the first three finishers in the exact order. And the gray had been a longshot so the payout was substantial. "Not bad," he said. "One hundred and sixty-four bucks on a two-dollar bet."

Dino chuckled. "She bet twenty. Raked in sixteen hundred bucks tonight."

"Good God!" Mark shook his head in disgust. "You made more money than me. Maybe now you can quit."

"Sorry to disappoint you, boss," Jessica said. "I'm not quitting."

He hid his spurt of relief. "Congratulations then. Lucky betting."

"It wasn't luck," she said. "I stayed up all night studying *The Form*. But at least now I can replace my stolen phone."

"I saw a kid running away," Mark said. "Did he swipe your cell?"

She gave a rueful nod. "I was watching Missy, barely felt anything. Just a tug—and poof, it was gone."

"He's young. Probably works with someone," Mark said. "I'll have a talk with Manuel. See what he knows. We can't have our top handicapper being hassled."

The smile she shot him was so grateful, he didn't add that her phone was likely long gone. Manuel didn't stoop to petty theft. And Mark hadn't recognized the bearded man. No doubt it had been lifted by an outsider, a random incident that was irritating but definitely not life-threatening.

CHAPTER SEVEN

Money bulged in Jessica's pocket as she crouched to check Buddy's legs. She stuffed the precious wad deeper, reassured by its presence. Just thinking about working for her grandfather almost made her sick. She'd hide the winnings in her coffee can later but right now, she wanted to savor the knowledge she'd earned it—on her own—and no doubt could do it again.

Numbers had always been a cinch. Now that she knew how to analyze *The Racing Form*, she was keen to bet again. Maybe she'd be able to raise enough to bankroll her own dog business. She gave a little fist pump, delighted she wouldn't have to borrow money from Gramps. Buddy stopped chewing for a moment and eyed her curiously.

She gave his neck a reassuring pat, thinking of Mark's statement that she'd been lucky. Sure, a bit of luck was involved, but she'd studied the horses' forms. It had been simple to narrow the race down to three or four contenders. A quick look in the paddock trimmed it further. And if Mark had a horse entered, it was bound to run in the top three—she'd checked all the trainers' stats, and Mark had one of the highest win percentages. No wonder her grandfather had entrusted him with Assets.

Voices rocked the barn. She stepped from the stall, frowning. Mark liked it library quiet; no one was supposed to ever yell or disturb the horses. Tonight though, two ladies with designer leather purses, Italian shoes and pink scarves giggled in the aisle as they followed Mark and Maria.

Must be the two owners who'd waved from the box. Maria said they always visited Missy after a race, bringing peppermints and insisting on taking the filly's connections for dinner. Apparently they enjoyed the day and, win or lose, relished every moment of the experience.

Jessica grabbed a rake, her mind scrambling as she tidied the already-spotless aisle. Maybe they'd invite her to tag along. It was always unbearably lonely in the evenings—she often raked five or six times just for something to do—and the thought of another meal of canned beans made her stomach churn.

"Our horse looked wonderful today, Maria. You braided her beautifully," the taller lady said.

Both Mark and Maria looked at Jessica.

"She helped with the braids." Maria shuffled uncomfortably and pointed at Jessica. "Showed me how to do it."

"It was no problem." Jessica paused and leaned on the rake. "Took a couple hours, but the extra time was worth it." However, she automatically rubbed her shoulder because the braiding had left a slight ache in her arm.

"Oh, dear. Missy didn't hurt you, did she?" The shorter owner stepped closer, studying the abrasions on Jessica's face.

"Oh, no. That wasn't Missy," Jessica said quickly, seeing the concern in the nice lady's eyes. "She's a very sweet horse."

"Well, I hope you join us for dinner. We really love the braids. It was such a nice touch."

Mark raised a sardonic eyebrow, but Jessica ignored him. Missy had looked beautiful and her owners liked it. Besides, Jessica really needed to be with people tonight. Mark didn't understand what it was like, isolated in the barn, alone with the horses. He always had people tagging after him, hanging on his every word, clamoring for his attention.

"I'd love to come." She quickly hung up the rake, hoping Mark didn't mind.

"Maybe Jessica should take us for dinner," he said softly. "She made all the money today."

She shot him a quick look of reproach. He seemed to think she was rich. Had yelled at her when she'd presented a sheet with ten horses' temperatures and asked if there were any more jobs she could do. Sometimes she didn't understand him at all. But at least he was letting her come.

"I just have to grab a sweater from my room," she said, gesturing over her shoulder, afraid they might leave without her.

"You actually sleep in there?" The ladies stared past her at the dark room, their revulsion almost comical. The tall one rallied quickest and turned to Jessica. "That is so sweet. Sleeping here with the horses, keeping our Missy safe. Mark is lucky to have an experienced horseperson like you."

Jessica glanced at Mark, wondering if he would announce she was totally inexperienced and, in fact, was only allowed to handle Buddy. However, his expression remained inscrutable although the corner of his mouth twitched.

Mark had made reservations at an Italian restaurant and bar across the street, and Jessica spotted many familiar faces when she stepped into the savory-smelling room. Clearly it was a track hangout with the requisite horse equipment and framed pictures decorating the walls. She detoured to the bathroom, lingering over the spotless washbasin, the endless supply of warm water and the sweet-smelling soap.

When she emerged, Dino leaned over a stool at the end of the bar.

"Mark said you're buying," he said with a grin, "and that I should drink as much as I want." His flushed face and the way he squeezed the smiling blonde beside him suggested he was diligently following Mark's advice.

"He's joking," Jessica said. "And you already owe me. Remember our bet on my very first day?"

"Yeah. I still can't believe he hired you." Dino shook his head. "You're not even flatulent."

Jessica stared in confusion, then edged away. She liked Dino—everyone did—but she'd learned long ago it was impossible to understand a drunk. She brushed past the giggling blonde, who seemed totally entranced by every word that came out of Dino's mouth, then rushed to Mark's table before he announced to the entire room that drinks were on her. Paying for the pizza tonight wouldn't be a problem. She'd made a lot of money betting and having company tonight was totally worth it, but she had a business to start. She couldn't afford to pay for everyone's liquor.

Maria, Mark and the two owners were already seated at a corner table.

"So nice of you to bring us here, Mark," the shorter lady was saying, glancing around at the horse pictures. "We feel like part of the racing community now."

"We definitely have the most handsome trainer," the tall one added, playfully squeezing his arm. "One we want to get to know much better."

Mark nodded but his smile was tight, and he looked at Jessica with obvious relief. "Ah, there you are. Where's Dino? Thought he was joining us."

"Thanks to your directive, he's guzzling his 'free' drinks at the bar, along with a little friend," Jessica said. "So you have us ladies all to yourself."

"Just the way I like it." But there was an edge to his voice, and she guessed the affable Dino usually served as Mark's buffer. Maria would certainly provide no help. She'd buried her head in the pizza menu, studying it with a concentration more appropriate to a five-star restaurant.

Mark stiffened every time the tall lady, Hilda, touched his arm, and Jessica's empathy surged. It was an awkward position. He had to please his owners but wasn't the type to flirt and definitely wasn't the type to enjoy trite conversation. Yet he'd always been kind, always fair, despite that moment of discomfort by the rail. She could certainly help him out tonight.

She leaned forward with a bright smile, distracting the lady hanging on Mark's arm. "Is that gorgeous scarf a Hermes? I love the color. It totally matches your silks."

It was a cinch to redirect the conversation and soon Mark's big shoulders relaxed, and even Maria lowered the menu and smiled shyly. The two ladies were delightful, and Jessica discreetly swiped her eyes when she learned they donated all Missy's race profits to the Cancer Society.

By the second bottle of wine, they confided they lived together as a couple. After that announcement Mark looked far more comfortable when they hugged his arm. At one point he even held Hilda's hand, comforting her when she spoke of her ex-husband and how he had fled following her breast cancer diagnosis.

"I'll braid Missy pink every race," Maria promised as the owners prepared to leave. Jessica scooped up the bill before Hilda could take it, but Mark overrode them all.

"I'll look after it," he said, extracting it from her hand. "Thanks, Jessica." He gave her shoulder a grateful squeeze before turning and calling Dino to the table.

"I'm driving Hilda and Dorothy to their hotel," she heard him say. "Don't let Jessica and Maria walk back to the track alone."

"I won't," Dino said, but he looked disappointed and shot a rueful glance at the bar.

"We're fine. Maria and I can walk home together," Jessica said as Mark headed toward the exit. Her shoulder still tingled from his touch, and she was absurdly disappointed when the door closed behind him. She wished he wasn't leaving yet; all the vitality seemed to seep from the room. She jerked her head away, afraid Dino and Maria might notice her growing interest in their boss.

"No, I'll walk you home." Dino sighed and shoved his hands in his pockets. "Even though I planned to invite that blonde with the nice laugh over to my apartment for a quick drink."

Maria snorted. "Some quick OTS, more like it."

"OTS?" Jessica frowned. She thought she knew all the racetrack abbreviations but couldn't remember ever hearing that one.

"Off-track sex," Maria said. "The only kind Mark allows. But since he told Dino to take us home, he'll have to postpone his party plans. Tough luck, Dino."

"Damn Mark's puritan rules anyway," Dino said with a good-natured wave to the girl propped on the stool. He linked his arms around Jessica and Maria. "No problem. I'll just switch to plan B."

"But it's after hours," Jessica said, feeling a little sorry for the blonde left at the bar who, despite her laugh, now looked quite forlorn. "Surely Mark can't tell you what to do?"

"Surely he can," Dino said. "He always worries about his employees. Which means we're heading back to the shedrow where there's no drugs, no alcohol and, unfortunately for you," he paused to give them both a quick squeeze, "no sex."

"But we don't want sex," Maria said, so loudly the people at the next table cranked their heads and stared. "Besides, Pedro just came so I'm staying." She pushed Dino's arm away and headed toward a smiling man in a red shirt.

"Let's go, Jessica," Dino said. "Maria and Pedro are practically married, so you're stuck with me. If you behave, I might let you cop a feel when we cross the infield."

She rolled her eyes, but it was impossible not to laugh at his totally irreverent grin, and they were both smiling when they left the restaurant.

A silver dollar moon lit the night. Still, Dino stumbled twice once they left the smooth walkway and cut across the track.

"Squeeze through the hedge," he said. "Then we can cross the infield. They know we use this shortcut. If this was Texas, they'd leave some lights on for us."

He was very drunk, Jessica realized. Probably wouldn't notice if she steered the conversation around to Mark, who was more interesting than any more ramblings about the state of Texas.

"So you left Texas and moved up here. How long have you worked for Mark?" she asked, ducking under the inner rail and stepping onto the turf course.

"We were both trainers in Texas. Mark was successful. I wasn't. My wife couldn't handle the hours. Up at four, asleep by eight, no parties, no vacation. Always about the horses. She hated the life. Hated the unreliable paycheck too." He hiccupped. "When your horses don't win, you don't eat and owners drop you for the next hot trainer. She took our ranch and I got a horse...and my roping saddle." He stopped so abruptly she bumped into his back. "Oh, man, what a lady."

"What lady?" She peered past him, straining to see through the gloom. Dino had more lady friends than any man she knew, but she'd never heard such admiration in his voice.

"Ruffian."

Of course. A horse. Jessica filled her lonely nights reading Mark's supply of racing magazines, and now knew all the illustrious Thoroughbreds. She edged up to stare at the headstone encircled with horseshoe-shaped shrubbery. "Is that the grave of the famous filly?" she asked. "The horse that never lost?"

"Yup. The only Thoroughbred champion buried at Belmont Park. She has her nose pointing to the finish line." Dino gestured to the left. "Broke down over there. Racing can be such a fucking heartache."

His voice was rough with emotion, and Jessica patted him gently on the arm. According to rumor, Dino had been a dedicated husband and she suspected he was thinking of his ex-wife just as much as Ruffian. "Smells like they've been doing some recent digging too," she said, trying to distract him. "Or using fertilizer."

"I don't smell anything. Come on. Watch out for the lake."

Jessica glanced at the fresh earth around the flowerbed then straggled after him. "So once you…left your ranch, you became a hotshot trainer."

"No, Mark came to Texas, cleaned me up and dragged me here. *Then* I became a hotshot assistant trainer." Dino's usual flippant tone had turned serious, and she peered through the gloom, trying to see his face. "He saved my ass," Dino added. "If it wasn't for his damn hiring policies, I'd probably never go back to Texas."

Jessica stiffened. She didn't think Dino resented her presence; he was nice to everyone. All the staff grinned when he walked into the shedrow, especially the girls. When Mark entered, they leaped to attention. "You hate that he hired me?" she asked in a small voice. "I guess you know who my grandfather is."

"Aw, Jessica, I'm glad he hired you. I love all women, every age, shape and size." Dino stumbled then laughed at his clumsiness, sounding more like his typical carefree self. "But Mark does skew to big staff."

"Why is that?" she asked. "At first I thought it was to better control the horses, but there are lots of little grooms in the other barns." Pretty little grooms too, she thought, especially that gorgeous Trish who paraded past Mark's shedrow every morning, tossing her hair and wiggling her butt. "So why is that?" she repeated, straining to see Dino's face.

"We like big women. Charlie's Angels, don't you see," he said. "Just a minute. Gotta piss."

She blew out a resigned breath, waiting as he turned and noisily relieved himself in the dark. He was definitely drunk—and the more he talked, the less sense he made. To her right, lights twinkled, marking the barn area. Fortunately they were almost there.

Dino stumbled from the gloom, adjusting his belt. "Charlie's wife was the first one to feed me dinosaur chicken," he said as though the conversation had never stalled. "Mark gave me my nickname. Everyone's called me Dino since I was eight, even Charlie."

"Charlie was Mark's dad?"

"Yup. Hired me to muck stalls." Dino's head dipped as he struggled with his buckle. "All the girls wanted to work for Charlie, and he couldn't refuse any of them. They weren't the best with horses, but his office saw lots of action. Hard on Mark though to know how his dad screwed." His voice turned hopeful as he swept a clumsy hand over her hip. "Mark doesn't mind what goes on out here. That's why I like to cut across the infield. He just doesn't tolerate sex in the barn."

She pushed his arm away, trying to think. It was clear now she liked grooming horses much more than dogs but it seemed she'd have to gain weight, a lot of weight, for Mark to want her as a permanent employee. But something Dino had said earlier in the bar was puzzling. "What did you mean about that flatulence thing?" she asked.

"Gassy Cathy." Dino's chuckle turned wicked. "Cathy didn't know much about horses, but she was damn pretty, so of course Charlie hired her. When Mark's favorite horse got loose in the feed, it was Cathy's watch. Unfortunately, she was busy banging Charlie, and it sounded like she'd eaten beans that night. So that's why Mark has a Three-F rule. Fat, forty and flatulent. Those kind of women are safe to have in the barn because they're not so attractive to us—"

"What?" Jessica swung around in disbelief. "You're kidding! That's the Three-F rule? Do you really think you'll lose your minds if a pretty woman is around?"

"Well, I dunno. Let's see." His head swooped as he tried to nuzzle her neck.

She twisted out of reach, still sputtering. She'd always placed a premium on physical beauty, knew you didn't have to follow rules quite so closely if you were pretty and receptive to a little flirting. Now she was attracted to a man who didn't want her around simply because of those very qualities.

And she was attracted to Mark. When he walked in the shedrow at exactly four-thirty every morning, her heart lurched. But what kind of oversexed moron didn't trust himself around women?

"Aw, Jessica." Dino stumbled after her, his voice thick with that husky timbre a man always had when he wanted sex. "We're both single adults. You could at least give me a chance here."

His clumsy attention wasn't welcome. However, she knew better than to piss off the assistant trainer so she edged silently into the dark, jogging to the right until his voice faded. She left the turf course and crossed back onto the dirt. The barns glowed a cozy welcome, and shadows drifted along shedrows as grooms checked their horses.

Home.

She slipped into the back of the barn with a weary sigh. Ten p.m. Incredible she now considered this hour so very late. Buddy was probably dozing, but she headed around the corner to his stall.

Movement flashed. *Whoosh*. Something metal rammed into her stomach, cutting off her surprised grunt. She hit the floor, flailing at the handlebars shoved in her gut as she stared into a panicked face. A familiar face. The kid from the track!

He scrambled up and dashed into the darkness leaving her sprawled beneath her twisted bike.

She rose more slowly, cursing under her breath, but the nimble kid had vanished. She turned back and yanked the bike upright, groaning at the damage. One broken spoke and a misshapen seat. Other than that, much the same—as battered as ever. She'd noticed the boy on her first day when he was slinking around the yard sale, and it was obvious he really wanted the bike. But he was a bit of a fool not to steal a newer one.

She grabbed the seat, trying to twist it back into position, but it was stuck, and she was too drained to rouse the required effort. Sighing, she left the bike in the aisle and turned toward Buddy, wanting to console herself with his solid presence.

He must have heard the ruckus. His head poked over the door, curious eyes heavy with sleep, and he stood obligingly while she buried her face in his neck. His warm breath tickled as he nuzzled at her pocket, searching for the peppermint she'd taken from the bar. But he waited patiently until she peeled off the cellophane wrapper.

"These are a different kind, fellow, but tomorrow is your big race. I'll get more then."

His velvety muzzle, now neatly trimmed, tickled her hand as he accepted the mint, and he pushed at her pocket, looking for more. She scratched him under the jaw until he forgot about treats and tilted his head, grunting in bliss.

She did a quick stall check. Hay, water and feed tub licked clean. However, anxiety pricked her when she eyed his flimsy legs. She'd never considered how small a horse's legs were, never thought about the stress they faced, the weight they carried. Until now. When it was his turn to race.

No wonder Maria had been tense. She sighed and headed for her room, tired but afraid she wouldn't be able to sleep a wink.

The white-faced chestnut in the stall on Buddy's right stuck his head out and nickered, hopeful for a treat too.

"I'll give you one tomorrow," she promised as she walked past. The chestnut kicked the wall in annoyance, and she flinched with guilt. Mark had told her not to give Buddy treats in front of the other horses, and now she understood why.

The chestnut kicked again, harder this time. Assets shoved his head over the door, ears pricked as he surveyed the aisle.

Her steps slowed. She didn't know much about the chestnut, but Assets was the barn's big horse. Every employee in Mark's barn was focused on helping the colt peak for the Breeders' Cup. If he hurt himself kicking the walls, all because of a silly peppermint, the entire staff would hate her.

Assets stared down the aisle, not deigning to look at her, as though aware of his elite status. He was fed first, galloped first, washed first, and the idea that another horse had received a treat must have been ludicrous. He snorted at the chestnut, shaking his head in displeasure, and turned away from the stall front.

She'd been holding her breath, but now it escaped in a relieved sigh. From now on, she'd feed Buddy unwrapped peppermints so the other horses didn't hear the cellophane. And she'd definitely go in the stall, as Mark had instructed.

She trudged down the aisle, collecting her bike on the way, and jammed it in her room. Her space was cramped, but she couldn't leave the bike outside anymore. Not with that kid lurking. First her phone then the bike. That pesky little kid really coveted her stuff.

"Kato," she called, checking for the cat. No doubt he watched from under the bed, wondering why she disturbed him with the clunking bike. She turned out the light and leaped onto the cot before he could bite her ankles. The lumpy mattress sagged in the middle but usually didn't keep her awake. Tonight though, tired as she was, sleep wouldn't come.

Images of Buddy's race dogged her, persistent and dreadful: Buddy refusing to go into the gate, Buddy bucking off his jockey, Buddy jumping over the rail. The race had her stomach in knots, bothering her more than any of her own competitions. In skiing, she had control. With Buddy, she had nothing. Nothing but braids.

She flipped her pillow, trying to redirect her thoughts. Mark's scowl when he wanted her to get cracking was oddly reassuring. But then the scowl shifted to his sexy smile, which was much too stimulating, and she was wide awake again.

The night sounds were distracting too. Horses thumped in their stalls, wind whistled on the roof, and just when she was about to give up on sleep, Kato emerged and curled against her chest. His contented purr was a tonic. She stroked his soft hair and let exhaustion push her into oblivion.

CHAPTER EIGHT

For the fourth time that morning, Jessica dropped a bucket, and the irritating clang of the metal handle made everyone scowl. She scooped it up, swallowed her nerves and wished the day would crawl faster. Post time was one, Buddy was in the third race, but it was only nine-thirty. It didn't help that she was tired, a bit hung over and that Dino was still mad she'd walked alone into the 'dark infield.'

"I was supposed to see you home safely," he'd complained. But the track had to be the safest place on earth. There was always someone in each barn, guards at all the gates, and since the sheikh's big horses arrived, security had intensified. Granted, she didn't know Spanish and often didn't know what some people were saying, but the vibes they gave off were always friendly.

Just yesterday she'd raced two guys to the track kitchen, beating them soundly. Lefty's old bike could really move when pushed, and their shouts of approval had made her feel like an elite athlete again. She wasn't riding her bike now though, not until the seat was straightened. Mark had been so busy this morning, she hadn't dared ask for help or bother him with a report about a sticky-fingered little boy.

She straightened Buddy's twice-cleaned race bridle and blew out another sigh.

"Nervous?"

She spun around and saw Mark studying her with his knowing smile, his hair ruffled as though he'd been running his hand through it.

She forced a shrug. "Not so much."

He always knew what she was thinking or maybe he heard the crack in her voice. "Come with me," he said gently.

She followed him into his office, where he left the door open and poured two cups of coffee.

"Milk?"

She nodded and took the chair he kicked out for her. This was the first time she'd been in his office on a social visit, the first time he'd ever offered her coffee. Usually he was scolding her for something, or she was nagging him for perks for Buddy. But today his office was a relaxing place. He had his desk set up so he could keep an eye on the wash rack, something she hadn't realized when she'd used triple the amount of shampoo for Buddy's bath.

The linoleum floor was cracked, but the wall was freshly painted and crammed with race pictures, except for an obvious gap in the middle. She relaxed with her coffee, enjoying the undemanding quiet. One of the many things she liked about Mark was that he was comfortable with silence. Comfortable with waiting.

"I'm amazed you're always so calm," she finally confessed, leaning forward and resting her mug on his desk. "I had awful dreams last night."

He raised a brow. "The one where the horse shows up in gaudy braids?"

"Are you asking me not to braid?" She grinned, feeling more relaxed than she had all morning.

He took a slow sip of coffee, studying her over the cup. "You know I don't like the braids," he drawled, "but do what you want. Something has given the old guy energy. Just be careful in the paddock. He can get pushy. I was thinking of asking Maria to help."

"No," she said quickly. Buddy was her horse. "Please," she added, "I'd like to be the groom in the paddock, the one who wears that little apron and leads him back after the race."

His amused smile made her entire body tingle. "It's called a bib, Jessica." His expression turned serious as he leaned forward. "Look, don't expect miracles today. And remember betting is always risky. Be happy if Buddy runs in the money."

"In the money?" she asked. "Is that first to sixth place?"

"For bettors, it's first to third. But for us, payout is top six. The purse is nine thousand dollars, so if Buddy runs fifth—and that would be a good result for him—his percentage is five.

Trainers get ten percent of the purse, and I give a percentage of that to the groom and hot walker."

She quickly calculated his payoff. Hard way to make a living. Now she understood why he'd been so disappointed when Maria's filly was nosed out for second.

He settled back in his chair. "That's why everyone wants the quality horses and at least one big owner. Being a public trainer means you spend as much time with horses and owners, but money is much tighter. And Jessica," he added, his astute blue eyes studying her face, "I'm recommending to Buddy's owners that this be his last race. He has a chance to go out sound and make a nice riding horse for someone. That means he'll likely be leaving tomorrow."

Her shocked jerk sloshed coffee on her thumb. Tomorrow! She didn't want Buddy to retire until after she left. There probably wasn't another horse in the barn that was quiet enough for her to handle. More importantly, Buddy had been a gentle and patient teacher. When she was lonely, she brushed him for hours. And though her room was now mouse free, she still napped in his stall.

A lump tangled in her throat. She averted her eyes, staring at the wall above Mark's head. She felt his concern but couldn't bear to look at him, afraid his empathy might shatter her composure. A garbage truck rumbled down the road, stopping to empty a clanking bin, and the smell of diesel drifted into the doorway. She coughed and swiped her eyes, pretending the smell bothered her.

"I guess a nice horse like Buddy deserves a second chance," she said.

"Atta girl." But the approval in his voice made her throat spasm.

"You have lots of win pictures," she managed, keeping her eyes fixed on the wall.

He seemed to know she was struggling. Shoving aside his charts, he rose and introduced her to the important horses in his life, adding colorful tales about various tracks and personalities. His stories were like a tonic, and soon she was nodding and feeling much better.

"Is that your dad holding the gray horse?" She pointed at a rugged man in a cowboy hat. Same crisp blue eyes and chiseled face, although she detected a weakness in the man's jaw that Mark didn't have.

"Yeah. The horse is Scrappy Cat, his first Grade 1 winner."

Mark's voice had hardened, so she quickly changed the subject. "Why is this space empty?" she asked.

Silence.

He looked down at her, studying her face as though uncertain what to say. Finally he traced the spot with a slow finger. "Reserved for a Breeders' Cup win. I really think your grandfather's colt can do it, Jess. It'll be the first time I ever had an entry."

It was also the first time he'd called her Jess, she realized, as she stared up at him. So close she could smell his aftershave, could smell the potent combination of leather, horse and male. She was tall but he was so much taller, so much bigger.

She automatically swayed forward, her lips parting with invitation, and somehow his mouth covered hers and she was pulled against his hard body. He tasted of coffee, virility and hunger—and, man, could he kiss. She clung to his ridged back, weak and off-balanced from what he was doing to her mouth.

A car honked, and he abruptly lifted his head. Dropped his arms and stepped back. "Christ, I'm sorry," he said.

"No big deal." She crossed her arms, hiding her hurt. She'd more than enjoyed it; he was an excellent kisser. Mind-blowing, in fact. But she'd never had anyone pull away with such obvious regret. Clearly he hadn't found her as appealing. Or maybe he was so accustomed to women, he'd grown impervious. Too bad, because she was definitely affected.

Still, she didn't want to be considered another fawning female, not like that persistent Trish. The floor still rocked slightly, but she was determined not to grab the desk for support. "It's race day." She forced a negligent shrug, her balance almost back to normal. "We needed a diversion."

He dragged a hand through his hair, something she'd noticed he did when stressed, and that disarming gesture made her feel slightly better.

"Nothing to apologize for," she added. "It was just a little kiss."

"Didn't feel so little to me," he said.

But his grim tone and the implacable way he walked her to the door, made her wonder why he considered a hot kiss such a very bad thing.

CHAPTER NINE

Mark shoved his hands in his pockets, hiding his restlessness as he awaited the arrival of My Best Buddy. Seven horses already circled the walking ring—Radcliff's runner included. Mark ignored the man's perpetual sneer and instead studied Radcliff's horse, a bay with a distinctive blaze, four white feet and red blinkers.

The bay was the favorite, and deservingly so. He'd been in the money his last five starts. Radcliff's weakness was his tendency to work a horse hard before a race. The media influenced him, and he loved to notch bullet works. It was unimaginable that Buddy would beat the bay, but maybe another in the field could.

Mark glanced hopefully at the number one horse, the second favorite. The sleek chestnut had speed and with the rail, he might lead gate to wire. "Good luck, Jim," he called to the chestnut's trainer.

"Yoohoo, Mark!" A woman's voice, too loud and too shrill, sliced the muted murmur of the crowd.

He barely winced, pasting on a smile before turning to greet Buddy's owners. Sophie and Devin Green were social climbers, using horses to chisel their way in, and how they came to own a gentle soul like Buddy was one of life's many ironies.

"Where's our Bobby horse?" Sophie asked.

Mark didn't bother to correct her. She never remembered Buddy's name. "Coming now," he said, hiding his relief as Jessica finally appeared at the entrance to the paddock.

She swept in like a movie star, last to arrive, her head held as high as Buddy's. And Buddy looked good too, so good for a moment Mark forgot his dismal record. The old gelding obviously blossomed from the attention Jessica lavished, and her confidence was infectious. Today Buddy simply exuded class.

The crowd hushed as Jessica and the purple-braided horse paraded around the walking ring. Even the towel sticking from her pocket was bright purple. Only she would color coordinate the groom's rag.

Buddy's owners turned silent for a moment. "Is that *my* horse?" Sophie finally asked.

Mark nodded, smiling as he watched the odd pair. Jessica and Buddy seemed to have stepped from another venue—a horse show or fashion runway maybe—and they strutted around like they owned the track. The other horses wilted, as though intimidated by Buddy's brashness.

The valet waited with the saddle, and Mark gestured at Jessica. She nodded and turned Buddy into the five hole. Now that she was close, he spotted her tension, the tightness of her mouth, the way she always raised her chin when she was frightened but bravely rallying for battle.

"Try to relax," he whispered. "He'll do okay."

She jiggled the bit, keeping the horse's attention as Mark adjusted the saddlecloth. "I'm not worried about Buddy," she said, "but I didn't get my bet down. And he's going to win today."

"He looks good—great, in fact. But this is a tough race." Mark tightened the overgirth. "And he hasn't won in a very long time."

"Today he will."

The conviction in her voice made Mark study Buddy with fresh eyes. Buddy's neck seemed thicker, his muscles more defined. Odd, but he seemed to swell when he was braided. It gave him attitude.

"Can't believe you're actually running that nag," a voice said behind them.

Mark didn't turn. He knew Radcliff was saddling in the slot next to him, had felt the trainer's hostile glares.

"Christ, even your dad raced better horses, and they were all dog food," Radcliff said. "Every one I claimed was sent to the meat packer."

Jessica's cheeks flagged with anger.

"Hear someone whining, Jessica?" Mark asked, keeping his voice calm, afraid any outburst would upset Buddy, or worse, attract the steward.

She gave a dismissive shrug. "Just some old guy making excuses." She turned to Radcliff. "Put your glasses on, Pops, so you can watch the purple-braided horse. He'll be the one leading the way."

Mark chuckled, glad she was in his corner. Her grandfather had mentioned she'd done some competitive skiing and, no doubt, she could talk smack with the best of them. Now Radcliff was the one red-faced with fury. The man was sensitive about his age, and somehow she'd guessed it. However, it wasn't wise to bait the vindictive Radcliffe—Mark felt a jolt of unease.

"Just ignore Radcliff, and tell Buddy to beat his horse," he murmured, only half joking. Buddy seemed willing to do anything Jessica asked. Usually he was a rascal to saddle, but today he stood like a statue.

"I will." Jessica lowered her voice. "But only if you promise to tell me what's going on between you and him."

"Deal," Mark said. "But only if Buddy wins." He never spoke about his father, except to Dino, but it was a safe promise. Buddy had little chance of beating Radcliff's horse.

A line of colorful riders marched from the jockey room with Emma Rae leading the way, her shoulders squared with purpose. "How do you want me to ride this guy?" she asked Mark, flicking her stick against her shiny black boot.

"He likes to stalk so keep him close. He's honest. If he's not running at the end, there's nothing left in the tank. Just take care of him."

Mark checked that Sophie and Devin were out of earshot. They wanted to win at any cost and wouldn't like his riding instructions. But Buddy was a grand old winner in his day; he always tried hard and deserved to go out sound. As an apprentice, Emma Rae was more likely to listen to instructions than the more experienced jocks, and her weight concession would help Buddy over Belmont's long, tiring stretch.

"Riders up!" the paddock judge bellowed.

"Watch out for the gray," Mark said as he legged Emma Rae into the saddle. "They might try to box you."

Emma Rae knotted her reins and scowled at Radcliff's jockey. "Yeah, that's a mean sonofabitch riding for Radcliff. Prick almost pushed my horse through the rail last week."

Jessica blanched at the idea someone might deliberately try to hurt Buddy, but she acted like a pro. She calmly led Emma Rae and Buddy through the tunnel to the track. No one would guess this was the first time she'd ever led a horse over.

She said something that made Emma Rae laugh, and Buddy tossed his head and looked pleased. The horse was really on the muscle now, prancing, neck arched, and some of the spectators pointed and checked their programs. It was obvious Jessica made Buddy feel special, and racing was as much about attitude as speed. When he was younger, he'd been the star of someone's shedrow, and Jessica's pampering clearly left him revitalized.

The trumpet sounded, and a familiar thrill slammed Mark as the post parade began. Jessica's face glowed with a shared excitement.

"Come watch the race in my box," he said impulsively. He handed her a twenty-dollar win ticket. "This will save you a trip to the windows."

"Thanks." She scanned the stub, her eyes sparkling. "So you think he'll win?"

"On paper he looks outclassed but—"

"But they're not racing on paper," she said. "And I can't believe how my stomach is flipping."

"Yeah, I can." He grinned. "My stomach does that too." He took her elbow, guiding her through the flowing crowd. This would work out great. Jessica was an excellent conversationalist and would be the perfect buffer against Sophie and Devin, self-centered idiots whose company always left him frazzled. Sophie was a pain in the ass and the way she'd flirted at their last dinner, in her husband's presence, had made both men edgy.

"Jessica, these are Buddy's owners, Sophie and Devin Greene," he said as they entered the box. "Jessica is Buddy's groom, and the reason he looks so dashing today."

Devin shook hands with Jessica, his guarded look fading. Few men would look at someone else's wife when they had a stunner like Jessica by their side. He gave Mark an approving nod, loosened his tie and turned his attention back to his drink.

Sophie's lips, however, flattened in a line of disapproval as she studied Jessica's casual clothes and the purple rag protruding from her back pocket. Jessica was either unaware or uncaring. She seemed absorbed in watching Buddy warm up, although it was difficult to tell. More went on in her intelligent head than he'd originally thought.

Probably she didn't care. She was one of his few staff members who wasn't intimidated by his scowl. Not because she didn't notice; it just didn't matter. Maybe since she was part of the wealthy Boone family, she possessed a sense of self-worth that was unaffected by clothes or setting or company.

"Mark's box has the best view," Sophie said. "Is this the first time you've been in the expensive seats?" Her tone was so patronizing, Mark's mouth tightened. If Sophie knew Jessica's last name, she'd be fawning over Jessica instead of talking down to her.

"Yes, it's my first time in this box," Jessica said carefully. "And it's my first time to ever watch a horse I've groomed myself. You have an excellent eye for animals. Buddy is wonderful."

Sophie preened at the compliment. "Yes, I definitely can pick them. But that horse is getting old, and Mark suggests retirement." Her preening faded to a moue of discontent. "It's embarrassing to see him lose all the time. I can't invite my friends to the races anymore."

"How horrible for you," Jessica said, but her voice had an edge, and Mark gave her shoulder a warning squeeze. "I'm sure if Mark wants you to retire him that would be best," she added.

He loosened his grip but left his arm slung over the back of her chair. Just in case she got testy again. Just in case Sophie made any more slurs about her beloved Buddy.

The runners were approaching the starting gate now, and Buddy was the bright light of the bunch. Even Sophie recognized him. Jessica leaned forward, clasping her hands as an assistant starter reached up and led him into the gate.

"He's in," Sophie said.

"Five to load," the announcer said.

Radcliff's horse balked and had to be circled but again refused to load.

"That's not fair." Jessica twisted in her seat. "Buddy has to wait in the gate, thinking it's going to open, and Radcliff hasn't taught his horse to load."

"Radcliff may not even have seen the horse run before today," Mark said. "He trains at a lot of tracks."

"You shouldn't defend him," she said. "Anyway, it doesn't matter. I can see Buddy's head, and he's standing quietly."

"Maybe he's napping," Sophie said, adjusting her binoculars.

Mark ignored Sophie's commentary. Jessica was tight as a fuse. He remembered watching his first horse run, an exhilarating but terrifying moment, and gave her hand a reassuring squeeze. She shot him a grateful look and squeezed back, gripping his fingers like a lifeline.

"They're putting a blindfold on that horse. He's in now," Sophie said.

Sophie's husband said nothing, merely clinked the ice cubes in his glass and stared across the empty infield. Clearly, horse ownership was his wife's idea. Once Buddy was gone, Mark would no longer be their trainer. He heaved a sigh of relief and checked the tote board.

Bettors liked Radcliff's horse, making him the two to one favorite. Buddy, in spite of his flashy braids or maybe because of them, was going off at eighteen to one. But Buddy didn't know he was a long shot. Jessica's loving care had him believing he was, once again, king of the shedrow.

Could be an interesting race.

He watched Jessica's face, understanding her tension, knowing how hard it was to pass a horse over to the jockey, knowing there was nothing else you could do, knowing she had an intensely kissable mouth—

"They're off!" the announcer called.

Mark's attention jumped back to the race, and he leaped to his feet as the gates smacked open. The five horse bumped Buddy when he lunged from the gate but Buddy fought back, grabbing ground like a linebacker. His sharp break put him near the front, sandwiched between a horse on the rail and Radcliff's speedy gray horse on his outside.

Mark was conscious of Jessica tugging his fingers as the horses charged down the backstretch. Buddy was fourth, just off the rail, and galloping fluidly. "Way to go, Emma," Mark murmured, checking the fractions. First quarter in twenty-three and a half seconds. Perfect.

Jessica leaned forward, straining to see the horses as they entered the turn. Both Sophie and Devin had rudely shifted sideways, completely blocking her view. Mark squeezed against his chair and pulled her in front of him. She was wiggly though, jumping and shouting as the horses rounded the turn with Buddy running a strong fourth.

"He can't get through!" she yelled, gripping his arm.

She was fresh and sweet and so engrossed with the horse, he gave her an impulsive squeeze. For Jessica, it wasn't about training percentages or money or prestige. She wanted it for Buddy.

And the horse seemed to share her desire. He looked like he had a ton of run left, but the gray had boxed him in and there was nowhere to go. Just give him an opening, Mark willed. For Jessica, for Emma Rae, for Buddy. And at the eighth pole, the front runner lugged out, and Buddy scudded through the opening like a purple missile.

Emma was really riding, pushing on his neck, urging him home. He drew alongside the leader, a blinkered bay. But on the outside, Radcliff's gray closed rapidly and it was now a three-horse race.

Jessica jumped up and down, pumping her arms, and even Sophie and Devin hollered. The old gelding was putting on quite a show. A third with this bunch of horses was quite an accomplishment.

"Go, boy," Mark said. "Just beat the gray."

But Buddy wanted to beat them all. He flattened his ears and dug deep, surging across the wire with a last gutsy effort, a winner by half a length.

Jessica turned, face radiant, and wrapped her arms around his neck. He dipped his head and kissed her, forgetting the crowd, the horse, the win. Her breasts brushed his chest, and he instinctively tugged her closer, didn't want to let go—

"My turn," Sophie said. Somehow Jessica was shuffled back and Buddy's owner sidled forward, smelling of wine and cigarettes.

He dodged her eager mouth and instead brushed his lips over her clammy cheek. "Congratulations, Sophie," he said. "We need to get to the winner's circle."

She looped her arm through his, abandoning her husband as she gushed about how she'd absolutely known Bobby was going to win today. Jessica grabbed Devin, who immediately brightened and set down his drink. Sophie's husband definitely had the better of this deal, Mark thought wryly.

They hurried down the steps, past sharp-eyed security and toward the winner's circle. Mark stepped out to catch Buddy as the victorious horse trotted back. Both Buddy and Emma Rae were streaked with dirt, but it didn't diminish the jock's gleaming smile or the way Buddy strutted.

"Congratulations. Good ride." Mark shook Emma Rae's hand as Jessica proudly led Buddy into the winner's circle. They grouped around the horse, cameras clicked and the presentation was made. Emma Rae twirled her stick and leaped off.

"Thanks for the ride, Mark. Those braids gave us luck. That gray sure didn't want to let us out."

"Radcliff is an old friend of mine," Mark said.

"Friends like that, you don't need enemies." Emma rolled her eyes, pulled off her saddle and strutted to the scales.

Sophie waved a manicured hand, keen to reclaim the spotlight. "We must celebrate." Her eyes flickered from Mark to Jessica. "I suppose you have a boyfriend you're busy with?" she asked hopefully.

"No boyfriend," Jessica said.

"You'll drive to the restaurant with me, Jessica," Mark said firmly, squashing any more of Sophie's manipulations. No way was he eating solo with Buddy's owners. Dino was trailering a horse tonight, and he needed someone to deflect Sophie. Besides, Jessica was enjoyable company, very enjoyable. With her around, dinner might be halfway fun.

He dragged a hand through his hair as anticipation jangled with the warning in his brain. Not only was she an employee, but she was also Boone's granddaughter, and he was starting to look at her in a most unprofessional way. Nothing he couldn't handle though. There were plenty of other women around, and there was no way he'd ever risk pissing off Boone. No way.

CHAPTER TEN

"I want to look good tonight," Jessica said as she and Maria mixed the evening grain. "Is there a yard sale anywhere? I need a dress."

Maria's face clouded with sympathy. "Is Mark making you to go to an owner's dinner? I hate those."

"Oh, he's not making me. I want to." She still bounced after Buddy's amazing performance, and the thought of eating a good meal only increased her excitement. Of course, it was apparent her role was to keep Sophie from plastering herself over Mark, thereby preserving owner/trainer relations. No problem. She could do that. But she also intended to eat and drink, in honor of Buddy, her very own wonder horse.

Maria banged the lid shut on the bin and tilted her head in open appraisal. "You're taller than most women around here. But Tricky Dick usually has something."

Must be a cross dresser, Jessica thought, nodding eagerly. Five weeks ago she would have been appalled at the idea of buying secondhand clothes, but as she propelled Maria out the door, all she said was, "Let's go see Dick."

Tricky Dick's dorm was in the west end of the backside, an area Jessica hadn't yet explored.

"If my bike was fixed, we could've ridden double," she said, conscious of Maria's labored breathing.

"I gotta lose weight." Maria patted her rounded stomach. "But then, Mark might fire me. He has no restraint around women."

"He's restrained around me," Jessica said, hating the wistfulness that crept into her voice.

"I expect he already has another woman. That scrawny Trish was the last I know of." Maria's voice faded as she ducked beneath a sagging clothesline.

"Trish sure is tiny," Jessica said, skirting a dripping cotton shirt. "Guess Mark likes his girlfriends small?"

"Yup," Maria said. "According to Dino, that's why he prefers big women on staff. So he doesn't mix them up." Her eyes narrowed as she glanced back at Jessica. "Although he must not like tall, skinny women either because he hired you."

Jessica blinked. She'd never been called skinny before. She smoothed her shirt, wondering if she'd lost any weight. But all her clothes felt the same, even her jeans, and, for sure, she'd never get any shorter. So if Mark had a preference for petite girlfriends, she was definitely out of luck.

She remained glumly silent as Maria pointed to a second-floor apartment. They clunked up the wooden stairs, and Maria rapped on a panel door.

A slender man with a hooked nose cracked the door open.

"This girl needs a nice dress, Dick," Maria said. "Can you help?"

"Come back Saturday. I'm busy arranging racks." He pointed over his shoulder at the mass of clothes behind him.

Jessica peered in, straining to see. "Oh, my. What beautiful things you have. Is that Dior?"

"Yes, an original." Approval brightened Dick's long face, and he waved them inside and slammed the door. "Okay, but be quick. What do you need?"

Maria gestured at Jessica. "She has to go out with fancy owners tonight and only has jeans."

"I see." He cocked his head and studied Jessica objectively. "Tall. Thirty-six inch bust. Good hips. Drop your pants. Let's see your legs. Quickly."

Jessica stared.

"Come on. Hurry." Maria shot an anxious look at Dick.

Apparently, Tricky Dick's time wasn't to be wasted. Jessica unzipped her jeans, raising her head as she stepped out, conscious of her ugly knee and daring him to comment on any swelling.

"Tiny waist. My, yes!" Dick cooed, clapping his hands. "And I have just the dress to show off those gorgeous legs."

He swept into another room and moments later emerged cradling a tiny black sheath. "Slip it on. I'll be back with the perfect shoes."

Jessica glanced down, relieved he hadn't commented on her swollen knee. Maybe it wasn't so bad. It hadn't hurt lately even though she hadn't seen her doctor since she'd moved to the track. She'd skipped the regular treatments her grandfather had insisted upon, since it was much too difficult to travel to the doctor's office.

"Hurry," Maria urged.

Jessica stripped and pulled on the dress, a Nina Ricci she confirmed after a peek at the label. "Where does he get all these gorgeous clothes?" she whispered.

"Donations," Maria said. "He resells on the Internet and gives all the profits to Anna House. He's a groom but spends his spare time fundraising. Lives somewhere else in the winter."

"What is Anna House? The money from Lefty's bike was for that too."

Maria smiled as she helped Jessica with the zipper. "It's our childcare center, named after Mr. Eugene Melnyk's daughter. He donated a lot of money to start it up. And now that my English is good, I can volunteer there. Oh, my!" She stopped talking for a second, her eyes widening. "You're beautiful!"

"Is it okay?" Jessica twisted, looking for a mirror.

Dick appeared in the doorway, jerked to a stop and let out a low wolf whistle. His eyes narrowed. Based on their very male gleam, Jessica decided she looked just fine.

"I'll take it," she said. "How much?" She knew it would be costly, but her coffee can had money, and she needed this dress.

Dick shook his head and shoved a pair of black stilettos in her hands. "My clothes are expensive. But track workers are welcome to borrow if they make a donation to Anna House and return the outfit clean and undamaged. Everyone needs to dress up sometime." He waved his hand. "Now, change and go. I'm behind in my cataloguing."

Despite his impatience, Dick's generosity was staggering. Jessica paused. The entire backstretch was supportive, more like an extended family than co-workers, and the urge to contribute swelled. She'd never volunteered before, thought it was something people did if they were bored or lonely, but maybe that wasn't true. After all, Mark helped his staff with English lessons, and he was the busiest person she knew.

"Maybe I could help with the cataloguing?" she asked, half expecting Dick to turn her down.

"That'd be nice," he said. "Tomorrow at eleven."

Her eyes widened in dismay. That was her nap time. But he studied her with open cynicism, as though expecting an excuse, as though aware she really was a selfish person.

"See you then," she said, surprising Dick—and herself.

CHAPTER ELEVEN

Mark grabbed his dinner jacket and strode from the office into the barn. Some feed and bedding still had to be ordered, but it was unlikely Jessica had anything suitable to wear and they'd need to detour for some hasty shopping. No doubt she had an elaborate wardrobe somewhere, but her fancy clothes certainly weren't at the track.

He checked the stalls as he passed, ensuring every animal was tucked in for the night, an ingrained habit developed from a lifetime of caring for horses. The sweet smell of good hay, the munching of contented animals, the serenity of a well-kept barn always filled him with satisfaction.

Assets stretched his neck out, clicking his teeth and pretending to bite. Mark stopped and opened the door, pushing the colt's head away until he behaved. Unfazed, the horse pulled at Mark's hand, eager for attention, just a bored colt eager to play.

"Play all you want—just keep winning," Mark said as he scratched Assets' jaw. He liked the colt's attitude. Assets was brash, precocious and fast. If he ran in the Breeders' Cup as he had in the preps, no one would catch him. Even the sheikh's powerful entry was thought to be running for second.

The colt quit trying to grab Mark's sleeve and stared regally down the aisle, looking every inch a champ. Only nine months earlier, he'd been green and undeveloped but now exceeded everyone's expectations, and he'd earned big praise for Mark's training program.

"Three more weeks," he said, giving Assets a final pat before checking his watch and reluctantly leaving the stall. Sophie and Devin had reserved a table for eight, not much time if Jessica needed something to wear. She'd mentioned Maria might help dig up a dress, but he guessed that was wishful thinking.

Bump. He rapped on her door, puzzled by the banging sound coming from her room. A vacancy had opened in one of the dorms, luxurious accommodations compared to the tack room, but she'd turned it down; he suspected it was because she wanted to stay close to Buddy.

Still...he glanced down the long aisle, noting the isolation. She'd lasted much longer than either he or her grandfather had expected. Boone was oddly quiet when Mark reported how well she was doing but, heck, the man must be proud of her. Even Mark was proud of her. She'd learned so much—

She flung the door open. "Oh, good. Can you help me with my bike? I've been whacking it with the hammer but the seat's still twisted."

His breath oozed in admiration, and he could only stare. It seemed she'd stepped from a sexy magazine—chestnut hair swept elegantly to the side, eyes dark and mysterious beneath the makeup, full and luscious lips—

"Please, Mark," she said, misreading his silence. "It will only take a sec."

He tore his gaze from her mouth and stared dumbly at Lefty's bike, propped between her legs. Jean-clad legs. Still, no restaurant would refuse her entrance. No maitre d' could possibly look beyond that stunning face.

"The seat's twisted." His voice sounded rough.

"That's right." She thrust a rusty hammer in his hand. "It's been busted since that kid tried to steal it. Remember, I told you and Dino all about it."

He kept his attention on the bike, but goddammit, she was gorgeous. He vaguely remembered her talking about some kid, but his brain often stalled around Jessica. He wiped his warm neck and stared numbly at the seat. "I doubt anyone would want this wreck," he mumbled, tossing the useless hammer on the cot. She was standing so close, he could see her bare toes, toes with happy purple-painted nails, peeking out from the bottom of her frayed jeans.

"But he did try to steal it," she said. "That's how the seat broke. Can you fix it?"

Anything for you, sweetheart, he thought as he wrapped his hands around the seat, trying to twist it back into position. But it only shifted an inch. Definitely stuck. He flipped the bike upside down.

"That's the trouble." He pried a black phone from beneath the coils. "Your cell was blocking it."

"That's not mine. My phone is pink. And the kid stole it." She grabbed her bike and straddled the seat. "That one must be Lefty's."

Mark pressed the power button, but the display remained dark. "No one knew Lefty's relatives. Maybe it lists some contacts. I'll hunt around for a charger and let the police know."

He slipped the phone into his pocket, watching as she bounced on the seat, clearly delighted with her bike's restoration. He'd never seen her with makeup or fancy hair, but now it was easy to imagine her entrenched in high society. She should be lounging in a Jaguar, not perched on a decrepit bike in a dusty horse barn.

"Ready?" he asked, more curtly then he intended.

"Yes. Thanks for fixing it." She scrambled off and propped the bike against the wall. "I just have to slip my dress on. No, Kato!" Her eyes widened as sharp needles stabbed his ankle.

"Christ!" Mark jumped, shaking his leg before realizing what it was, then bent down and gently unhooked the beast from his pants. "This kitten turned into a guard cat."

"Sorry." She laughed and scooped up the cat, dipping her face in his gray hair. "Kato just has a thing about attacking ankles, but he's really quite cuddly. He sleeps with me every night."

"Lucky cat."

Her eyes widened at his impulsive comment but she didn't step back. Her mouth, that delicious mouth with the pouty lower lip, thickened. He swallowed but couldn't pull his gaze away, couldn't stop staring at the delicate curve of her neck, the sweep of her chest, the way Kato's indolent paw rested on her breast. Christ, now his own hand twitched.

Kato twisted and leaped to the floor. Mark gulped and stepped back, anchoring himself against the door and resolutely locking his gaze on her forehead. "You found a dress to wear then?" It was a struggle to push the words past his dry throat.

"Yes. I just have to slip it on."

He nodded, backed out and shut the door. Jammed his hands in his pockets, annoyed at his reaction. Wished she'd leave the track then wished she wouldn't. Fucking impossible situation.

A car idled outside, its brake lights casting an eerie red glow over the shedrow. Welcoming the distraction, he strode to the end of the aisle, but the vehicle powered away in a cloud of gas fumes. He swore, resenting that his horses had to breathe the mess.

Probably another reporter. In spite of the tight security, visitor flow had tripled and with a Breeders' Cup favorite, it would only get worse. Tomorrow he'd hire a full-time guard to keep the gawkers away, to ensure his staff and horses weren't disturbed.

Down the aisle, a door closed. One good thing about Jessica was that she dressed fast. Actually there were many good things about her. He pivoted and his hands, still crammed in his pocket, fisted at the sight. His first thought was that a model had been dropped into the middle of his shedrow, and it was fortunate his staff wasn't around to be distracted. And then he simply stopped thinking and just stared.

Her dress was black and molded to her curves, showcasing shapely legs that didn't seem to stop. Creamy shoulders, no straps. Generous breasts strained at the fabric as though eager to escape, as though eager for his hands to free them.

"This just gets worse and worse," he muttered.

She didn't pretend not to understand, just gave him a teasing smile and patted the black jacket slung over her arm. "If I'm too hot for you, boss, I can always add the jacket."

"Best slip it on, sweetheart," he said, no longer trying to hide his slow perusal. "At least give me time to adjust."

Dinner dragged. Ever since Jessica removed her jacket, Devin's gaze had been riveted to her chest; it was a struggle to concentrate on Sophie's prattle. That man was a rude lout, Mark thought, as Devin passed Jessica the salt, practically drooling as he peered down her dress.

Sophie squeezed Mark's fingers, reclaiming his attention. He forced another nod, unable to garner much interest in her mind-numbing chatter.

"And we are so pleased to have you for our trainer. Penny Bremner, she's the president of our society, told us you had a horse running in the Breeders' Cup. When she heard you trained our dear horse, Bobby, she decided she must come and watch his next race."

"I thought you agreed to retire Buddy." Mark laid down his fork, using the maneuver as an excuse to escape her clinging fingers.

"Oh, but he ran so well today, and I do want my friends to see him win."

Mark folded his napkin, appetite lost. He nodded at the hovering waiter to remove his plate. "The horse can't keep going," he said. "Buddy's running on guts alone. He's had fifty-six starts. Let's just be grateful for what he's accomplished and do the right thing."

"Oh, pooh." She flicked her hand in dismissal. "One little race won't hurt. Not with a trainer like you. One more race, and then maybe we'll sell him as a riding horse."

Jessica's arm brushed Mark's wrist as she leaned forward. "How much do you want for him?"

Mark shot her a warning look before turning his attention back to Sophie. "The best way isn't to sell but to place them with an adoption facility. They can retrain and take the time to find a suitable home. It ensures a good future."

"But if we can make money selling, I'd rather do that." Sophie's voice rose. "I don't want to just *give* him away."

"How much do you want for him?" Jessica repeated.

Mark's mouth tightened as she leaned past him, ignoring his signal to back off. Damn. Now she had Sophie thinking money instead of a simple retirement.

"You really like my horse," Sophie said, looking at Jessica for the first time that evening. "How much, I wonder?"

Jessica's gaze flickered, and Mark saw the panic in her eyes as she realized her mistake. "I just want him to have a good home." She shrugged and fingered her wine glass, but the damage was done.

"You'd probably get a thousand, maybe two, off the track," Mark said reluctantly. "Buddy doesn't have the movement for dressage, but he might make a nice hunter."

"So you're saying his value as a racehorse is zero." Sophie's lips compressed. "Okay. I'll sell him to your groom for two thousand dollars, but only after one more race."

"Then I'm sorry," Mark said. "But I won't train Buddy. You can move him to a different barn tomorrow."

He ignored Jessica's gasp but felt her hand tighten around his knee in a desperate plea. Sophie plopped two sugar cubes into her coffee and stared with stony eyes.

He crossed his arms and leaned back, equally inflexible. Jessica's hand rested on his leg, but she remained silent as though aware they were in the middle of negotiations. Her fingers edged up his thigh, but he concentrated on holding Sophie's stare.

"I don't want to move Buddy to another trainer, but I promised my ladies' group a day at the races," Sophie said. "Surely you can agree to one more race?"

"Not fair to the horse." Mark shook his head, trying to ignore the sensual movement of Jessica's hand. Buddy had seemed a little stiff after the race. No obvious pain or swelling, just a shortness of stride. Nothing the track vet would notice. Still, it worried him. And it would be nice if the horse retired on a win. No, he wasn't budging on this call.

Jessica's fingers drifted, tracing a circle on his thigh, and his thoughts scattered. Just an inch to the left, he willed. He crossed his arms, fighting the urge to grab her wrist and place her hand in a more satisfying position. The little minx. Sophie wasn't the only one deep into negotiations.

"One more race and I promise to sell him. Two thousand dollars," Sophie said, "no matter how he runs."

Mark remained motionless, caught between the two women. He wanted to tell Sophie to shove her last race. Wanted to tell her to consider the horse. But most of all he wanted attention for his throbbing erection.

"All right," he finally said, blowing out a shattered sigh. "I'll train him. One more race." However, resentment thickened his words, and the knowledge that he'd been swayed for all the wrong reasons made him ball his napkin in disgust.

Jessica bounced at the front of the walkway as they waited for the valet to deliver Mark's car, her euphoria only slightly tarnished by the fact that she didn't have two thousand dollars.

Asking her grandfather for a loan wasn't an option. He'd claim it breached their agreement and use it as an excuse to drag her into his company.

Yet two thousand dollars wasn't entirely impossible. She had almost fifteen hundred remaining from her track winnings and, with a paycheck or two, could scrape the money together. She continued bouncing, ecstatic she'd talked Mark into keeping Buddy.

Well, maybe not exactly *talked*. The sexy dress she'd worn had helped. He was a typical man after all, although she feared he affected her much more than she did him. His presence always left her exhilarated—a wonderful feeling but usually better if shared. She tilted her head, letting the crisp air fan her cheeks, feeling intensely alive and eager to discover what the rest of the evening might bring.

Whispers caught her attention. She glanced sideways, watching as two women ogled Mark. As usual, he was oblivious, face impassive under the canopy. Jessica gave them a knowing smile. She'd deliberately left her jacket off in spite of the cool air, but Mark hadn't looked at her, hadn't even spoken since they'd left Sophie and Devin's table. He was definitely zoned out, no doubt thinking of horses.

Still, it had been an enjoyable evening, despite being stuck with Devin. The salmon was delicious, the wine unending and, best of all, she'd managed to keep her horse. The thought of Buddy being walked to another trainer's barn tomorrow had filled her with panic, and she'd been desperate to sway Mark.

She shot him a grateful smile, but he only stared down the street, watching as his car eased to the curb. A wiry attendant with a nose ring jumped out. Mark opened the passenger door, his gaze hooded as she slid in. He tipped the valet and joined her in the car, still silent as he accelerated away from the restaurant.

Jessica felt a twinge of unease as she studied his flat mouth, the way his hands gripped the wheel. He seemed angry even though she'd done her job—chatting up Devin all night, leaving Mark free to humor Sophie. The car's speed increased; she twisted in the seat, scanning the blurring sign posts.

"Isn't that the exit to Belmont?" she asked.

"I assumed you were going home with me."

She gave a haughty sniff. He hadn't spoken for ten minutes yet had the arrogance to think she would accompany him back to his bed. Without an ounce of sweet talk which, she admitted, was all she really needed. "That's quite an assumption."

"I assumed that was your hand under the table," he said dispassionately. "That you were trying to show me something."

His detached tone hurt, and she crossed her arms. "I was just showing you how I feel about Buddy. It doesn't have anything to do with how I feel about you. Or Devin," she added, guessing that lumping him with Devin would hurt any man's ego. "So you can just turn—"

She was abruptly tossed forward, gravel ricocheting as he veered into a rutted parking lot. The seatbelt dug into her shoulder—her sore shoulder—but Mark didn't seem at all concerned. His voice was crisp and unapologetic as he switched off the ignition.

"Then perhaps you better explain how you feel about me," he snapped, "now that I agreed to run Buddy against my better judgment. Feel clever playing your little games?"

Ah, ha. So that explained his anger. He hated to think a woman could influence his decisions. It hadn't been a game though. She'd been desperate to keep Buddy but would never have stooped to such behavior with another man. It was Mark's attention she wanted as much as the horse. The knowledge scared her, and she hid her feelings behind a condescending tone. "If a woman's hand on your leg blows your mind, then I understand why you prefer to hire big people. I have control but you really need to practice yours, maybe—"

His body slanted, blocking out the road lights and then his mouth covered hers, hard and punishing. One hand held her head in place, the other trapped her arms, and she couldn't move, could hardly breathe. But at her muffled protest, his mouth immediately gentled. Turned coaxing, teasing, until her lips parted.

Ah, this was better, much better. He was such a wonderful kisser. She sighed and arched toward him, her arms slipping around his neck as she surrendered to the hardness of his body, his minty taste, the sureness of his hands when they unclipped her seatbelt.

His tongue mated with hers and when his bold hand caressed her breasts, it felt so right. He peeled down the top of her dress and his fingers stroked her nipple, sending out waves of pleasure while his mouth sizzled a trail from her neck to her chest.

She moaned and arched against him, not caring that he'd rolled her dress to the waist, that he was sucking her breasts, that he'd quickly filled her with a throbbing need.

The sudden slap of cold air was shocking.

She opened her eyes in confusion. Mark had settled back in the driver's seat, staring straight ahead as he turned on the ignition.

"I'll take you back to the track now," he said.

She stared at him in disbelief then lowered her head, fumbling to replace her dress. The fabric was clingy, her fingers awkward as she tugged it into place. She jammed her arms in her jacket, holding it tight, needing protection against the chill. And her shame.

He drove fast, threading through traffic as though eager to be rid of her. A red Explorer cut in front of them, and he slammed on his brakes, tossing her against the dash.

"Fasten your seatbelt," he said. Nothing more.

By the time they pulled onto the track grounds, her embarrassment had swelled until she wanted to shrink into the seat. The car stopped near the barn entrance. She grabbed the door, fumbling with the handle, but the lock depressed with an ominous click.

"Let me out," she said, her voice surprisingly level. "You proved your point, and I deserved it. No need to humiliate me any further."

He turned, his face enigmatic in the shadows. "I want you to quit."

Panic balled in her throat. Only three weeks left, and he was going to fire her because she'd been stupid, impulsive and lovesick. Her grandfather would win. She'd end up working at Boone, reliant on his every whim. Controlled by him.

"I can't." She almost choked on her desperation. "Please. I have to finish out the meet."

He shifted in the seat, his voice flat. "I don't know why you're so keen to prove something to your grandfather, Jessica, but everyone has options."

"Not when you have no money."

"You're a smart girl. Hard worker. You don't need your grandfather's money. And you already have connections...I really don't want you here."

She squeezed the door handle, his words exacerbating her plummeting self-worth. She couldn't even hold her first job, a manual job she enjoyed. Hell, a job she loved. "Please don't fire me." She swiveled, looking directly at him for the first time since he'd stopped the car.

"I'm not going to fire you. *You* haven't done anything wrong."

The bleakness in his voice made her feel guilty but at the same time, she pushed her advantage. She had to stay until Breeders' Cup, the last weekend of the meet. "Then you promise you won't fire me?"

He stared straight ahead, silent, his fingers gripping the steering wheel. Finally he turned to her. "I won't fire you, Jessica. But don't test my control again." He pressed a switch on the panel of his door, and the locks rose. "There's not much left."

His gruff warning sent a thrill shuddering through her. She opened the door, somewhat mollified by the knowledge he wasn't unaffected. She turned to say good night, but he'd already stepped from the car.

"I'm going to sleep in the office," he said. "In four hours we'll have to get up."

Something rustled in the fallen leaves, startling them both. But it was only Kato who scampered from beneath the trees, wrapping himself around her ankles and greeting them with a plaintive yowl.

"You rascal." She scooped him up. "I thought I locked you in my room."

"You did." Mark turned and stalked into the barn.

Yawning, she and Kato followed him down the aisle. The rich food and alcohol, combined with their intense bout of kissing, had left her drained. Her shoes, so jaunty and energizing earlier, pinched her feet, and the prospect of kicking them off and slipping into bed was wonderfully appealing.

Her gaze drifted to Mark. He looked different now, focused and remote as he checked each horse. Inconceivable that only thirty minutes ago, his mouth had been on her breast...it had been rather nice.

"Damn!"

He stopped so abruptly, she rushed up with Kato curled in her arms. "What's wrong?" she asked.

"Quiet." He backed her up, his hands on her elbows as he pressed her against the rough boards. "Wait here."

He walked to the end of the aisle and vanished around the corner. She hesitated, but he was out of sight and curiosity egged her forward. She inched to the spot where he'd first stopped.

"Oh, God." She dropped Kato on the ground and stared at the destruction.

Her door was smashed. Her tiny room—her home—in shambles.

She entered slowly, bursting with indignation. Her clothes were scattered, the cot flipped. Even Lefty's bike was wrecked, with five broken spokes and a slashed seat. Worse, her coffee can of hard-earned money—Buddy's money—was overturned and empty.

"I'm going to kill that kid!"

Mark appeared in the doorway, his face alight with relief. "The horses are all fine."

She sank to her knees, overcome with a sense of violation. It was great the horses were fine, but his priorities were very clear, and it only highlighted her insignificance.

"Much taken?" he asked as he tried to straighten Lefty's mangled bike.

"All my money." She fought her despair as she scooped a bra from the floor and tossed it into her duffle bag.

"I'm sorry." He gave up on the bike and urged her to her feet. "Come on, it's late. Nothing can be done now."

"But this is my room. Where I sleep." She shivered in revulsion. "And that kid touched everything."

"What kid?"

"That kid. You know, the same kid. He was here before, trying to steal my bike."

"Okay. I'll call track security." He gently pushed a strand of hair off her face. "But I don't think a kid could have broken the door. It had to be someone bigger. They ripped the room up looking for money. Good thing you weren't here."

She shivered, unnerved, realizing she might have met the intruder if she hadn't been with Mark. He was standing so close, his eyes dark with concern and another emotion she couldn't read, and she had to fight the impulse to burrow into his safe chest.

Safe, with a man whose driving concern were horses.

Her tiredness was making her melancholy. And fearful. She stepped back, irritated with herself. "Would you help me straighten the cot so I can go to sleep?" she asked. "I'll clean up in the morning."

He shook his head, slipping his arm over her hip, and guiding her past the battered door. "I'll stay here and talk to security. It's time they take this seriously. You can sleep in my office tonight."

She tried to argue, but he shushed her, and she was much too tired to bicker. Besides, after spending weeks in a cramped tack room, his office would be like the Ritz. She might even be able to sleep in. "Do owners' dinners count as overtime?" She limped beside him, trying to keep up in her ridiculously high shoes. "Maybe count for an extra half-hour of sleep?"

"This kind of night does."

"*This*, meaning the break-in? Or *this*, meaning the kind of night where the boss embarrasses the employee in his car?"

He brushed a finger gently over her cheek. "Maybe a little of both," he said.

CHAPTER TWELVE

Mark yawned, stretching in his office chair. His mind felt like mush, and he knew he hadn't been sharp for the morning gallops. He scowled when Dino dropped another stack of invoices on his cluttered desk.

"Add thirty dollars to Buddy's invoice," he said, scanning the farrier's bill. "Horse lost a shoe and had an extra visit."

"Right." Dino's voice muffled as he bent over the calculator and made the adjustment. "Guess that'll finish up Buddy. You have a new horse for his stall?"

"Not yet. Buddy's racing one more time." Mark gulped his coffee, hoping it would flush away his guilt.

Dino lifted his head, his eyes narrowing. "Thought you wanted to retire that horse? Thought you could persuade Sophie of almost anything."

Mark yanked his side drawer open and rummaged for a stapler. It seemed Miss Jessica Boone was also adept at persuasion. Last night, he'd been thinking with his dick, a damn poor way to make decisions. Clearly it wasn't just his dad who suffered from impaired judgment whenever he got close to a pretty woman. "Where's the stapler?" He slammed the drawer in frustration and shuffled the mounds of paper.

Dino picked up the stapler and slapped it in Mark's hand with a knowing grin. "Did Sophie get to you last night? She's not a bad-looking woman. Just give her what she wants. Take her out and bang her."

"Great way to lose horses," Mark said. "Clients don't like trainers banging their wives." *Or their granddaughters either.*

He absently picked up a beanie bag, squeezing the paperweight in his hand. It was round and firm, yet soft, much like Jessica's breasts. His gaze drifted to the cot where the imprint of her head was still visible. He realized he was still squeezing the bag and tossed it on the filing cabinet with a disgusted snort.

Dino had moved to the doorway to sip his coffee and watched as the last set of horses were bathed. "Why is she so hot?" he asked. "Obvious reasons, of course, but probably it's her spirit."

No need to ask who Dino was referring to, and Mark resisted the urge to join him. It was always fun watching Jessica bathe Buddy; invariably more water ended up on her than the horse. Usually he placed Buddy in the first set so it was cold when she washed him—cold enough that she wore a vest—but today he'd deliberately scheduled Buddy last so she'd have more time to sleep.

"Does she have her vest on?" he asked, trying to concentrate on the list of upcoming races.

"No, just the long-sleeved purple shirt. Not the high one with the buttons, the one with the low neck."

"Jesus, Dino. You know all her clothes?"

"Most of them," Dino said unapologetically. "I'm single now, and I like women. Unfortunately, she's not into casual sex."

"How do you know that?" Mark's voice sharpened.

"I tried, walking her home one night. She was no fun at all."

Satisfaction warmed Mark, satisfaction and a curious relief. He crossed his arms behind his head and tilted in his chair. She'd been fun with him, lots of fun. Course, last night she'd been drinking. And last night she'd wanted something.

"Leave the employees alone," he said, sharper than he'd intended.

Dino twisted, raised a curious eyebrow and stared at him over his mug. "Just not in the barns, right? Not at the track?"

"Not anywhere with Boone's granddaughter," Mark said.

"Okay." Dino gave a good-natured shrug. "But you can't keep the other guys away. Lately more men hang around our shedrow than sit in the kitchen."

Mark scraped his chair back, brushed past Dino and strode to the wash pit. It didn't help that the feed man lounged against his truck, watching Jessica with rapt attention.

"Buddy's finished," he said to Jessica. "Take him inside."

He scanned her shirt. Not really transparent, but her clothes were somewhat inappropriate. Tight, clingy stuff that was fine on the streets, maybe fine on other women, but not on her. It wasn't anything specific. He couldn't even yell at her for breaking the dress code. Clothes just couldn't hide that gorgeous body.

She wrinkled her nose, bent over and placed a hand on Buddy's chest. The back of her jeans tightened, hugging her curves, and her T-shirt lifted, revealing a full half inch of creamy skin. "No, Buddy's still warm. I better walk him a bit longer," she was saying. Arguing with him. Probably thinking she could do whatever she wanted just because he had the hots for her.

"Get the horse inside. Now," he snapped. He wheeled and stalked into the shedrow. Could hear Dino's chuckle, felt Jessica's hurt bewilderment but didn't turn around.

He wasn't like his father. Just because she had a pair of beautiful breasts that she'd let him handle last night didn't mean she could waltz around the barn doing whatever she wanted.

"Is that horse wrapped yet?" he yelled at Carlos, aware several grooms were looking at him. Assets wheeled in his stall, agitated by the unusual noise. *Perfect.* Let's get the colt all excited so he'll run like shit in the Breeders' Cup—the Breeders' Cup, when millions of people are watching, and a trainer's ability is on display.

But the shedrow was a mess, and he couldn't shut up.

"Maria, the aisle is filthy. Who left this helmet on the ground!" He kept walking, circling the shedrow, whipping his barn into shape. Everyone was slacking. Two of the race bridles hadn't even been hung properly.

Dino caught up to him, still grinning. "Three more weeks of this. Christ, we'll all have ulcers."

Mark sighed and blew out a rueful sigh, knowing he'd been unfair. "Tell me again why I want a Breeder's Cup runner?"

"Not just a runner. You got the favorite. Everyone's watching you, boss."

"Fuck off, Dino."

"I need money." Jessica buried the metal scoop in the oat bin then diligently measured Buddy's rations. She'd learned that horses had notoriously weak digestive systems; it didn't take much to start stomach cramps, and the ensuing colic could be fatal. "Quite a bit of money," she added. "The shithead who broke in last night cleaned me out."

Maria didn't ask a single question, just dug some crumpled bills from her back pocket. "Here's twenty-four bucks."

Jessica's throat tightened, and she turned away for a moment, blinking rapidly. Maria was so generous, so quick to share everything she owned. Like many at the track, she lived for the moment and didn't give a hoot about last names, background or education. So poor yet so happy.

And she was too, Jessica realized. In fact, track life was so absorbing she hadn't thought about skiing in weeks. Maybe she'd never been committed. After her dad died, her mother had shipped her off to private school. Skiing had turned into an outlet, a way to get attention by excelling. Coaches and teammates had become her surrogate family, and she hadn't wanted to give them up, despite the manipulations of her grandfather.

And now she had new family which included a wonderful horse and a wonderful friend. Her eyes itched, and she kept her head averted, pressing at the molasses pump until dark sweetness drenched Buddy's feed. The rascal wouldn't eat his glucosamine or MSM if it wasn't covered in molasses and sprinkled liberally with brown sugar.

"I'll have another fifty-five dollars when Mark pays my bonus," Maria added, misinterpreting her silence. "You can have that too."

Jessica impulsively dropped her bucket and enfolded Maria in a grateful hug. "You're one of the best friends I've ever had," she said, swallowing the persistent lump in her throat, "but unfortunately I need a lot of money. Two thousand dollars. Enough to buy Buddy."

"Oh, no." Maria stepped back, eyes wide with dismay. "You can't fall in love with the horses! They'll break your heart, every time. And how can you afford to keep him?"

"I can't, but Mark said there are adoption farms that will find a nice home. A place where he won't have to race anymore." Her voice cracked. "I can talk to them too and tell them how much Buddy loves molasses."

"But two thousand dollars? That's so much money." Maria leaned against the bin, her eyes dark with worry. "I suppose we could try stooping."

"Stooping?"

"You know, checking betting tickets that people throw away. The clubhouse is the best place. Good stoopers can make a bit of money. The trick is to memorize the race results so you can sift through them faster."

"Is it legal?" Jessica asked.

"It's not illegal, although security doesn't like it. We'll be careful though. We can head over there after you get back from Dick's."

Jessica grimaced and checked her watch. Almost eleven. Too bad her bike was wrecked. It was a long walk to Dick's although her knee felt amazingly good, so good she could probably run. Mark had even commented that she no longer limped. Weird, she felt better than when her doctor treated her. It'd be great if Dick had some real running shoes, and she could burn off the calories from last night's feast.

Last night. She didn't want to dwell on *all* the events. The most important thing was she could buy Buddy. She wasn't going to brood about her busted bike or ransacked bedroom or stolen money. Or how Mark's kisses made her toes curl.

Her breasts tightened just thinking of him. She'd barely talked to him this morning. Everyone had scrambled, trying to avoid his foul mood—everyone but Dino who seemed to find it amusing. Yet Mark had been thoughtful enough to let her sleep late, and spending a night in his quiet office had been like staying at a five star hotel. When she'd finally wakened, the second set was on the track and the door to her tack room already repaired. He'd scheduled Buddy for the last set of the morning so she had more time to sleep.

"You have a dreamy look on your face. Horse or a man?" Maria asked.

"Horse," Jessica said, shoving thoughts of Mark firmly from her head. Besides, Dick expected her to show up to work, not to be daydreaming about her gorgeous, slave-driving boss who possessed a surprising core of kindness.

*

Jessica smoothed her hair back and rapped on Tricky Dick's apartment door. Footsteps thumped, and the door opened.

"Come in." Dick gestured and stepped back. He wore a white high-collared shirt tucked into a black tutu belt, and his purple pants had no fly. "I didn't think you'd actually show."

"That's harsh." She arched an eyebrow but actually appreciated his honesty.

He smiled, not unkindly. "Dear, I know the smell of money, and you're not the sort to unpack boxes. So tell me, who designed my trousers?"

"Prada."

"Very good. Now what about my paisley scarf?"

"Gucci, I think."

"You'll do." He gave a satisfied nod. "I need each box unpacked and racked, separated by design. About half are unlabeled knock-offs. Those are the ones you need to identify. Mary from downstairs will take pictures later. Questions?"

"No coffee, no get-to-know-you chat?"

He made a rude gesture before swooping down the hall. "My phone list includes twenty society ladies, the most influential in New York, who need charities like Anna House to support. And I have to reach them before they send their money and clothes elsewhere. But if you perceive your coffee as critical, by all means, dear, go make one."

"Maybe later," she said, spotting a Veneta jean jacket that would be perfect for cool autumn mornings. She scooped it out of the box, fingering the jacket with admiration, then reluctantly hung it on the rack and dug back into the cartons.

She liked the job and worked fast. Enjoyed unfolding each garment and guessing the origin and where it would fit in Dick's Catalogue of Fine Clothes. And when dust tickled her nose, she muffled her sneezes, aware he was on the phone, patiently explaining Anna House's role and asking for support.

His voice was smooth, cultured and assured as he spoke of charity dinners and benefit auctions. And he was a master at name-dropping. She smiled, imagining the people he called. No doubt they pictured Dick as a member of their elite, living in a home like her grandfather's, and that perception made a difference. She calculated Dick—he introduced himself as

Richard—had a forty percent success rate, and it was fascinating to hear his spiel.

Time sped. At one point, Mary, a lady with bulging biceps, charged in carrying a camera and a tattered cardboard box. Jessica emptied the box on the floor, scattering an assortment of belts, cummerbunds and a plastic duck.

"We never know what's in the boxes," Mary said, rolling her eyes and rushing off.

Jessica rubbed a kink in her lower back as she mentally itemized the articles. Best to hang them all, she decided, so Mary would be able to take good pictures for the Internet. Kato might like the squeaky duck.

At some point Dick finished his phone work, so the apartment was quiet except for the clicking of her hangers and the shouts and laughter that filtered in from outside. Maybe Dick had gone to the kitchen to make coffee, she thought wistfully. They'd been working for at least three hours, and she still had the stooping thing to do with Maria.

However, when Dick reappeared, she gaped, thoughts of coffee forgotten. His neutered image had been replaced with an empowering Armani suit with a definite masculine look. She gave an admiring thumbs up. "You must be Richard now. Definitely not Tricky Dick."

"It's all about appearances, my dear," he said, with a faint blush. "This one works best when I speak at the ladies' luncheons."

"Yes, I imagine you're well-received," she said dryly.

He ignored her smirk, adjusting his jacket as he stared down at the road separating the apartments. "Is that man waiting for you? When I first saw him behind you, I assumed he was a gardener, but his clothes are too clean. Odd he's still there."

"Who are you talking about?" She joined Dick by the window and studied the man slouched against a corner apartment. Beard, slit of a mouth and the same hostile expression she'd seen at the paddock. He had a garden rake in his hand, but he definitely was watching Dick's door.

Flustered, she backed away from the window. A chill attached to the back of her neck. "I've only seen him once before. Is he part of the Mexican Mafia?"

Dick laughed. "Not unless they recruit from the Middle East." He grabbed the camera Mary had left and snapped several pictures. "Did you buy anything from that guy? Do you have anything he wants?"

She shook her head. "Nothing like that. And the only good stuff I had was a bike and my phone, but his kid took care of that. Stole my money too. It took me twenty minutes to fill out the police report."

Anger propelled her back to the window, and she pounded on the glass. The man's eyes shifted from the door to her face, holding her gaze for an instant before he snaked around the corner and disappeared.

"My, my, you're bold." Dick chuckled and closed the window, carefully checking the lock. "Why don't I drop you off at your place. Barn or apartment?"

"Barn, number forty-eight."

"Ah, the esteemed Mark Russell's stable."

"You know him?" she asked as she pulled her boots on.

"Let's just say he arouses my lust."

"Mine too." She gave a glum sigh.

Dick's perceptive laugh made her feel much better, and she enjoyed their candid conversation on the drive back. The man was difficult to slot, so she stopped trying. He worked as a groom for the spring and fall meet but lived at his own house in the winter. Fundraising for Anna House seemed to be his main interest, and his selfless commitment left her awed and humbled.

He pulled his panel van in front of the shedrow with a flair appropriate for a limo. "You did an excellent job today, dear, and you're welcome to borrow clothes for any future event." He glanced at the barn's drying rack. "I see you washed the dress. Hand washed, I presume."

"Definitely," Jessica assured him, glancing at the tiny dress now flapping between two immense horse blankets and a motley line of leg wraps. "Let me know when the next batch of clothes arrive. I enjoyed it."

"As did I. Thank you for contributing." He leaned over and kissed her cheek. "And I'll make some inquiries about your mysterious admirer. I have his picture now. Do be careful. Don't go walking in the dark."

She nodded and slid from the van then watched as it rumbled down the road. She'd missed her nap and was bone tired, but the realization she'd contributed to a worthy cause made her warm with satisfaction. Maybe she wasn't as useless as her grandfather believed. She bounced toward the entrance, jerking to a stop when she saw Mark and Dino.

"Wish I was the man who put that smile on your face." Dino grinned and adjusted his cowboy hat, his gaze sweeping her with his usual admiration.

"Wish it was a man too," she said, "but I was volunteering." She glanced at Mark. This was the first time she'd been close to him since last night and her nerves jangled; it was difficult to forget that hard body. He wore a blue sports jacket that matched his eyes and if he was tired, it wasn't apparent. "Thanks for letting me sleep in this morning," she added.

Mark's slow, deep smile made her stomach flutter. "You deserved some extra hours," he said. "Besides, I need you this afternoon."

"Okay," she said calmly, but her heart jerked in her chest.

Dino chuckled. "You showed up at the wrong time, Jessica. Everyone else is hiding."

"Because Mark was in a bad mood earlier?" she asked.

"Partly." Dino shot Mark a told-you-so grin. "But mainly because there's a TV crew coming. And a guy from some magazine who wants pictures of our very own illustrious trainer."

"I see." She tried to hide the wistful note in her voice, but for most of her life she'd been the one in the limelight, the one the media clamored to interview. She missed it. A white van with the *Sports Illustrated* logo on its side slowed, and she automatically smoothed her hair.

"You look fine," Mark said. "They just want a couple of workers in the background."

"I don't like background," she said mournfully, turning away from his perceptive smile.

A sandy-haired man wearing cargo pants and sporting a flamboyant moustache hopped from the passenger's seat. Gary Timmons! She'd recognize him anywhere. She squared her shoulders. No doubt he'd want to ask her some questions too, maybe talk a bit about sports injuries and career changes. This would be cool after all; now Mark would see she was good for more than just background.

Gary had interviewed her several times before, once after a World Cup final. He'd also been the first to request an interview after her spectacular fall. She'd refused, of course, unable to accept her ski career was crushed, but now she was ready, eager even, to grant an interview.

Gary walked across the gravel, and she beamed her most welcoming smile. He reached past her and pumped Mark's hand.

"Thanks for your time, Mark," he said. "We just need a few pictures to go with the November article. Maybe we can get the girl to hold the horse."

The girl? Her smile slid away. Something wrenched deep in her chest.

"You okay with that, Jessica?" Mark asked, his gaze pinned on her face. "Keep Assets in the barn. He'll stand better there."

"Sure," she mumbled, ducking her head in shame. Naturally Gary didn't recognize her. She was a nobody now, her status drained away when she lost her position on the team. Ironically, when she was finally able to talk, nobody cared to listen.

She slunk down the aisle, feeling small, wounded and unwanted, while the three men laughed and chatted by the door. A horse nickered—it was Buddy, watching over the stall guard. She detoured, and he shoved his neck out, pressing his forehead against her chest in complete and absolute trust.

She stilled. It was the first time he'd ever done that. Usually he didn't like his head constrained. Mark thought he'd probably had his ear twisted so would always be a little head shy. She slowly reached up and rubbed the inside of his left ear. A big quiver enveloped his entire body, but he kept his head against her chest. She was even able to press her lips against his satiny forehead. Wow. This was a complete breakthrough.

"We need that horse today, Jessica," Dino called but the impatience in his voice didn't dent her delight.

"I'll be back later, Buddy," she whispered. "And I promise to find you a good home with someone who'll love you. Someone who will be gentle with your ears and feed you lots of peppermints."

Smiling, she floated down the aisle to Assets' stall. Hurdling down a mountain didn't seem nearly as important as saving a grand old fellow like Buddy, and she'd be making some lucky person very happy in the process. She hummed as she slipped a chain through Assets' halter and led him into the aisle. The colt jigged a bit, but it was nothing she couldn't handle. She did notice Mark tensed when Assets rocked back on his legs and tried to rear.

"Good work," he said as she snapped the colt's nose, pushing him off balance and maneuvering him safely back to the floor.

Gary kept a cautious distance and eased around the restless horse, snapping pictures and moving quickly. "Feisty fellow," he said. "Is this the horse everyone thinks will beat the sheikh's runner?"

"He should give a good account of himself," Mark said.

Gary grinned, motioning Mark to step closer to Assets. "You people are so superstitious. I did a Derby story last year, and the trainer wouldn't mention the word winning. What's up with that?"

Mark shrugged. "Too many things can happen to ever expect anything from a horse. You do your best. And hope."

Gary flipped open a coiled notepad and checked his notes. "You're thirty-one, one of the youngest trainers to ever have a favorite in the Breeders' Cup. And you're from Texas, certainly not the center of blue-blooded racing." He glanced at Dino's hat and gave a wry grin. "Everyone will be watching your horse on the last Saturday in October. Some hope you fail. How do you handle that kind of pressure?"

"Good assistant. Good staff," Mark said, his mouth tight.

"Come on." Gary waved his pad in frustration. "Give me something interesting. Something people will want to read."

"At night, he sneaks into the barn and feeds Assets peppermints. And sometimes he croons to him. It actually sounds like baby talk." Three heads twisted to stare at Jessica. "I hear him because I sleep right over there." She pointed at her tack room.

"Perfect," Gary said, scribbling furiously. "Anything else you can tell me, young lady?"

"The young lady's leaving now," Mark said as he lifted the shank from her hands. But though he was frowning, his eyes looked amused.

She smiled and retreated to her room, quite content to be dismissed, although it still irked that Gary hadn't recognized her. It was nice to stretch out on her cot and ignore the cluster of voices. Mark's training regimen was somewhat confusing anyway: all the talk about doing their best, good staff, slow progress. His method definitely worked, but it seemed to center around patience, just watch and wait for the horse to mature. So different from skiing where it had been push, push, push.

She punched her pillow and caught the lingering smell of Mark's aftershave. Maybe he'd think of her when he smelled the pillow on his cot. The notion gave her some satisfaction since lately he'd dogged her thoughts with irritating persistence.

Something rustled, and she thumped the floor with her foot, scaring the mouse back into its hole. Kato generally wandered the backside during the day; he didn't join her for naps, so she and the mice had reached a practical agreement. She wouldn't scream if she didn't see them, and she always made lots of noise so they'd have time to skedaddle.

Anyway, there was little hope she'd be able to grab a nap. Mark had three horses racing today, so their grooms would be returning soon and making all kinds of racket. She crossed her arms behind her head and studied the new lock gleaming on her door. Mark hadn't skimped, she'd grant him that. No one would ever get past that massive deadbolt. It did seem rather pointless though; she had no money left to steal.

Hopefully stooping would replenish her Buddy Fund. *Stooping.* She liked how the word rolled over her tongue although it sounded like back-breaking work, and was unlikely to be listed in any career manual.

She flipped open *The Racing Form*. Betting also seemed an easy way to make money. Child's play, really. She'd cashed in big before—no reason she couldn't do it again. The lively gray filly that occupied the stall two down from Buddy was running in the sixth race. She'd been working well and Carlos, her groom, was exceedingly confident.

Mark was letting Emma Rae ride again. Jessica ignored the little twist in her chest. It was only natural for Mark to give Emma Rae more mounts after she'd done so well with Buddy. She was a good jockey too, although it was tiresome how she dropped around the barn every morning to chat with Mark. Jessica always felt like a giraffe next to the petite jockey.

It would be fun to be small. To race. She blew out a sigh, staring blankly at the pages of *The Form*. Jockeying was an exciting profession, and the riders always looked wonderfully snazzy in their crayon-box colors. She often caught herself watching them, unable to hide her wistfulness. And it seemed Mark really did prefer little women. He and Emma Rae were always laughing—

Rap, rap.

"Come in, Maria," she called.

But the door swung open, and Mark loomed in the doorway. "You're supposed to keep it locked," he said, inspecting the new hinges with a critical eye.

She tossed aside *The Form*, dropping her feet to the floor without even checking for mice. "Who's paying for that expensive lock?" she asked.

"Hadn't thought about it," he drawled. "Guess I'll deduct it from your pay."

"But that's not fair." She rose to her feet, glancing over her shoulder at her empty coffee can. "Whoever uses this room later will keep it. I shouldn't have to pay for fixtures. Besides...I'm sorry but I can't afford it."

"Relax." His voice softened. "I just wondered if you were okay for money after the break-in. Obviously not. I'll have Dino advance some cash."

His thoughtfulness was touching, but he'd turned to leave before she could clear her throat and thank him. Just like her family, quick to dole out money but always in a hurry to rush away. "Aren't you going to pay overtime for last night?" she called, hoping he'd linger a bit longer.

And that got his attention. He slowed to a halt, his ridged shoulders tightening beneath his shirt. He turned and studied her with such intensity the air between them crackled. "Jessica," he said softly, "I just wish I could afford you."

Her jaw dropped, but he walked out the door before she could think up a suitable reply.

CHAPTER THIRTEEN

"So someone is drunk or careless and throws away a winning ticket?" Jessica turned away from the horses entering the paddock for the sixth race and looked at Maria. "Stooping seems kind of mean," she added.

Maria snorted. "It's not mean at all. We're not hurting anyone. Besides, the people who throw them away don't know, and it beats having a good ticket swept up in the garbage. Just memorize the race results, especially if there's a scratch or disqualification."

Jessica nodded, but her attention had leaped to Mark, who'd just walked into the paddock with Carlos. She jangled with anticipation, buoyed by his statement in her room. Maybe tonight she'd see him at the bar.

Maria's elbow poked her. "What'cha looking at? You're practically drooling."

Jessica's cheeks warmed, and she averted her head. "Just Carlos and his filly. She sure looks ready. Who do you think will run second?"

"Don't know. But don't bet on the two horse. Pedro knows the horse's groom, and he said the mare's a bit sore."

"Then why are they racing her?"

Maria rolled expressive brown eyes. "Don't be naïve. The track vet will scratch any obvious lameness, but lots of horses run when they're a little sore. I have some aches and pains myself, but I still do my job."

"Mark doesn't race sore horses," Jessica said.

"Not now. He's worked his way up to better animals. Purses are bigger, so he doesn't have to race them as often. Assets is running for two million, and all his connections will get a piece. Carlos is so excited he can't sleep."

Jessica glanced back at Carlos who led the feisty gray filly around the walking ring. She remembered when he'd dropped his superior attitude and finally acknowledged her presence. It was the same day she'd caught Assets. The same day Mark had let her use his Jacuzzi.

She hadn't realized how important her grandfather's colt was to the barn. Hadn't understood about all the different kinds of races and horses, and the wide range of purses. However, it didn't need to be a big race to bet, and Buddy certainly didn't care how she earned his purchase money.

Handicapping seemed simple—she'd made a lot of money when Missy last ran—and Dino had kindly advanced her two hundred dollars from next week's paycheck. She'd already analyzed the entries. Now though, she needed extra time to study *The Form* since Maria had cautioned not to bet on the two horse.

She stared at the numbers, trying to choose her second horse. Number ten, Mark's gray horse, for sure, but she needed a second one for her exacta. The jockeys paraded out, and it was obvious she had to hurry, but panic made her brain stall—the past performances blurred together in an information overload.

"Wow, look at the six horse. His groom sure turned her out nice," Maria said. "And I also like the one horse and the seven horse."

Jessica tried to block Maria's comments—she didn't like the one horse who seemed to quit running when things didn't go her way. However, Jessica felt like she was in a math test, and the teacher had just announced time was almost up. She glanced at the thick-chested man next to her. Could see his program spread against the rail. He'd circled three horses but not Mark's runner. Maybe he knew something she didn't?

"Who do you like in this race?" she asked, flashing him a friendly smile.

"I'm betting on the jockeys." He slurped his drink and wiped his chin with the back of his arm. "Highest percentage on top."

"What about Mark Russell's gray? How can you ignore that horse?"

"Apprentice jockey and a girl. No way I'm betting that combo." He snorted, spraying beer and belligerence. "The trainer's probably using the jock so he can get a little ride himself."

"That's ridiculous!" she snapped.

"Yeah, well, you asked for my picks, lady. Don't get huffy if you don't like them."

She rolled her eyes and edged closer to Maria, who leaned over the rail and yelled at Pedro. Maria's partner led number nine, a white-blinkered horse who pranced and chomped at the bit. Saliva dripped from the mare's mouth, and Jessica heard the grinding of her teeth as she jigged past.

"Who's that?" Jessica asked, deciding the horse was either unhappy or just very keen to run.

"You've met him," Maria said, completely discounting the horse. "That's my fiancé, Pedro,"

Jessica laughed and let her frustration seep away. Clearly she was taking this handicapping business way too seriously. The sun was shining, ten gorgeous horses paraded in front of her, and the camaraderie of the crowd needed to be enjoyed.

She shoved *The Form* back in her pocket and leaned against the rail while Maria continued to heckle Pedro—who flashed Maria an adoring smile every time he circled.

"I see why you two are always slipping off to your apartment." Jessica grinned. "How long have you lived together?"

"Two years, and we still don't get much napping done. But I wish *he'd* find some afternoon entertainment." Maria twisted, shooting a wary look at Mark. "Boss been yelling at everyone lately. Told me I wasn't raking the aisle right. Even Dino got in shit for flirting with the masseuse."

Jessica's smile faded. Mark had yelled at her too. She just ignored it, sensing something was bothering him. But she hoped to be the new woman in his life, and the idea of being dismissed as afternoon entertainment was rather demeaning.

"So I guess Mark doesn't take his girlfriends to dinner or shows or anything like that?" she asked wistfully.

"Doubt it. They pretty much have to fit his schedule. There was an ESPN woman who was perfect for him. She worked early mornings so they could hang out at his place in the afternoons. I read all about it in the *Track Tattler*. Oh my, look who's working for Radcliff's barn now." Maria leaned further over the rail, her voice rising. "Don't forget to cool that filly out, Trish," she hollered to the blonde leading the nine horse.

"Trish works for Radcliff now?" Jessica's mouth tightened with distaste as she searched for the trainer's distinctive white hair. "I don't see him here."

"He might be at the Keeneland sale or racing at Churchill. Trish will fit right in with Radcliff. He doesn't care about horses either so long as they make money. God help a horse that breaks down in *his* barn."

Jessica watched the composed blonde as she led a dainty chestnut filly with three white legs. Trish seemed a capable handler, although Jessica had heard rumors she'd been responsible for Belle's colic.

"I read in the *Tattler* that another girl from our barn went out with Mark too," Jessica said. She'd read no such thing, but she hoped to keep Maria talking. "I assumed it wasn't true since Mark doesn't usually date girls who work for him..." She let her voice trail off pretending the subject was of little interest.

"Oh, he does once in a while," Maria said. "He just doesn't do anything on track. Keeps everything private. No one really knows what Mark does. The *Tattler* likes to gossip about all the good-looking, single trainers."

"I see," Jessica said. She stared across the paddock watching Mark pause to talk to a little girl on crutches. He gestured at Carlos, who immediately guided the gray filly close to the rail. The girl leaned over and patted the horse, then looked up at her mother. The girl's toothy grin, her utter delight, made Jessica's throat spasm.

A simple action on Mark's part, but Jessica knew she'd never been so thoughtful with ski fans. She'd taken their cheers for granted. Yet no matter how Mark's horse ran today, to cheers or jeers, the joyful look he'd put on that little girl's face was priceless.

She swiped the corner of her eye and jerked her attention back to Maria. "So? When do we start stooping?" she asked, her voice gruff.

"Soon. See that group over there?" Maria pointed. "Where the woman has a Canadian T-shirt and the men have souvenir glasses? Lots of people clean their pockets when they're standing in concession lines. Be a good place to start."

They waited until the jockeys were boosted onto their horses and had filed into the tunnel then edged around the drifting crowd. Jessica bent over, scooping up every ticket she could find, concentrating on the ones in clumps. It was hard enough to keep track of one ticket, she reasoned, and the clumped tickets would be harder to check. People might make more mistakes.

"I got one," she called in glee. Race three, ten dollars to show on number six. She pulled out her *Form* where she'd scribbled earlier results. There'd been a disqualification, and number six had been placed over the number four horse.

"Yeah, that's a good one." Maria peered over Jessica's shoulder, her voice sharpening with envy. "Should pay at least ninety bucks."

"We can split it," Jessica said quickly.

"No. Finders keepers," Maria said. "Racetrack code."

"At least let me buy you a beer."

"The beer's too expensive on this side of the track. I brought some from home." Maria reached in her pockets and pulled out several large clear bags, plastic gloves and two cans of Bud. "Take the bags and gloves for later."

Jessica shoved the plastic in her pocket, deciding to rush up to the clubhouse after the last race. The owners' boxes would be the perfect place to stoop. She opened her beer and took a complacent sip. Ninety dollars every five minutes; at this rate, Buddy would be paid for by the end of the day.

"Are you ladies going to watch the race or just drink?" Mark's amused voice sounded behind them.

Jessica jerked around even as Maria's sharp elbow jabbed her in the ribs. However, she didn't need the warning to know Mark wouldn't like what they were doing. "We're just trying to decide who will run second," Jessica said. "We're pretty sure you'll win."

"Nothing's a sure thing," Mark said, "but this is probably the best race to bet. Six, nine and ten should be finishing strong. Did you get an advance from Dino?"

She nodded, but the ticket from race five burned a hole in her pocket, and her cheeks warmed with a guilty flush.

"Okay then, you're good for money?"

She nodded again, wondering why she felt so tongue tied.

"All right," he said. "Well, I'll see you tomorrow."

She and Maria watched him stroll away, past the security guard and into the elite trainers' section.

"Man, that was weird," Maria finally said.

"What?"

"He has a horse warming up on the track, and he's not watching her. And he stayed to give us betting tips. He never gives tips. Always says to bet only if we don't need the money."

Jessica shrugged, wishing he'd invited them to his box. Hopefully the filly's owners were men or else very old, very married women. Probably Mark and Carlos would be having dinner with them tonight. Maybe Emma Rae would join the group too.

She beelined toward the rail, resolving to check his box and find out exactly what sort of owners Mark was entertaining. But Maria ran up, grabbed her arm and propelled her towards the betting windows. "This way, kid, and bet big. If we're lucky enough to get advice from the boss, we'd be fools not to take it."

They studied the fluctuating odds and after two minutes of heated discussion settled on a ten-dollar exacta box six, nine, and ten, and a fifteen-dollar trifecta with Mark's horse on top.

"Which horse did he say would run second?" Jessica asked Maria, to the exasperation of the harried mutual clerk.

"He didn't say," Maria said. "Better box them. It'll cost more but will cover our ass."

Jessica tried not to wince as she handed over the last of her two-hundred-dollar advance. It was a huge bet, but the payout would make it all worthwhile.

They rushed to the front of the grandstand, breathless and excited, arriving with only four minutes to post. Maria pushed in by the rail but Jessica lingered behind, scanning the collage of faces in the reserved boxes, trying to spot Mark and his owners. No good, too many people. A sea of swarming faces stared down at her.

She turned to the well-dressed man beside her. "Sir, could I borrow your binoculars for a moment?"

"Sure, but I want them back for the race."

"Certainly." She looped them over her head and pressed them against her eyes. They were the cheapest glasses she'd ever used. Everything looked tiny, and she rolled the dial repeatedly, trying to put the distant faces into focus.

"They work better if you look through the other end," Mark drawled. "Who you looking for?"

She gave a guilty start and quickly returned the binoculars to their owner. "I heard Brad Pitt was up there," she said.

"Really? Didn't see him." Mark looked distracted as he stared over her head at the starting gate. "Come on, baby. Get in."

The urgency in his voice startled her and she swung around, horrified to see their gray filly twisting from the gate, refusing to load. Aw, damn. Her bet.

"Get your butt in there!" she yelled, squeezing closer to the rail. The horse had to load. Her money was riding on Carlos and his filly. She held her breath as the jockey dismounted. The gate crew produced a blindfold.

Mark studied her face. "I assume you have a bet down," he said dryly.

"Yes." Her fingers tightened around the rail. "Next week's salary."

"What!" He grabbed her arm, tilting her around so he could see her face. "Jesus, Jessica, sometimes you scare me."

Jessica shrugged, but she was scared as well. They both watched as the stubborn filly was led in circles. She could feel Mark's tenseness, the tightness of his grip, the absence of his breathing and then realized she wasn't breathing either.

But finally the filly entered the slot, and the gate crew slammed the door shut. An assistant starter whipped the blindfold off, and the crowd cheered.

Jessica relaxed a notch and heard Mark sigh.

"She likes to stalk, so hope for a good break," he said. His arm had loosened although it was still looped over her hip.

"And the other horses you mentioned?" she asked not turning around, not wanting to do anything that might make him move his arm. "Where should they be?"

"They're closers. Break isn't so important."

Jessica kept her eyes glued to the gate, willing the gray to break clean. She felt more confident now that she knew the racing scenario required. Her sports therapists had taught to always envision the perfect run, but she wasn't sure how she could possibly envision three horses.

Maybe she could picture the jockey silks: blue, striped green and yellow. If the colors crossed the finish line in that order, she, Maria and Buddy would have a very successful day.

"They're off!" the announcer yelled as the gates burst open.

Colors churned. A white-blinkered horse from the seven hole broke like a rocket then disappeared from sight as a crowd of horses fought for position.

The crowd groaned, a weird simultaneous sound. She stretched on her toes, struggling to see what had happened. Something bad, judging by the way Mark's arm clamped around her waist.

"Damn. Rider's off," he muttered.

Jessica twisted, staring at the large screen. Mark's gray filly still ran gamely in third, but something looked strange. And then she realized—the saddle was empty.

"Do they need a rider for the race to count?" she asked, her voice cracking.

"Yeah. Steve's up though. Looks okay."

Jessica stared blindly at the group of horses, now led by Mark's riderless gray, who galloped gaily around the turn, reins flapping as she pulled away from the pack. Little good that would do.

"Why did you pick Steve to ride?" Her voice rose. "Why not Emma Rae, or someone who can at least stay on?"

"Stop thinking of yourself." Mark dropped his arm, and she immediately regretted her thoughtless words. "It's hard to stay on when a horse stumbles. It's also dangerous for everyone out there. No one knows what a loose horse will do."

"Well, your horse is going to win the race." She sighed. "And it won't even count."

The jockey in striped green silks made a huge run on the outside, closely followed by the jockey in yellow. They couldn't catch Mark's riderless gray though, who crossed the finish line ten lengths in front. The perfect finish—all three horses on her betting ticket—except the filly had no rider.

Carlos materialized beside Mark with a beige cooler over his arm. They left her and walked onto the track, talking animatedly. An outrider snagged the loose filly, turned and escorted her back to the waiting group of trainers and grooms.

The outrider grinned as he passed the reins to Carlos, and the prancing filly looked so proud of herself, Jessica felt like screaming. She looked around for someone who shared her frustration, but Maria was draped over the rail, slapping hands with a beaming Pedro. Clearly, they were both delighted with the race results.

The inquiry sign flashed but when the ambulance rolled up and Steve hopped out, his shrug was self-explanatory. Mark patted Steve on the back, grins all around.

"Russell has his horses running so fast, the riders need seatbelts," the man on her right grumbled.

Ah, an understanding ear. Jessica waved her betting stubs in disgust. "I would have had the trifecta if that rider hadn't fallen off."

"Yeah, well I would have had the Pick Six," the man said. "Twenty thousand smackers down the tubes." He snapped his fingers in disgust and walked away.

"Mommy," a young voice called. "The horse I patted came first! She's so fast she didn't need a rider to whip her."

Jessica spotted the little girl on crutches. Ketchup stained her tiny face, but didn't hide the brilliance of her smile, and Jessica felt a rush of shame. The filly had run well. Even a little girl recognized it. If Jessica hadn't bet every dollar she owned, as well as her advance, she'd also be proud.

Squaring her shoulders, she smiled at the girl and trudged to the concession stands. Clearly handicapping wasn't the cinch she'd first thought, and stooping would probably be the best way to fill Buddy's coffee can.

"Yuk." Jessica flipped over a darkened ticket, wrinkling her nose at the wad of tobacco stuck in the middle. Lemonade, beer stains, even mustard were okay, but she didn't want to touch anything that had been in someone else's mouth.

Race fans still trickled from the clubhouse but an army of stoopers had appeared, armed with clear plastic bags and gloves. A lone photographer snapped pictures of the deserted track but so far, security hadn't bothered them.

She bent back down, shuffling along the concrete as she scooped tickets into her bag. She had the rhythm now—shuffle, drop, scoop but it would be much easier if she were short like Maria.

"How you doing, kid?" Maria called. "It's almost dark, and I'm meeting Pedro to celebrate his win. Think I'll go back and get cleaned up."

Jessica shook her bag, letting the stubs settle. Half full. "I'm going to stay a bit longer," she said. "Maybe check upstairs."

No way was she walking back with Maria. It was nice that Pedro's horse had won, but Jessica was still slightly bitter about Steve falling off. She didn't want to hear any more replays of that particular race.

She climbed the concrete steps and shoved the door open. Amazing how fast the building emptied. The escalator was motionless, so she bounded up three staircases and pushed through several doors until the concrete changed to plush carpet.

This was the place to be. Millionaires' row. She scooped quickly, working through the elite boxes that extended onto a balcony high above the track. A garbage can clinked—another stooper perhaps, or else cleaning staff. She ignored her aching back and scooped faster. No telling what riches she'd pick up here, but she needed to grab them before others did.

The garbage can clinked again. Someone must be concentrating on the stubs in the numerous metal bins. She'd tried that earlier but found it too messy. Must be a newbie. Smiling with a pro's complacence, she glanced into the adjoining skybox.

Her smile flipped to dismay. A young boy rammed a half-eaten hotdog into his mouth; his other hand clutched a container of greasy fries, and he wolfed the food as though starving. Concern pushed her closer, her steps absorbed by the thick carpet.

He twisted, sensing her presence. They stared in shock.

"You," she said, recognizing his face. He moved first, leaping sideways trying to evade her grip, but anger blasted her forward, and she grabbed his arm. "Where's my phone? Why'd you bust my bike?"

He muttered a torrent of words, waving the hotdog, eyes large in his thin face. His arm was bony beneath the filthy shirt, and her anger dissolved. Oh God, he was skinny.

"It's okay," she said quickly. "I don't care about the phone. Or the bike. It's okay."

He didn't seem to understood her words, but he obviously sensed her softening. Keeping a wary eye on her face, he rammed the hotdog in his mouth, no longer trying to bolt, seemingly more concerned she might steal his meal.

"It's okay," she repeated. She wished Maria were here to translate. She thrust her hands in the air and backed up a step, trying to show she didn't want his food. Watched helplessly as he rummaged through the garbage. Witnessing his hunger made bile rise like a sour wave in her throat.

A door slammed, and the rims of the boy's eyes flashed a startled white. She reached out and touched his arm. "Don't worry," she said softly. "I'll get you more food. I'll help."

But he was having a complete fit now, backing up and staring at the door, muttering such a high-pitched, incomprehensible string of words, her grip tightened. "I need help," she called, afraid he'd bolt.

"Where are you?" a man yelled. "I hear the boy. Is he with you?" The voice was harsh with a heavy accent, and doors slammed as he moved along the skyboxes, checking each room, moving toward them. Moving fast.

The sharp smell of urine cut the air. The boy's arm trembled beneath her hand, and she glanced down, shocked at the stain darkening the crotch of his jeans.

"Do you know that man? Is he your father?" Her voice cracked in dismay. What sort of fear would make a kid piss his pants?

Impulsively she reached out and turned the door lock. Moments later the handle shook. The boy edged back, his eyes swinging from the door to Jessica. He raised his arm and made a slashing gesture across his throat.

"This is our skybox. We're finishing our drinks," she called, trying to inject some righteous annoyance.

"Open the door. Give me the boy." The door handle rattled, and the voice thickened with frustration.

"What's your name?" She wiped her sweaty palms on her jeans as her gaze scrabbled around the room. Dirty plates, race programs, glasses. No phone.

"Open the door," he said. "No one will be hurt."

Okay, this wasn't good. No one ever said that except in the movies, and it was always a lie. She jerked away from the door, pressed a finger to her mouth and pointed to the sliding glass doors at the front of the box. The boy nodded and slid them open.

"Just a minute," she called brightly. "We'll be right out." She grabbed her plastic bag of tickets, holding it out from her body so it wouldn't rustle, and joined the boy by the balcony overlooking the track.

She slid the door wider, letting in a rush of dark and chilly air. The boy bolted to the left, but she grabbed his arm and pointed to the right. The balconies connected, and they vaulted over the railing, her adrenaline so pumped she kept pace with the nimble boy as he crossed two rows of boxes.

Silence now. The man had stopped pounding on the door. Must have already circled to the next box. She grabbed an empty wine bottle, tossed it in the opposite direction, then pulled the boy between the chairs as glass shattered.

They huddled in a ball, pressed into the grimy floor, watching as a figure swooped onto the balcony. Only five boxes away, not nearly far enough. Oh God, what was in his hand? Something glinted. A knife? Her breath leaked in a gasp of disbelief, and she flattened against the floor, oblivious to the discarded nachos rammed against her cheek.

Maybe it's a beer can. Not a knife. Please, God, not a knife. Someone made a whimpering sound, and the boy's hand pressed against her mouth.

Shit, she was making that noise. Okay, deep breaths. She tried to steady her breathing and think, but they were stuck. Too high to jump, and the back doors of the skyboxes all opened onto the same corridor. She squeezed her eyes shut, afraid the man would feel her gaze. Willed him to walk in the opposite direction. He'd already checked these boxes; surely he'd go the other way.

The boy pressed against her, his hand still rammed against her mouth. I'm the adult here, she told herself. She opened her eyes, removed his hand and gave it a reassuring squeeze. If only she had her cell phone, she could call for help.

The man turned and vanished into the skybox.

She sucked in a shallow breath, trying to gather her courage, knowing they had to move. Pushed herself up on shaky legs and tugged the boy behind her. They sidled along the balcony, through a sliding door and into the adjoining box.

Similar to the first. No phone. But there had to be a fire alarm in the corridor.

122

The boy balked when she reached for the doorknob, but she forced a reassuring smile. There was no alternative. They had to leave. Once the man reached the end he would simply search the remaining boxes. He'd find them, stuck like rabbits in a hole.

She pushed the door open a crack and peeked up the corridor. To the right, thirty endless feet, perched a red alarm box. To the left, a staircase, headed down. She was a fast runner. So was the kid. A door opened, and she jerked backwards, holding the door, holding her breath. A dark shape flashed in the corridor then disappeared into the last skybox.

She grabbed the boy's hand and tugged him across the corridor toward the steps, the bag of tickets bouncing against her leg. They bolted downward—third floor, second floor, bottom.

God, where were all the people? She yanked the kid to the left. Saw a man with wispy gray hair pushing a mop. But he was too feeble, too stooped.

"Call security," she yelled, her voice breathless as they streaked past. "There's a man with a knife in the skyboxes."

"You stoopers shouldn't be up there." He shook his head in disapproval and turned back to his shiny floor.

She ran out the side exit, around the paddock and toward the security booth with the kid sticking so close she could feel his ragged breath. Usually she resented the security guards and their anal need to check credentials, but tonight the lights of the guardhouse were a welcome beacon.

She charged to the booth and pressed against the grilled window, weak with relief. "A man chased us," she panted, "and he had a knife. A really big knife."

"Can you describe him?" The guard swiveled in his chair, leaned forward and picked up a pen.

"No, just his voice."

"How did you know he had a knife?"

"Shiny." She squeezed her eyes shut, overcome with emotion. God, her throat hurt, and it was so hard to breathe. Everything was okay now though. The security guards had radios; they'd catch this creep.

"Was it another stooper?" The second guard set his thick sandwich on the desk and stepped closer to the window, his voice rising as though she had trouble hearing. "Maybe it was a shiny plastic bag."

"Maybe it was someone working an area you wanted," the first guard added.

"No, no! It wasn't like that. Listen, do you speak Spanish? Because this boy was with me. He'll tell you." She glanced over her shoulder, but the kid had vanished.

"Hey, k-kid!" She tried to yell but her voice squeaked, and trembles wracked her body. She frantically turned back to the guards. "You have to find him. Help him."

The two guards exchanged glances. "Can we see your credentials, miss?"

She fumbled to unclip her card, but her hand shook and her fingers were too cold, the blackness around her too malevolent. She sensed the man's presence. Knew he was out there, watching. Knew it with a certainty that made her sick.

"Please. Just find the boy. Quickly." She stared over her shoulder, weak with fear. "He's all alone. We have to help…" She could no longer hold back her wave of nausea and bent over and vomited.

CHAPTER FOURTEEN

Mark smiled at the pretty waitress, switching to English to order another round of Corona then back to Spanish once she'd left.

"And with the rest of the cash, I will bring up my mother and younger brother," Carlos announced. "What'cha doing with your Breeders' Cup money, boss?"

Mark shrugged and grabbed his pen, uncomfortable with the topic. Dino and Carlos had already spent every dollar Assets might make. Mark wasn't overly superstitious, but he didn't like to fool with karma either. Racing luck was fickle, and the fastest horse didn't always win, just like his gray today.

He scribbled another notation on his training sheet. "I want to concentrate on the filly's gate work," he said. "The starter wasn't happy. Steve said she spooked and came out of the gate ragged. Then stumbled."

"She sure ran tough though." Dino's voice faded as his attention drifted to the bar. "Is that Trish over there? She's looking damn good."

Mark glanced over his shoulder. Several people from the track had drifted in, including Trish, all gussied up. Maria and Pedro were huddled over the bar, although he didn't spot Jessica's regal head. She and Maria had struck up an unlikely friendship considering Maria's aversion to rich white folk. And Jessica—he sighed just thinking of her. There was simply no sense guessing what she might do or who she'd do it with.

He turned back to the table and added another notation. Smelled Trish seconds before she squeezed in beside him. He tried not to stiffen but wondered if horses disliked strong perfume as much as he did. Jessica always smelled of herbs and flowers, a fresh smell that Buddy obviously liked. Of course, Buddy liked everything about Jessica.

He'd also noticed Jessica didn't eat much meat, bought a lot of salads and hated anchovies. Maybe Buddy liked that she didn't smell like a meat eater. Or maybe it was her voice Buddy liked. Or the confident way she moved...

Jesus. He shook his head, annoyed he wasted so much time thinking about Jessica.

"Working, Mark?" Trish asked, her voice coy.

"Yeah. In the middle of a meeting." He flipped over his barn notes before she saw them.

"Good evening, Trish. How's everything in barn thirty-nine?" Dino grinned. "Hear your new boss is a bigger prick than Mark."

Trish's smile tightened, but she nodded hello to Dino and Carlos before turning back to Mark. "Thought you'd like to know my barn has a nice three-year-old dropping in class," she whispered. "He runs next week. Probably a good claim."

"Trish, stop." Mark raised his hand. "Don't tell me that stuff. You work for Radcliff now. At least show him some loyalty."

"But my loyalty is to you." She leaned closer, her voice lowering. "I keep telling you I'm sorry about what happened. That one mistake—"

"One mistake, but a huge one," he snapped, irritated Dino and Carlos were grinning like fools, hanging on Trish's every word as they checked out her low-cut shirt. They'd love it if he rehired her. As if Jessica wasn't enough.

And wouldn't that be chaos. Trish and Jessica in the same shedrow—double the distraction, double the trouble. He shuddered and grabbed his beer.

"I've been having trouble sleeping since you fired me." Trish leaned closer, and her leg pressed against his thigh. "Lost a few pounds."

"You look good," he admitted, letting his eyes drift over her undeniably lovely body.

"I think so too," Dino added, while Carlos nodded with so much enthusiasm he spilled his beer.

"Look, we're at a work meeting here, Trish." Mark scowled at his two employees who were obviously thinking of everything but work.

"Then let's talk later." She squeezed his arm and rose from the seat "Once you finish your work. Or tomorrow afternoon. I'll be around. Whenever you want."

Dino chuckled, watching Trish's cute butt wiggle away. "You must feel a little sympathy for your old man now. He had these kinds of opportunities every day."

"He was married, and he was a prick." Mark flipped over his worksheets.

"Well, you're not married." Dino's gaze remained locked on Trish. "And she's sitting by herself. It's mean not to cheer her up. I think she feels really bad about Belle."

Even Carlos, whose tendency to hold grudges was legendary, nodded.

"Yeah, she feels so bad about Belle she didn't yet ask if the mare recovered," Mark said, effectively silencing the two men. "No rain is forecast for tonight, so we'll go ahead with Assets' work," he added. "Four furlongs, first set tomorrow. This is huge."

His phone vibrated. He scowled at the interruption but checked the display. Security. "Just a sec." He flipped open his phone, listening with growing irritation as a guard explained a stooper had been caught posing as his employee.

"Look," he interrupted. "Just deal with it. ID theft, whatever. I don't care. Whatever your policy is." He flipped his phone shut and looked at Dino. "Track security. Christ, why are they calling me." Shaking his head, he returned to his notes. "Same company we used in the spring is sending us a barn guard. Starts today, twenty-four seven. Unless one of you wants to sleep there?"

"I will if I can bunk with Jessica," Dino said. Carlos nodded, grinning so wide his lip stretched over his broken tooth.

Mark flipped his pen in exasperation. Women loved Dino, and if they helped his friend forget his ranch and busted marriage that was fine. But Mark didn't like the idea of anyone sleeping with Jessica...and Dino was a charming bastard. "No more jokes," he said, avoiding Dino's amused gaze. "But it's been a long day. Go relax. We'll continue this in the morning. I'll check the horses on the way home."

He rose and shoved the notes in his briefcase, ignoring Trish's lingering gaze. He wished Jessica were around. She was a great buffer; other women tended to step back when they saw her. Good horses had that effect too. The really great runners had a fearlessness, an air of invincibility that made other horses back away.

He nodded at Maria who gave a jerky wave and ducked behind Pedro. Five years and she was still intimidated by him, no matter how approachable he tried to be. She couldn't speak any English when he first met her. Now she talked as snootily as Jessica.

He walked over and shook Pedro's hand. "Congratulations on the race today. If we couldn't win it, I'm glad your barn did." He smiled at Maria. "Saw you feeding Buddy tonight. Is Jessica off somewhere?"

"No, no," Maria stammered. "She's probably working in her room."

Maria sometimes mixed up words when she was nervous so he switched to Spanish, hoping to put her at ease. "I'm assigning Missy to Jessica and giving you Belle, the filly Trish rubbed. Belle is running in the undercard on Breeders' Cup weekend," he added.

Maria's eyes widened as she realized the purse money involved. "Thank you, boss." Her smile deepened.

Pedro thumped her back in hearty congratulations.

"You deserve it. You're a hard worker," Mark said. "I appreciate how much you've helped Jessica."

"But I like her."

"I do too," he admitted, turning away. Trish was still posed on the stool but busy talking with the bartender, and he slipped out the side door with a sense of relief.

"Everything's quiet in the barn, sir." The guard, spiffy in his crisp khaki uniform, flipped open the logbook. "Last visitor was Carlos, who checked the horses at six."

"And another check by Jessica at eight?" Mark asked as he glanced down the aisle at Assets, who played with his hay net and now had long stalks stuck in his forelock.

"No, I haven't met Jessica yet," the guard said.

Mark frowned and looked in Buddy's stall. Jessica spent a lot of evenings with the horse and sometimes was a little sloppy with her time, but she'd never missed a night check. He strode down the aisle and rapped on her door. No answer.

128

Kato brushed against his leg, impatient to get in. He turned the knob, and the door opened. Damn. Over two hundred dollars on a new lock, and she didn't bother to use it. Kato bolted to his empty dish then turned, arched his back and yowled indignantly.

Mark stepped into the room, grabbed the cat food and dumped a pile into the dish. It was just an old horse stall but now so stamped with Jessica's presence, he felt like an intruder. Her busted bike was propped against the wall, serving as a drying rack for T-shirts and incredibly wispy underwear. He jerked his head away.

Buddy's win picture hung in a place of honor above the head of her bed, but the rest of the walls now had beautiful pictures of their own. He sank down on the cot and studied the artwork. It was apparent now who cut out the pages in his magazines. Clever how she'd arranged them. The fields ran together, making it look like an endless window and giving remarkable depth to the tiny room. The end wall was the view from the clubhouse, but her emphasis was on horses running free in green fields and not racing at a track.

Papers crumpled beneath his leg. He shifted, pulling them out. Just notations on today's results written in her elegant writing. Race two, photo, runners three, nine, seven. $$$$$ Check betting machines. Race three, disqualification, two, eight, five (five moved to the win $$$$. Ask Maria about gloves. Lots in first aid kit.)

His gut spasmed, and he thrust the papers aside and leaped to his feet. Scrolled through his display and frantically called the guardhouse. "That stooper. What was the name on the stolen credentials she had?" he asked.

"Jessica Boone."

"Damn. Look, just tell her I'm sorry, and I'll be right there. She's one of mine."

"Too late. Our policy is to turn them over to the police. And you did say—"

"What station?" His hand squeezed the phone.

"Jamaica. It's on the corner of Ninety-first and—"

"I know where it is." And at least the station chief there was a friend. He snapped the phone shut and rushed down the aisle, past Assets, who shook his head in irritation, past the curious security guard, and into his car.

He called the station while he weaved through traffic. A clerk answered the phone, huffed a moment, then reluctantly put him through to the chief. They began their usual negotiating.

"For this one—eight tickets on Breeders' Cup weekend," Bruce Connelly, the station chief said, sounding rather complacent, as though aware he held all the bargaining chips.

"Come on, Bruce. Only four. And the seats might not be together."

"Not much fun if they aren't together. And I need at least six. Especially if I drop two counts of resisting arrest. She pushed one of the officers, and they both ended up in the mud."

"All right. Six seats. But I'm picking her up now." Mark closed his phone, sped the last half mile, and charged into the station.

He signed every form the scowling clerk shoved in front of him then waited by the steel-enforced door. Someone with filthy jeans and muddy hair was escorted from a side room, but he kept his gaze on the door, fighting his guilt. If only he'd taken the time to answer the phone, if only he'd listened to what the guard was saying—

"Mark?"

He swung around, too stunned to speak. Jessica? Christ. It looked like she'd rolled in the mud. And maybe something else, he thought, catching the unmistakable smell of overripe food. If Bruce's officer looked half as bad, it explained why Bruce wanted six tickets.

"I gather you had some trouble stooping?" he finally managed. Her lower lip wobbled, and he stepped forward and wrapped her in his arms. "It's okay, Jess. Everything's okay." He tried not to breathe too deeply.

He nodded at the impassive guard and carefully escorted her down the hall.

"Wait." She twisted. "They have my bag. Can you get it?"

"Sure. We're going to the counter anyway. You can sign for your purse and stuff there." He led her to the hard-eyed clerk, reluctant to let her go. She seemed subdued, shaken by her arrest. Her unnecessary arrest.

The clerk reappeared with a disapproving scowl, slapped down a watch, some coins and not a purse, but a huge, transparent bag of betting stubs. She gave Jessica a look of disdain and passed the bag to Mark as though it were tainted.

"Good job, honey," Mark said loudly as he slung the bag over his shoulder. "You got a nice pile here."

"They threatened to throw it out. All that work." Jessica's lower lip trembled. "They handcuffed me and wouldn't let me find the boy...I might have got a little mouthy."

"That's my girl." He shot the clerk a dark glower. "Let's get out of here."

He clipped her into the passenger seat and pulled a horse blanket from the back seat. The blanket was new and white and immaculate, compliments of a recent stakes win. But he only hesitated a second before tucking it around her filthy body.

"Thank you for getting me," she said, and promptly fell asleep.

He drove directly to his house, waking her only when he pulled into the driveway. She didn't argue or ask questions, and his concern grew as she followed him, zombie-like, into the house.

"What happened to you, honey?" he asked as he pulled off her boots, stiffening when he saw her laces had been confiscated. Damn. They'd given her the full treatment. A muscle ticked in his jaw, and his guilt mushroomed. A visit to a police station could soften all but hardened criminals, and Jessica was certainly no criminal.

"What happened?" he repeated.

"A man chased us. A man with a knife." She stared at his face as though doubtful he'd believe her.

"You and Maria?"

"No. Me and that poor little boy." Tears welled in her eyes and when she reached to wipe them away, her entire arm shook. "He was so scared. I was too. I hope he's okay..." Her voice trailed off and he held her, soothing her, trying to absorb the trembles wracking her body.

"Everything's okay," he said. "We'll talk later. You're safe now."

He scooped her up and carried her down the hall and into the bathroom. Turned on a stream of warm water. "A quick bath, then bed. You can tell me all about it in the morning."

She stared, unmoving, her face a stiff mask. "He ran off. I just don't know if he's okay."

"Aw, honey. Nothing we can do now." He unbuttoned her shirt. "There, can you do the rest?" he asked.

She nodded again but struggled with the snap on her jeans, and her look of helpless panic filled him with concern.

"It's okay. I'll do it." He tugged down her jeans and underwear. Picked her up and plunked her in the water. Tried not to look or respond, but it was damn hard.

"Bubbles, I think," he muttered. He grabbed an old container from under the sink and dumped in the entire contents. Turned the jets on until blessed suds frothed over her body. Only then did he unpeel her soaked shirt and bra. He tossed them on top of her soiled jeans, then grabbed a washcloth, leaned over the side and scrubbed. Her tense muscles eased as he rubbed her shoulders and when he worked shampoo through her tangled hair, she leaned back and closed her eyes.

A pink nipple peeked from the swirl of suds and he palmed her breast without thinking, massaging it beneath the water. Aw Jesus, she felt good. He wanted to climb into the Jacuzzi with her. It was clear they shared a powerful attraction, and she wouldn't be around long enough to create complications. She wasn't a motor mouth and, unlike Trish, would never neglect a horse. But sex wasn't what she needed or wanted, not tonight. She'd looked so frightened, so exhausted, and she obviously trusted him.

And so did her fucking grandfather.

However, his hand didn't want to leave her slick breast—it touched, explored, caressed. Her eyes opened, and a slight smile tilted her mouth.

"Found some dirty spots, did you?" she asked.

"Yeah." His voice thickened. "Real important spots. Just give me a sec." He cupped both breasts, watching the water lap around them, feeling a hot possessiveness toward this naked woman in his tub. A woman who was fighting to keep her eyes open and preoccupied about some unknown kid.

He jerked back, swallowing a spurt of shame. Turned and grabbed a towel. Helped her from the slippery tub then wrapped her tightly, afraid to linger with the drying. She swayed so he scooped her up and carried her, still dripping, into his bedroom.

"Sleep now. We'll talk in the morning." Before he hauled the blankets up, her eyes had drifted shut.

He closed the door, dumped her clothes in the wash and headed for his spare room. It would have made more sense to put her there. Now he had to set the other alarm, but the idea of having her in his bed was rather appealing even if he wasn't in it with her.

He blew out a sigh and set the clock. Already two a.m.—only an hour and a half before they had to get up. Assets had a big work scheduled. He certainly hoped the colt had a better night's sleep than he and Jessica.

As usual Mark woke at three-thirty, one minute before the alarm sounded. He rose, transferred Jessica's clothes from the washer to the dryer and showered. He quietly opened his bedroom door and approached the bed.

She lay in the same position as when he'd tucked her in last night. He shook her shoulder. She felt limp, lifeless, and his heart kicked. He should have taken her to the hospital, had her checked out. But he felt her pulse, checked the steady rhythm of her breathing, and his relief was so great he backed from the room, deciding to let her sleep another precious hour.

He made a pot of coffee and checked the weather. Perfect. Logged onto the track and watched the live cam of the dark oval. At four thirty he still didn't have the heart to wake her and called Dino. "I'll be a little late. Make sure Assets is ready to go in the first set. I'll meet you at the gap. Put wraps on his hind. No blinkers."

"What's up?" Dino asked. "Car trouble?"

"Jessica trouble. Better have someone look after Buddy. He can walk the shedrow today." His voice hardened. "Let me speak to Maria."

Maria's voice was cautious at first, but it strengthened as she denied any knowledge of a kid or man with a knife.

"Then this incident happened after you left," he said. "After you took her stooping."

Maria must have heard the disapproval in his voice because she stopped speaking.

"It's not your fault, Maria." He sighed. "Stuff just happens around her." He hung up and dragged a hand over his jaw. Returned to the bathroom and spent extra time shaving. At five-thirty, he grabbed her clean clothes and re-entered the bedroom, deliberately loud. There was absolutely no way he could linger any longer.

She'd moved slightly. Her hair now fanned the pillow, and the glow from his clock radio illuminated her face. A bruise darkened her cheekbone, and her lower lip was swollen. She looked like a street fighter—beaten, subdued but oddly heroic.

He lowered himself into the chair, holding her clothes and studying her face. Old Man Boone had a helluva granddaughter, and if he believed the backside would send her scurrying home, he had no idea of her grit.

But she needed sleep. Would've been spared the whole police ordeal if he'd only taken a minute to talk with security. There was no real reason why he had to be present for Assets' work. Dino was immensely capable. The work would either go well or it wouldn't. And Jessica needed him much more than Assets did.

He left the bedroom, deliberately taking her clothes with him, and picked up his phone.

Dino's voice rose with disbelief. "You're not coming? You feel okay?"

"Yeah. But I just can't make it," Mark said. "Call me after the work."

He stretched out on the sofa and for the first time in five years, missed a training day.

CHAPTER FIFTEEN

Jessica woke in an unfamiliar but truly comfortable bed. Her gaze jerked from the ceiling and skittered around the masculine room. Aw, shit. Afternoon already? The clock said one o'clock, and sunshine filtered through the drapes. Clearly she'd slept away a big chunk of time, several feedings at least, and she hadn't arranged for anyone to look after Buddy.

She must be at Mark's house, in his huge bed. But if she'd slept with him, regrettably she couldn't remember. She did remember he'd dumped her in the Jacuzzi and sloshed water over her head. Probably hadn't used conditioner.

Her hands swept to her hair. Oh God, it felt like a rat's nest.

The bathroom was down the hall, and she needed to creep to it unseen. Hopefully Mark was at the track. Odd, he hadn't woken her, but maybe the guards had confiscated her credentials. It hadn't been wise to resist arrest. Maybe she no longer had a job, and her grandfather was sending a car to pick her up. Maybe the police were pressing charges just like they'd threatened.

A wave of emotion engulfed her—she'd been so scared, so helpless, and those people had made her feel like scum. They'd refused to help her look for the boy, impatiently cuffing her when she'd insisted they find him.

She shoved aside her jumbled thoughts and eased from the bed. No sense trying to speculate; she had to regroup. A meshed shirt was thoughtfully folded on the chair. She slipped on the shirt, examining it doubtfully. An old exercise shirt, maybe? Great for workouts but the holes didn't give much coverage, and the bottom of the shirt only reached mid-thigh.

She listened by the door. Didn't hear anything. Pushed it open and tiptoed down the hall.

Mark stepped from the kitchen, a steaming coffee mug in his hand. "Good morning," he said. But his gaze drifted to her hair and the side of his mouth twitched, the way it always did when he was trying not to laugh.

Heat flamed her cheeks. She stared at him, vulnerable, embarrassed and overwhelmed with gratitude. It had been the scariest, most frustrating night of her life and he'd rescued her. She wanted to burrow into his arms, but it was clear he didn't feel the same way—despite the skimpy shirt, all he was looking at was her messy hair.

"Thanks for everything last night." Her voice quavered. "I've never been in jail before."

"The police dropped all charges."

"Oh, that's nice." She edged along the wall, desperate to escape, afraid she'd cry if he looked at her any longer with those empathetic eyes. "Where are my clothes?"

"I washed them. They're drying."

"Thanks for that too. I really need to use the bathroom now." She eased past him, wishing for a bag to pull over her head.

She showered quickly and joined him in the kitchen with renewed composure. At least her hair was back to normal.

He handed her a cup of coffee. "Tell me about last night."

"Right. But you promised you wouldn't fire me." She gulped and studied his face over the rim of the mug. He didn't seem mad, but he wasn't smiling either.

He slid a glass of orange juice and two pieces of generously buttered toast in front of her. "I want to know about the man with the knife."

"Didn't see him very well." She bit into the delicious toast, then took another quick bite, realizing she was hungry. "It was dark," she added. "But he spoke English with an accent."

"What about this kid? Did he know the man?"

"Yes, but the boy doesn't speak English. Not much anyway." She stopped chewing and stared at Mark. "He's the same kid who tried to steal my bike. He was so hungry. And so scared of that man. The guards didn't believe me."

"I'll alert Child Services. They'll look after him. The sooner we catch the kid, the sooner we can identify the man."

136

She lowered her toast on the plate. *Catch the kid?* It sounded as though they were looking for a criminal. She wanted to help him, not pack him off to some agency.

"It seems like a dream now," she said. "But it really happened." She couldn't find a napkin so licked the butter off her fingers. Mark's gaze lingered on her mouth, and her breath quickened. Such a kind, capable, gorgeous man. Surely he'd help the boy.

His denim shirt emphasized the blueness of his eyes, the broadness of his shoulders. She dragged her attention back to her toast, even though her appetite seemed to have disappeared...or moved in another direction.

"I don't think you should keep working at the track." His voice hardened. "There's nothing left for you to prove, and I'll certainly tell your grandfather that."

She forgot she didn't want to ogle him and jerked her head up. "But I have to finish the meet. Once I do, Gramps is giving me money to start my own business. I'll be independent. You don't understand how controlling he is."

"You're not independent if he's giving you money."

"More independent though," she said, hating the truth in his words. "We Boone women tend to be useless, and he takes great satisfaction in reminding me of that fact. I have to get away."

"So you really are broke?"

"Actually, I might be very rich once I sort through my tickets." Flippancy was the only way to hide her despair. "Where are the stubs, by the way?"

He gestured down the hall, but his voice softened as though aware she was struggling. "Is that bag the extent of your plan to raise money for Buddy?"

"Yes, unless my boss gives me a raise."

"Not likely," he said, but she noticed how his eyes drifted to her chest. He seemed different this morning, much more relaxed than he was at the track. And he was definitely getting an eyeful. This meshed shirt was truly hooker-worthy.

She shifted in discomfort, tugging it further down her legs then realized the holes now highlighted her breasts. She tried crossing her arms. However, he continued to look relaxed, like it was no big deal she sat in his kitchen, like he was used to seeing her half naked.

Damn. Maybe they did have sex. But surely she'd remember something? She hoped she hadn't missed it. "Okay," she said, giving up and lowering her arms. "Did we sleep together last night? Because I'm sorry, but I just don't remember."

A smile creased his face. "How would you feel if we had?"

"That it was unmemorable, and you must be a dud."

"I'm not a dud," he said.

His voice carried such implicit promise, a shiver of excitement swept her. She swallowed, feeling disadvantaged with her damp curling hair, her nakedness beneath the scanty top. However, she crossed her legs, trying to match his coolness.

He abruptly leaned forward, his smile disappearing as he traced a finger over her swollen lip. "I noticed this earlier. Who hit you?"

"No one. I bumped the ground." She tried to ignore the quiver created by his touch but felt the jolt right to the tips of her toes.

"The police? Were they rough?" His finger stilled, and his voice had an odd quality, almost scary.

"No," she said quickly. "It was my fault. I wanted to find the boy first. They were trying to put me in the car. We...scuffled a bit. That's when they put me in handcuffs."

"Oh, Jess. I'm so sorry." His finger remained on her bottom lip, his eyes darkening as he stared at her mouth. His focus was so intense she could feel his heat. And his desire.

She swayed forward.

His eyes shuttered, and he dropped his hand and leaned back. "I don't want you stooping again. I'm sure your grandfather doesn't either."

Regret laced his voice, but he wasn't looking at her anymore—in fact, he was studying his watch. She stared in dismay, certain he'd been about to kiss her. She didn't understand his mixed signals...and then she realized. Of course. He was worried about Gramps. He'd never risk angering his most important owner. She tried not to smile; however, knowledge was a powerful thing.

She leaned back in the chair and stretched her legs, aware the meshed shirt was very revealing. And that Mark was tempted. He just needed reassurance—and a new approach. "Oh, Gramps never worries about what I'm doing. Or who I'm doing it with."

She circled her knee with a slow finger. Mark liked Thoroughbreds so he probably appreciated long legs, and she certainly had those. "I used to be a skier until I wrecked my knee," she went on, "but he wants me to forget about that life." She picked her words carefully as she pretended to examine her knee. "He wants me to go out with other guys...forget about my old boyfriend."

Mark's breath hissed as he jerked forward. "He *wants* you to forget a boyfriend?"

"Yes," she said quickly. "He wants me to meet other guys. Have some fun while I'm at the track."

"Fun?" Mark's voice had thickened.

"Casual fun, casual friends," she said, remembering all she'd heard about Mark's aversion to anything or anyone that might distract him from work. She stopped tracing her knee when his hand stilled her fingers.

"So you're looking for something casual, something temporary?" His voice was hot with hope and sexual hunger. "And your grandfather wants that too? You both want that?"

"That's right," she said. "We're temporary kind of people."

"Temporary is great." He grinned then, his relief so obvious it ripped her heart, but already his hand had slipped under the bottom of her shirt. "Then maybe I can be of some assistance after all."

He circled the sensitive skin on her inner thigh, and her misgivings scattered. It shouldn't be that hard to rein in her feelings. She'd learned a lot from Anton. She could keep things light too. Pretend this was all part of an agenda.

She forced a jaunty chuckle. "And maybe you can help me buy Buddy." Her voice trailed off as his hand moved higher on her thigh.

"Okay," he said. "So this is all about Buddy. That's good. I understand now." It was good he understood because she couldn't concentrate on his words, not when his wicked massage left her gasping. "But two thousand dollars is a big chunk of money," he added.

She couldn't speak, couldn't think, not while he was doing that wonderful thing with his hand.

"A lot of money, don't you think?" he prompted.

She was mortified her brain was stalling, mortified her breath escaped in pants. "Maybe you could just buy me a coffee then," she managed.

His chuckled and his left hand slid around her bottom, holding her in place, while his other continued its brazen massage, between her legs now, working its magic until she writhed against his hand. "I'll buy you all the coffee you want, honey," he said. "I just need to know this isn't about a horse."

"No," she gasped, wishing he'd unbutton his jeans and quit talking. She no longer even knew what they were talking about.

"I'd be delighted to help you forget your old boyfriend."

"Who?" she squeaked.

But he nudged her legs wider and dipped his head. She shattered in seconds, quivering as he held her in place, riding out her waves until she collapsed, boneless against the chair.

She stared, enjoying her delicious lassitude but resenting the satisfied look on his face. Resenting how, once again, he'd so easily aroused her. "Don't look so smug," she said. "It's been a year."

He chuckled and began unbuttoning his shirt. "Must have been a helluva boyfriend. Sounds like I have a lot of work to do."

She straightened her poor excuse for clothes and leaned back in the chair, watching as he pulled off his shirt. Clearly his exercise equipment wasn't just for show. She liked his rippled abs, how his chest hair tapered into the waistband of his jeans, and totally understood why Trish was so reluctant to give him up.

And then he scooped her up, and she stopped thinking as he carried her into his bedroom and dumped her on his wide bed.

His belt buckle clinked. She watched the intricate play of his muscles as he yanked off his jeans. Her gaze dropped lower and she gulped. He was big—big everywhere.

"Let's get that shirt off, honey." His eyes darkened with primal intent as he reached down and tugged it off. "Skimpiest shirt I could find, but it's gotta go," he said, his breath an appealing mix of coffee and male hunger. He lowered himself over her, covering her mouth with a possessive kiss until their tongues entwined like familiar lovers.

She ran her hands over his contoured chest, savoring his hardness, enjoying the kissing. His mouth nuzzled the side of her neck as his knowing hands roamed her body, searching, feeling, caressing her intimately. Minutes later she writhed with fresh need.

He paused and reached toward the bedside table. Slid the drawer open in an obviously practiced move and removed a condom. He was back over her soon enough, using his knee to separate his legs, and she gripped his shoulders and arched against him.

He entered fast, thrusting deep, and she wrapped her legs around his thighs, abandoning herself to the hot, hard feel of good sex. Great sex, she amended as he adjusted her legs higher over his hips, driving deeper, harder. And that was all he wanted, she reminded herself, but his gaze held hers as he shuddered above her and when he kissed her, so tenderly, her arms tightened around him and she didn't want to let go.

He rolled over, pulling her with him, silent for a moment as he pushed a strand of hair off her face. "No more stooping, okay, Jess. I'll buy Buddy for you."

"That's okay," she said quickly. "Just help me…ah, forget my ex."

He was silent for a moment. "I would very much like to do that," he finally said, running a possessive hand over her hips.

She kissed his chest, slick with sweat and the smell of pine soap, but his hand now palmed her right knee. She tried to wiggle away remembering how her grandfather had called it misshapen. However, he held her still, massaging the swelling. "This was the accident that made you stop skiing?"

"Yes. Last race of the year."

"Bummer." His fingers skimmed over the sensitive area behind her knee sending jolts to her nerve endings, and from his expression, he didn't seem to think it was ugly at all. In fact, he touched every inch of her, watching her reaction, until she quivered under his slow touch.

She could feel he was aroused again and couldn't understand why he lingered. She was more than ready. She tried to pull him on top, but he was so very strong and far more patient than her. She reached out and fumbled in his drawer. Found another condom and ripped it open. His breath caught when she rolled it on. She tried to go slow, shocked by her desire, but finally he pulled her on top, holding her hips as she straddled him.

He slipped a finger between them, splaying his other hand across her bottom, playing her until she gasped with pleasure and wiggled against him, desperate for release. He slowed, moving his attention to her sensitive breasts, controlling her until she gave his shoulder an impatient nip.

"In a hurry, are you." He growled and flipped her over, hooking her knees around his hips then filled her with his thrusts. She gripped his back, their bodies rocking in perfect rhythm as waves of sensation built. She heard her single cry of release, but it was overpowered by his groan and they collapsed in a tangle.

She held his hand, their hearts beating as one. She didn't want to let go. Didn't ever want to leave his bed. He was silent for a long time, his other hand caressing her neck. She looked into his dark eyes, wondering if he had felt it too, an intense connection that left her speechless.

"We gotta go," he said.

She swallowed. Even managed a careless nod.

"I'll use the shower in the guest room," he added. "You can have the Jacuzzi but hurry."

"What about my clothes?" she managed, relieved her voice sounded completely normal.

"They're ready, on top of the dryer."

She propped up on an elbow. "But you said they were wet."

"I lied. That bath almost killed me last night. Thought I deserved a peek."

"I didn't think you noticed the holes," she muttered.

"I notice everything about you, Jess," he said, so sweetly she didn't feel quite as rejected, and she let him tug her from the bed and propel her down the hall.

She washed and dressed quickly, pulling her clothes on with only a faint grimace. One mustard stain marked the front of her shirt, but he'd done a capable cleaning job. Skilled at everything— unlike her, she thought with a pang.

She joined him in the kitchen. He was dressed only in jeans, hair still slick, as he whipped together two peanut butter and jam sandwiches. His muscles rippled when he reached for a plate. Ridges, he was all hard ridges. Normally she wasn't into Rambo men, more accustomed to lean, skiing silhouettes but she liked him shirtless, liked seeing his magnificent body, and her admiring sigh leaked out.

He glanced up. "Allergic? I don't have much salad stuff. But want something else?"

"No, peanut butter's great. Unless you have a Mars Bar tucked away somewhere. I always like a bit of chocolate …afterwards."

His boyish grin made her heart lurch, but he only kissed her cheek and shoved the sandwich in her hand. "Eat in the car, okay. I want to be in time for the night feed."

"Right," she said, washed with an inexplicable sadness. She found her bag of betting tickets and moved to the front door, nibbling on her sandwich while she waited. He reappeared, fully dressed, briefcase in hand, swallowing the last of his sandwich.

His mouth tightened when he spotted her garbage bag but he didn't say a word, merely waited for her to step outside. Then he locked the front door and followed her to the car.

She'd tossed her bulging bag of tickets in the back and slipped into the passenger seat before she noticed the stink. "Gosh, something smells." Wrinkling her nose, she lowered the window and sucked in the fresh outside air. Couldn't remember his car smelling so bad.

He didn't say a word, only lowered his own window and backed the car from the drive.

And then she realized. "Oh, the smell…that was from me?" Her voice was small, and she remembered she'd been crawling over discarded food. That she'd vomited and rolled in the mud. She must have been a mess.

She shrank against the seat, feeling small, It was amazing he hadn't put her in a taxi last night. Even more amazing that he'd taken her home and kindly cleaned her up. "I guess I didn't thank you enough," she said.

"Oh yes, you did." He reached over and gave her knee a reassuring squeeze. Suddenly she didn't feel nearly so bad.

Traffic was heavy but steady. He drove fast, checking the time and adjusting the volume on his phone while he spoke to Dino, giving her a perfect chance to study him. She liked his hard jaw, his lean cheeks, how his thick brown hair curled at the back of his neck. The way he handled the car, his staff, the way he handled everything.

143

But she didn't like it when he skirted the gate behind the clubhouse and veered down a wide road toward the paddock entrance. She fiddled with her seatbelt, her nails tapping on the metal buckle, when she realized where he was going.

A security guard rushed from the guardhouse. "Here are her credentials, sir. Sorry about the mix-up."

"It's not me who needs the apology." Mark's voice hardened, and he pointedly kept his hands on the wheel. "It was my fault too. I should have checked your call."

The guard peered in the window, spotted Jessica and hurried around the car to the passenger's side. "Here are your credentials, miss. We're very sorry about the misunderstanding." His gaze slid to the stuffed plastic bag on the rear seat then bounced back, his expression carefully blank as he returned her laminated pass.

She gave a regal nod, but neither she nor Mark spoke again as he drove to the backside and parked in his usual spot close to the office. He switched off the ignition and turned to her. "I've shuffled some horses," he said. "Starting tomorrow, you'll be rubbing a second horse, My Silent Miss."

"Missy!" Jessica jerked in delight. "And the fun New Jersey ladies? Does that mean I'll see them again?"

"It does. In fact they'll be more delighted than you. People like you, Jess," he said. "They like you a lot."

She smiled, buoyed by his approval, then deflated. "Oh, but what about Maria? I can't take her horse."

"No problem. I already assigned her your grandfather's filly. Last night, in fact. Maria can fill you in on your new horse." His gaze settled on her mouth. "Just make sure you finish up by lunch each day. I'd like to spend time with you in the afternoons, if you're agreeable."

So it wasn't just a one-shot thing. Her heart raced. He was looking at her too, drinking in her face as though he really liked her. She tilted her head, pretending this new arrangement required substantial thought then smiled back. "I'd like to see you too," she teased, "but I'm just not sure how it's going to work out. I'm pretty slow, and you just doubled my workload."

He didn't kiss her—she knew he wouldn't at the track—but he *did* touch her knee. "Then I'll un-double it." He spoke with the assurance of a man in complete control. "Or else rub the damn horse myself."

CHAPTER SIXTEEN

Jessica brushed Buddy, feeling slightly guilty Maria had been forced to look after him during her absence. And Buddy liked a strict schedule. Little deviations worried him.

"So how long did he walk the shedrow this morning?" she asked again.

"Twenty minutes, and I put him on the hot walker for another thirty." Maria shrugged. "I didn't have much time. This place was nuts. Dino was running around, giving orders, enjoying being the boss. And I think Mark was with a woman. He's in a really good mood. Was anyone with him when he picked you up at the station?"

"No, just him." Jessica ducked over Buddy's leg and checked his wraps. She'd pretended she hadn't been released from the police station until a few hours ago, and the deception weighed heavy. But Maria had a rigid view of the hierarchy, slotting owners and trainers in distinct categories. She didn't tolerate mixing. Jessica's forehead broke into a cold sweat at the prospect of losing her only real friend.

"I think I saw that kid today," Maria said. "The one who got you in all the trouble."

"Where?" Jessica asked, scratching Buddy on his muscled shoulder. There were bags of peppermints in Mark's office, and she intended to snag a few, to compensate Buddy for her absence.

"He was hanging around the kitchen dumpster. Now that Mark told security to keep an eye out, they should catch him quick enough."

"There must be something we can do." Something ached in Jessica's chest. "Couldn't Anna House help him?"

"No, that's a daycare for track families. Your kid's a runner." Maria yawned and buttoned her jacket. "I'm going home. Pedro and I were out late last night. Oh, and we got real security guards now. The day one is old and grumpy, but the night one is real nice." Maria turned and bustled down the aisle, calling out a greeting as she passed a guard in a spotless khaki uniform. Must be the friendly one, Jessica decided, feeling rather melancholy as Maria rushed out the door to join Pedro.

There was no sign of Mark. She could wander around and see if his car was still in the lot but, like Maria, he had things to do. People to see. Afternoons were his preference for socializing, not nights when he tended to work. She certainly couldn't stalk him. But after her long sleep, she wasn't at all tired, and the approaching darkness only magnified her loneliness.

Loneliness and a slightly used feeling. Which was totally ridiculous, she told herself quickly. She squared her shoulders, determined not to feel sorry for herself. The guard might be good company and if she went to the kitchen for supper, the walk would fill up some of the solitary evening. There were also some issues of the *Tattler* and *Thoroughbred Times* to read, although Mark grew irritated when she cut out the pictures. Plus, the betting tickets needed to be sorted. Yes, there was plenty of stuff to keep her busy.

She strode down the aisle with renewed purpose. "Hi," she said to the guard. "I'm going to the kitchen. Want a coffee or anything?"

He swiveled, stared for a moment, then straightened from the doorway with pleasing enthusiasm. "No thanks," he said. "I have a coffee thermos right here. Be glad to share though."

Maria was right. The guy was nice with a cute smile, and it was reassuring to have someone around at night. "Maybe I'll join you later."

"Hope so," he said, and she felt his gaze as she exited the shedrow.

His open admiration made her feel less alone. More appreciated. This was the type of man she knew how to handle. Unlike Mark, who didn't care about anything but horses. He'd dumped her as soon as they returned to the track, was probably out eating and laughing with other owners, other trainers, other jockeys. Wouldn't give her a thought until tomorrow afternoon, when he wanted her in his bed.

She glanced over her shoulder as she walked down the road, and the security guard gave an enthusiastic wave. He didn't know she was broke, inexperienced and had no real friends. Noise drifted from a row of apartments. She kicked at a rock, feeling more isolated as laughter and music blended in the distance.

She didn't meet anyone on her walk to the kitchen. Inside it was quiet, almost sleepy. She ordered the evening special, three dollars and ninety-nine cents, carefully counting her precious change. A few people were scattered in chairs reading tote sheets and stable notes, but their muted conversations were in Spanish. On earlier occasions when she'd tried to chat, they had either looked at her blankly or just nodded and edged away. It was better when she was with Maria, but so far she hadn't been able to join their fraternity.

After placing her order, she ducked into the women's bathroom. The public bathrooms by Mark's barn were sporadically maintained, so she always slipped some toilet paper into her jacket pocket in case of a dreaded paper shortage.

When she emerged, the gentle-eyed cook passed her an overflowing plate wrapped in foil. He didn't speak much but always served extra, and she guessed he either felt sorry or else appreciated her awkward attempts at Spanish. She hadn't deviated from the evening special ever since one of her comprehension blunders had resulted in an odd supper of melted cheese and onions. She no longer had money to cover food mistakes.

Maria had said the night cook was saving money for a scooter. Well, Jessica was saving for a horse, and she knew what it was like to try to fill a can. Her coins clinked in the tip jar, earning the cook's grateful smile and no doubt some extra food on her next order. She picked up a free copy of the *Tattler* and walked out the door with her hands loaded.

The night was black, the sky dark with low-lying clouds, so she avoided her usual short cut and followed the street lamps along the roadway, determined not to check over her shoulder, determined not to think of men with knives or how she and the boy had been forced to flee from a homicidal maniac.

But her stride quickened until she was almost jogging. She did check behind her once, prompted by the sensation that someone watched, not a really spooky feeling though, not like outside the security booth when she'd sensed the man's evil presence. No, this time the shadows had a different feel. On a hunch, she pivoted and waved her food. "Hey kid. Come on out."

No one appeared, but she sensed someone was there, and Maria said the boy had been spotted by the kitchen dumpster. She cut around to the back of barn forty-seven and sat beneath a big gnarled tree, out of the light but accessible. Peeled back the crinkling foil and sniffed.

Yum. The powerful smell of fish and chips filled the crisp air. Already her mouth watered, and she wasn't starving. She chewed slowly, biting off small pieces of fish, taking her time, watching the shadows. A flutter of movement, and the boy was there, crouching beside her like an old friend. She smiled. He smiled back.

She gripped the paper plate, fighting her urge to wrap him in a relieved hug. *He was safe.* The security guards, the police, even Mark, might think she'd exaggerated, but both she and the boy knew the knife man was evil.

She controlled her wave of emotion and handed the boy a big piece of fish. He wolfed it down with a heart-wrenching lack of chewing then crossed his thin arms over his T-shirt and shivered, all the while staring hopefully at the food.

Seconds earlier she'd been hungry but seeing the solemn-eyed boy smothered her appetite. He was cold, ravenous and needed help.

Waving the plate, she motioned for him to follow then circled to the front of the shedrow. The guard remained propped by the door, so she eased around the back and slipped into her room, the boy dogging her heels. She gestured for him to sit, passed over the plate of food and ran to the tack room, afraid he might vanish if she dawdled.

She hurried back with two horse blankets and a large jacket. It was doubtful anyone would miss the blankets—Mark won so many coolers the barn bulged—but the jacket was a beautiful soft leather with AQHA World Champion on the back. She had no idea what the initials meant, but the symbol showed a cowboy on a horse, and it was the warmest item in the tack room.

The kid's face still pressed against the plate as his grimy fingers rammed the remaining food into his mouth. But his pace had slowed. And he definitely needed a bath. She tried not to curl her nose, didn't want to remember how Mark had endured a similar stench from her. But there was no way the boy's clothes could stay in this tiny room. The air was already too stale.

He finished the food and shifted to the blanket, where he sat cross-legged, wary but with no obvious inclination to bolt. She passed him the jacket. When he pulled it on over those awful clothes, she gave a silent apology to its owner.

"I'm Jessica." She thumped her chest. "Do you speak Spanish?" It was clear he didn't speak English. Maybe Maria could talk to him in the morning, find out his name and where he lived. She hoped it wasn't with that horrible man. Little wonder the boy had run away.

The kid nodded, but she sensed he didn't understand. Judging from his eager expression, he was conditioned to please. "How about French?" she asked, switching languages. They'd taught French at her boarding school in Switzerland, but it was Anton who'd helped perfect her street lingo, and she was very fluent.

He smiled and nodded.

"You speak English too?" she asked.

When he nodded again, she sank onto the cot. The kid was smart. She remembered his look of approval when she threw the glass, but he certainly didn't know English or French, and it would be tough to wash his clothes if she couldn't explain why she wanted him to strip.

She blew out a sigh, burdened by the unusual weight of responsibility. She could call Mark and hand the boy over, but his solution would be to call Child Services. And if the man with the knife was his relative, there was a horrible chance the boy could end up with a slit throat.

A scratch at the door made them both jump.

"Probably my cat." She rose and cracked open the door. Kato ran in and jerked to a stop, back arching when he spotted the stranger. The boy just laughed and flicked his fingers. Kato pounced and soon was alternately purring and biting at his feet.

They were both young, full of energy, and their playful antics knocked over her bag of stubs. She reached down and rescued the bag, but a few tickets escaped through a claw hole and drifted to the floor. The boy picked up the tickets, passed them back, and an idea blossomed.

Maybe he could sort tickets. It would keep him busy and give her time to scrounge around for some clean clothes. Plus the thought of sifting through the bag for winners, all by herself, was somewhat daunting. It would be lovely to have help.

She ripped up some sheets of paper and made eleven different headings with 'Race' and 'Race Number' on the top. The last pile was more complicated. She didn't know how to sort the daily double or combinations so just made a happy face for that bunch. The boy watched as she picked up a ticket, pointed at the words 'Race Three' and placed it in the third pile. He caught on after the fifth ticket, nodding and sorting so eagerly his hands hopscotched over the piles.

Perfect.

She rose, flushed with relief, thrilled she wouldn't have to sort through the staggering amount of discards by herself. It wasn't really work, just something to keep him occupied so he wouldn't run away. And it would give her time to figure out a way to clean him up.

When she gestured she was leaving, he barely glanced up. She pulled the door shut and rushed down the aisle, expertly dodging Assets' obligatory nip, slowing only to give Buddy a quick pat.

The guard turned with a welcoming grin. "Coffee time?" he asked.

"Not for a while. I have to take a shower first." She tugged at her lip, studying the lighted bathrooms across the road. From the guard's vantage point, he could easily see the door, and if the boy protested, the guard would check in a flash. She wasn't ready to turn the kid in though—not yet. At least not until Maria talked with him.

She turned back to the guard with a conspiratorial smile. "My boyfriend is staying with me, a jockey. He likes loud music when he showers. That won't bother you, will it?"

"Not a bit." The skin around the guard's eyes crinkled with amusement. "You two can make all the noise you want. By the way, my name's Terry."

"I'm Jessica."

"Oh, Mr. Russell dropped by when you were out. He had to go to a meeting but left something for you." He reached down and passed her a white plastic bag.

She slowly opened the bag and peered inside. Her heart thumped. A giant Mars Bar. The biggest, thickest one she'd ever seen. A lump clogged her throat as she clutched the bag to her chest, grinning foolishly. He hadn't forgotten her after all.

The guard was staring so she bounced toward the bathrooms, swinging the bag, unable to stop grinning.

She pushed open the bathroom door, turning cautious. The building was deserted, silent except for a dripping shower and the rhythmic plunking of water on the worn tiles. A navy blue sock and a shrunken bar of soap blocked the drain. She checked the men's side for any abandoned clothing, but the smell of urine made her gag, and she backed out of the doorway in disgust. But one sock wouldn't clothe a kid, and Dick's apartment was too far away to recruit his help.

She turned, uttering a quick prayer for forgiveness, and headed toward the apartment complex behind the bathroom. The wind was up, a good drying night, and the clotheslines were full.

It was eerie, sneaking beneath the flapping clothes. Squares of light shone from the tiny apartments, but no one seemed to be watching. She grabbed a pair of jeans, the smallest ones she could find, along with a brown sweatshirt, and clipped her last ten dollars on the clothesline, hiding the money beneath a pair of ratty socks with a hole in one heel.

She stashed the borrowed clothes behind the door of the women's bathroom and headed back to collect the boy. No sense in alerting him to his bath. It was doubtful he'd be enthusiastic.

She eased open the door to her room but he barely looked up, his gaunt face set in concentration. He'd definitely made good progress with the ticket stub sorting. Race eight was the biggest so far, and clearly the little guy was saving her a ton of work.

She slipped a bottle of shampoo behind the waistband of her jeans then tapped him on the shoulder, motioning for him to follow. He rose so quickly, she was humbled by his trust.

However, his steps turned reluctant when they neared the bathroom, and he abruptly balked and tried to slink away.

"It's okay." She grabbed him by his arm and propelled him into the building.

When she slammed the outer door, his protest rose into a sharp torrent. She held her finger against her lips but he ignored her, flapping his arms and yelling words she didn't understand. Yelling so loudly the guard would surely hear. She backed against the door, folded her arms and began belting out every raunchy locker song she could remember.

After a few minutes, he stopped yelling, sullen but blessedly silent. She stopped singing, pulled out the shampoo and borrowed clothes, and tossed them at his feet. Pointed at the shower.

He shook his head.

She pointed again but he only crossed his arms, shook his head and stuck out a stubborn jaw. There wasn't really much else she could do. No way would she manhandle the poor boy.

She jammed her hands in her pockets, frustrated and defeated. Felt the thick Mars Bar. Ah, an ace in the hole. She pulled it out, brandishing it triumphantly, watching as his eyes lit up. When he reached for it, she pointed to the shower and the clean clothes.

He gave a resigned shrug and stepped behind the curtain. Chocolate. Always effective.

He was quick, emerging from the shower in minutes, his gaze fixed on the bar. The new jeans were too long so she rolled them at the ankles then stuffed his old clothes in a plastic bag. He needed a belt, but there was always lots of baler twine around. She'd improvise. When she rewarded him with the Mars Bar, he ripped the paper off with his teeth, devouring it with much lip-smacking.

She felt a slight pang as the bar disappeared— her first present from Mark—but corrected herself. 'First present' implied longevity, something Mark didn't want...and neither did she, of course. However, she couldn't resist picking up the torn wrapper and tucking it into her back pocket. Nothing wrong with a little keepsake.

The boy was sweet and tractable again, ready to follow her back to the barn. His hair gleamed, his face clean except for a ridge of chocolate staining his lips and teeth. She could see Terry by the door of the shedrow, craning to see the bathrooms, so they detoured round to the back and slipped into her room unseen.

Kato had curled on the cot, scattering two piles of betting tickets in the process. The boy groaned. She grinned, resisting another urge to wrap him in a hug. He was such a cute kid. Not bad company either, but she had a few trust issues that needed to be resolved.

She grabbed a piece of paper and drew a picture of her cell phone and a question mark. Held it up. He ducked his head and looked scared, so she put it away. Obviously he was the fleet-footed kid who'd swiped her phone, so maybe the man by the paddock was the same man with the knife. The same creep who'd followed her to Dick's. A chill skittered down her spine.

It was possible the man had credentials and lived on the backside. She no longer had a workable bike, and the idea that their assailant lurked around the barns made her gut clench. Especially if he were looking for the boy.

She wheeled and bolted the door, glad Mark had ordered such a heavy-duty lock. Glad the new guard, Terry, was around during these solitary nights.

The boy had already curled up under the blankets, his face relaxed in sleep. She eased a purring Kato off the tickets and checked the piles. The kid had done excellent work and if she could keep him another night, he might finish the sorting. It wouldn't hurt to wait one more day before telling Mark. Get a few meals into his stomach. Find him some better-fitting clothes.

But her chest banded with panic, and she gave a hard gulp. After being robbed, she was penniless. She'd already blown next week's pay, and her options were limited. Mark didn't want her stooping, and clearly betting wasn't as simple as she'd originally thought.

She tried to stack tickets, but her fingers were clumsy. Buddy and now the boy—both needed her. And never before in her insulated life had money been so important yet so very, very scarce.

CHAPTER SEVENTEEN

Horses stomped, eager for breakfast, jolting Jessica awake. Grumbling, she rolled over to check her alarm. Four o'clock. Twenty minutes to shower and dress. She sat up and gently shifted Kato's warm body. The cat must have left the boy and joined her sometime in the night. She switched on the light. Stared in dismay.

The boy had vanished. Worse, both blankets and the fancy leather jacket were gone too. So he was either searching for another sleeping spot or had bolted. His dirty clothes were here though, still stuffed in the white plastic bag, so perhaps he planned to return.

Voices drifted through the door. She scrambled from bed, realizing she'd soon see Mark. She'd been so busy with the boy, she hadn't indulged in her usual brooding-over-the-boss time. Being at his house yesterday now had a surreal quality. She remembered his bed, but the rest was a little hazy, although her breasts tingled with traitorous warmth.

She rushed to the shower, throwing Terry a friendly greeting. When she finished, she jogged around the barn and in the back entrance, just in case Mark had arrived before she was suitably dressed. She flipped her hair in a ponytail and grabbed her favorite striped shirt off the handlebars of the bike, pausing for a moment to survey its damaged metal frame.

She'd hinted to both Mark and Dino that Lefty's bike needed repairs, but neither of them had rushed to fix it. Very inconvenient because if the knife man was skulking around, speedy transportation was essential.

She burst from her room, buttoning her jacket, and checked the board. Her new horse, Missy, was scheduled to gallop with the first set and Buddy with the third. She liked to think Mark had split them up to give her more time, but it was probably just a coincidence.

She entered the stall, speaking softly to the filly. Missy stared and flicked her ears, as though surprised her groom was no longer Maria. Jessica checked her over, unwrapped her bandaged legs and brushed her until she gleamed.

"Good morning, Jessica." Emma Rae's pretty face appeared over the stall guard. "I'm galloping this filly today. Anything I should know that will help me earn points with your boss?"

"Can't think of anything," Jessica said, embarrassed to admit she barely knew the horse. "Good of you to get up early to gallop."

"Mark suggested it. And you know he always gets what he wants."

Jessica's head shot up and she stared at the jockey, searching for a hidden meaning. But Emma Rae seemed focused on Missy.

"I'm tired this morning, so please tell me she isn't flighty," Emma Rae continued as she tightened her safety vest. "Last night Mark also said I should cut back on the drinking and lose a couple of pounds."

Pain twisted Jessica's gut at the realization Mark had been with Emma Rae last night. "Celebrating something?" she asked, surprised her voice sounded so level.

"No, but he promised to put me up on your Buddy horse for his last race, and then Buddy's being retired. So maybe we can celebrate then."

Mark appeared, silhouetted in the entrance to the barn and hollered for the first set.

"Come on. Tighten that girth," Emma Rae urged. "I have to keep Mark happy."

Jessica stopped Missy in the aisle and boosted Emma Rae into the saddle. She pasted on a smile, watching the effervescent jockey join Mark at the end of the shedrow. He didn't glance in Jessica's direction, just nodded at each rider as they passed him at the entrance.

She grabbed a pitchfork and cleaned the mare's stall, working mechanically, telling herself she was overreacting. Mark met with different people every night, all kinds of people, all of it necessary for work. And, yes, Emma Rae was pretty, bubbly and single, but that was no reason to be jealous.

She'd never worried about Anton…who was now engaged to her best friend. She scooped up such a huge load of soiled straw, it almost tipped the muck bin.

"There's a big box of donuts in the tack room," Maria called as she rushed past. "Hurry, before the best ones are gone."

Jessica hung up her pitchfork and followed Maria. Her stomach had growled for the last hour, and yesterday's peanut butter and jam sandwich seemed weeks ago.

"Oh, wow, look at this." She stared in glorious indecision at the generous box of donuts, unable to decide between a glazed or chocolate. "Who brought these?"

"Mark, I think. He's in a super good mood. Assets had a bullet work yesterday."

"Assets worked yesterday?" Jessica blinked in confusion. "But Mark wasn't here…I mean…I heard he wasn't at the track yesterday morning."

"He wasn't. He must have been doing something really important to miss Assets' work. And to bring us all donuts today."

"Yeah." Joy warmed Jessica's chest. She grabbed a chocolate donut, wrapped the glazed one in a napkin, and hummed as she left with Mark's donuts clutched in her hand.

"Want me to cool out Ghost?" Carlos asked.

"No, send me Jessica," Mark said. "Tell her to bring a helmet."

Jessica appeared five minutes later, a battered helmet tucked under her arm and a wary look on her beautiful face. "I didn't know we needed helmets to walk a horse," she said.

"You're going to ride." He adjusted the stirrups for her legs. "Then maybe you'll be more understanding of your jockey."

Her eyes widened, and she backed up. "Is this punishment because I blamed Steve for falling off? Because I totally understand now that betting is risky. And so is riding."

"Mount up."

"This actually isn't a very good time for me. I was just about to knock down all the cobwebs, and Dino has those boots he wants cleaned." She took another step backwards. "Besides, I've seen Ghost on the track. He's much too fast. I'm not sure what

Gramps told you, but I'm really more of a pony rider. A very little pony."

Her face paled and she tugged at her lower lip, but several grooms were in earshot. Had heard him give Jessica an order. He already gave her way too much slack. It was impossible to back off now.

"Please, Mark," she continued, her eyes as wide as saucers. "I really don't want to ride. The last time I did, the pony rolled and squashed my leg. It wasn't the least bit enjoyable."

"Climb on now," he said quietly. "Job requirement."

She set her mouth and stepped up to the saddle, but her expression was mutinous.

"Hands on the horn, toe in the stirrup and step up. Don't kick him in the rump when you swing your leg over."

"What happens if I do?"

Mark smiled. "He'll buck."

"My old boyfriend is looking better and better," she snapped but stepped on with surprising grace. He even had an opportunity to admire her long legs without anyone guessing.

"Sit up and relax," he said, leading Ghost down the road and away from the watchers. He gave her a few minutes to settle before glancing back, and from her ecstatic expression it was obvious she was already hooked. "How you doing, honey?" he asked gently.

"Oh, Mark, I love this."

"So you don't want to get off?"

"No, this is fine. But maybe you could release the reins and let me ride by myself." She gave him such a beautiful smile, his chest tightened, and he was glad he'd been able to think of an excuse to get her alone.

He obligingly released the reins. She had a relaxed seat and good balance and soon was jogging circles like a pro.

"Loosen your reins a bit more," he called. "Ghost has a curb bit and is well-trained. He'll do everything better if you leave him alone."

He propped his hip against a tree, ignoring the insistent vibration of his phone, and simply enjoyed her happiness. He should have realized she was a superb athlete after that incredible snag of Assets. It was clear in the way she moved, her easy grace, her toned body and the way she could wrap her legs around his back—

He straightened, filled with urgency. "Finish up and walk him back to the barn now. Ghost needs his lunch. And so do we."

"Could I ride him later this afternoon?"

"If we get back in time." But he had no intention of coming back until four-thirty. He'd been thinking of her all morning, staring at his horses but not really seeing them. Dino had been the one to notice the bay gelding was a little off, and that wasn't good.

Observation was the most important element of training, not only of the horses' physical appearance but also of their emotional and mental state. They needed balance in every area. When he was younger, he always had his horses physically ready but hadn't been so attuned to their mental needs. Now he accepted that all aspects were equally important.

Buddy was the perfect example. Jessica's loving care had the horse thinking he was the main man again, and the gelding bounced with energy. Of course, it couldn't be sustained. After fifty-six races, Buddy had more than his share of aches and pains. But they only needed to nurse him through one more race, and then he'd earn his retirement.

Mark hated the idea of pushing another race on the old fellow, but Buddy was safer with him than any other trainer. And Jessica loved the horse. She'd be devastated if Buddy wasn't in his barn.

She pressed a rein against the left side of Ghost's neck, turning him neatly on his haunches. "Show off," he called, secretly impressed she was such a quick study. He could tell she'd always need a challenge, something to keep her stimulated, and although skiing was out, riding might be an option. With her grandfather's backing, she could train and compete in any discipline she chose.

"There's an English saddle in the tack room," he said. "It's bigger than the exercise saddles. Tomorrow you can try that. But you're a naturally relaxed rider, so you might prefer western."

She tilted her head, as though giving it serious thought. "Well, let's see. What clothes would be more fun? The flashy western shirt and silver buckle, or the black velvet helmet and skin-tight breeches?"

"I vote for the breeches," he said, staring up at her, high and saucy on his horse. And completely out of reach. She wore a striped shirt, and purple lines banded her breasts. He'd always admired her body, but now that he knew what was underneath, it was increasingly difficult to keep his hands in his pockets. "Time to dismount," he added, his voice gruff. "You can loosen the saddle here and lead him back. That way we can pop him in the stall and get to my place."

"In a hurry, boss?" She flashed him a teasing smile.

I'll let you find that out for yourself, he thought.

Traffic crawled, but it gave Mark time to finish his never-ending paperwork. He'd shoved a pen and notebook in Jessica's hand, bribing her with thirty minutes in his Jacuzzi if she updated while he drove. Since he intended to join her in the tub, he considered it an excellent arrangement.

"Sixty days at the farm. Okay, Doc." He reached out and adjusted the car speaker. "What about the stifle x-ray? The owner wants to sell and is calling every hour."

He listened intently then cut the connection and glanced at Jessica. "Got that? Sixty days' farm rest for Bridge Token. X-rays not ready yet on the Smart Strike colt."

She nodded. "And you want to call the farrier about glue-on shoes for the new two-year-old and check with the racing secretary about changing the conditions on Friday's race." Her voice lowered as she flipped through his scribble of notes. "Plus, call Emma Rae."

"I met with Emma Rae and her agent last night, along with Steve," he said. "So the jockeys are taken care of."

He didn't know what he'd done to deserve such a beautiful smile, but she seemed relieved, happy about something. And he liked to see her happy, didn't like the loneliness that clouded her face when the other workers rushed off to their apartments or thoughtlessly excluded her with their Spanish.

However, she simply didn't fit. She was a penniless groom sleeping in a stall but walked and talked like an owner. Her sheer class made people uneasy. Maria, bless her heart, had smoothed Jessica's way, but there would always be a chasm—an even deeper one if people guessed she was sleeping with him. And God help them, he wanted her too much to care.

160

He turned in his driveway and switched off the ignition. Heard her stomach growl. "Damn, I'm sorry, Jess. I should have stopped and grabbed you something to eat." He and Dino always met for a big meal in the morning, but the grooms were far too busy.

"Maybe we could make a couple peanut butter and jam sandwiches?"

Her hopeful expression made him feel like a jerk. He hadn't given her time to run to the kitchen, and she'd probably only eaten a donut or two. Tomorrow he'd bring Egg McMuffins, enough for everybody so no one would guess who he was really trying to feed.

His jaw hardened as his annoyance at Boone spiked. The man was utterly callous, dropping his granddaughter into the backstretch. Setting her up to quit in despair. Instead, she'd coolly handled everything thrown at her and developed into a pretty good groom.

He grabbed his briefcase, locked the car and followed her up the steps. The noon sun was warm, and she'd removed her jacket. Her jeans molded to her curves and when she slung the jacket over her shoulder, her shirt lifted, revealing the soft skin on the small of her back.

God, he was horny. Since he'd had to keep his hands off her all morning, he indulged in a quick grope of her rear while he inserted the door key. She twisted in surprise.

"Just brushing off Ghost's hair," he said, reluctant to admit how turned on he was. He followed her inside and kicked the door shut with a thud. Passed her the bootjack then tugged off his boots and caught up with her in three quick strides. Slid a hand around her hip and nuzzled her neck.

"You're going to have to feed me first if you expect top performance," she protested. "At least a sandwich."

"Okay, but one kiss first," he murmured, inhaling her fresh smell.

"No, I'm not falling for that—"

Silencing her with his mouth, he teased the corners, exploring the curve of her lips until her mouth parted. He slipped his tongue in, gentle at first then more persuasive, until she fused to him in a way that left him breathless. "I expect more stamina today," he managed, sliding a hand over her breast, hiding his need with some flippancy of his own.

"And I expect lunch," she added, but her voice had turned husky, and he knew he was getting to her. He slipped his hand beneath her hair, holding her in place, deepening his kiss until her mouth turned soft and pliant. He dawdled with her breasts then drifted lower. Ran his palm up the inside of her leg and cupped her, until her fingers gripped his shoulders and she arched against his erection.

"Unbuckle my belt, Jess," he said, needing to know she shared his desire—the hell with food.

She yanked the buckle open, fumbled endlessly with his zipper, but at last her warm hand held him, stroked him, until he couldn't think of anything except this maddening woman who was tilting his world. He fumbled in his back pocket for his wallet and extracted a condom. She snatched it from him and kneeled down, teasing him with her mouth as she tugged it on. Teasing him even more. *Jesus.*

"Uncle," he finally croaked. Her eyes held his as he flipped her onto the floor and tugged her jeans off. Spread her legs and thrust. Heard his groan, knew he was rushing but couldn't slow. She was slick and wet, and he felt like he hadn't had sex in a year.

He felt her telltale quivers and grabbed the back of her thighs, spreading them further so he could ram deeper. Felt his own release coming, shuddered and collapsed with her.

It was almost impossible to move, but he mustered the energy to shift to his side, pulling her to him, keeping her close. She burrowed into his chest. He pressed his lips against the top of her silky head but didn't say a word, couldn't, just twined his fingers around the back of her neck and held her.

They both must have dozed. When a horn tooted outside, she stiffened and tried to pull away.

"Lots of time yet," he murmured, pressing the sensitive spot on her lower back that he'd already learned made her arch into his chest. "Let's move to the bedroom."

She blew out a teasing sigh. "The Labor Board isn't going to like this. What about the Jacuzzi and sandwich?"

"You can have anything you want. Afterwards. Now please, just run along to bed."

"Anything? Like a hamburger or something?"

"Oh, babe, you drive a hard bargain." He probably would have given her Assets to groom if she'd asked right now. Which was the reason it was never smart to sleep with employees. It clouded judgment and pissed everyone else off. Right now, he didn't give a damn about pissing off anyone, including Boone or Dino or the rest of his staff.

But she'd already risen and sauntered down the hall, bare legs flashing, and he caught a peek of her beautiful ass. He hadn't even got her T-shirt off and she acted like they were finished, passing his bedroom and disappearing into the kitchen. He wanted her again but this time he'd have more control, slow down and linger. He just needed more time.

He found his jeans beneath the coffee table and pulled out his phone. Checked the time. Damn. Already three-thirty. If he did manage to coax her back to bed, there definitely wouldn't be time for a bath and a meal. Not unless he found someone to look after her two horses and Dino supervised night feeding.

But she'd been working hard. Deserved a little break. He dragged his hand over his jaw and made an impulsive decision. Called Dino but felt torn as he made the request.

She was rummaging in the fridge when he walked in. "Find anything good?" he asked as she added thick slices of cheddar cheese to a huge plate of crackers.

"Here." She shoved the plate across the counter. "Quickest I could do, but it still leaves me twenty minutes for the Jacuzzi. I'm taking a rain check on the other ten minutes and," she shot him a defiant look, "I'm taking any leftover cheese and crackers home."

He had a sinking feeling in his chest as he looked at the mound of cheese, and forgot about telling her that she had the night off. Payday was a week away, but she'd already been given an advance. However she was clearly worried about food. Had been crushed when Steve fell off and wasted her bet.

"You need money?" he asked.

"No, I'm fine," she said quickly. Too quickly. "And I'm sorting my tickets. There's bound to be something there."

"You're broke. You should have told me." He picked up a cracker, twisting it between his fingers. She rubbed a second horse now. Maybe he could justify a raise. Still, she was already close to what Maria and the other grooms were being paid, and they had three horses. He snapped the cracker in two, realizing this was exactly the mess his father had created with his womanizing.

Her lips were slightly puffy from their lovemaking; he watched as she popped a piece of cheese in her mouth. "I know I'm a problem for you." Her intelligent eyes were so empathetic, he felt lighter even though she quite definitely *was* a problem. "Guess your Three-F rule makes sense," she added. "Dino filled me in a little when he was drunk." Her voice softened. "Tell me about your dad."

He turned and snagged two beer from the fridge. "Not much to tell. He's dead now, died in a car accident, but he was a charmer and the girls loved him, including Radcliffe's wife. I doubt Dad ever said no. Always lots of activity in his barn—grooms, hot walkers, riders. Even owners."

He tried not to flinch, remembering his guilt at facing his mom, fresh with the knowledge of how his father really spent afternoons at the track. It had been difficult to hide the disgust he felt for his father, difficult to shield her from the truth. He'd always agonized, wondering if he should tell her. But, she'd found out on her own soon enough.

"Racing is hell on marriages," he added. "Hours are long, and sex in the afternoon is tempting. It's a good stress reliever."

"So I'm a stress reliever?"

"More of a stress creator, I think," he said bleakly.

"And do you have other stress relievers…on the go?"

"God, no." He rose and turned his back, uncomfortable with the way she leveled those big eyes on him. "You're more than enough for any man," he added.

"Good." She swept her beer off the counter. "Because I refuse to be a groupie, and I notice you have condoms all over the place."

"Which will be required if you continue flashing those bare legs."

She rolled her eyes and headed down the hall. "I'm going to the Jacuzzi before you renege on our agreement. Can't waste any more time talking."

"Of course not." He hooked his beer and followed. "But that

hot water tap has been tricky. You're going to need my help."

Jessica woke from a deep nap and glanced at the clock, seven fifteen p.m. She stretched contentedly against Mark's chest, soothed by the beat of his heart, loving how his arms tightened possessively.

"Thank you," she whispered, pressing a grateful kiss against his chest, not sure if he was even awake. However, she felt delightfully languid after the hot Jacuzzi, the lavish steak dinner and the surprise night off as well as his exceedingly generous lovemaking. He certainly knew his way around a woman's body. Already his drowsy hand stroked her breast, touching her the way she liked. The way he knew aroused her and countless other women.

She tried not to move, but the thought of other women made her stiffen. "How can you feel like more?" she muttered.

"Tired, babe?" His voice was husky with sleep. He probably couldn't remember her name, she thought sourly, always calling her *babe* when they were in bed. She wanted to twist away from his confident hand, but it had already moved to massage her lower back. She often had a knot there; she closed her eyes and sighed, automatically arching until her breasts flattened against his chest. He worked his fingers over her back, releasing every spot of tension, rubbing until her angst eased along with her aches.

He tilted her head and brushed her mouth with a gentle kiss. "Why don't you sleep here tonight? I'll find a way to sneak you past everyone tomorrow."

"How do you usually do that?"

"Don't know," he said. "Never had an employee stay overnight before."

"Good." She didn't intend to say the word aloud, but a bubble of happiness dragged it from her mouth.

Didn't matter though since he no longer seemed to be listening. His hand had wandered between her legs and she automatically rose to meet him. His bold mouth explored her chest, moving lower, turning her compliant with practiced skill.

She saw his satisfaction as he brought her to a shuddering climax but didn't care, didn't mind when he flipped her over and entered from behind, grasping her hips and holding her in position until he collapsed with a sigh.

"So, you'll stay," he said a few minutes later, tucking a strand of hair behind her ear. He was breathing hard but obviously wasn't as incapacitated as she. Her bones felt soft as butter, her mind like mush and it was incredibly tempting to sink back into the comfortable bed and sleep—or not—beside him.

But it was possible the boy hadn't run away, and she'd been fretting about him as the night deepened. Had he fled or was he wandering around the backside, even now watching the kitchen? Needing food? Needing her?

Plus, she had to escape Mark. She was beginning to crave him as desperately as any drug. His knowing touch sent jolts rocketing through her body, and already they molded to each other like longtime lovers. He even draped her the way she liked: her head on his shoulder, his leg over hers, his hand splayed over her hip.

He was going to be hard to forget, she realized with burgeoning panic. And she was beginning to care way too much.

"It's tempting to stay, of course, but I can't. I have stuff to do. I need to stop at Walmart too," her words came in an embarrassed rush, "if you don't mind lending me thirty bucks?"

"Okay." Eyes hooded, he crossed his arms and settled against the pillows, all sexy and disappointed male. "I'll drive you home whenever you want."

"Then I'll have a quick shower and leave." She leaped from the bed and didn't look back, didn't want him to see how hard this was. She grabbed her clothes, balled them up along with her fraying emotions and fled the room.

The lady ahead of Jessica in the checkout line searched through her bulky purse for one last nickel. Jessica peered over her shoulder, checking the front entrance, praying Mark wouldn't enter and spot her with boys' clothing stuffed in her arms. How long had she been in the store? Five minutes, maybe ten?

"I only need some tampons and stuff," she'd said, as she thrust him his phone. "You can use the time to make some more horse calls. I really prefer to shop alone." His face had hardened and she knew she'd hurt him, but there had been no other way to keep him from accompanying her.

166

Clink. At last the sluggish lady found exact change, dropped a nickel on the counter, and moved on. Jessica sagged with relief as the cashier bagged her purchases for the boy. Safely bought.

She rushed from the store and back into Mark's car. He was talking to the horse masseuse when she slid into the passenger's seat, and she tucked the precious bag on the floor beside her feet.

"Okay, Shelley, massage him again tomorrow," Mark said, "but I want the chiropractic work immediately following his jog."

Shelley's reply made Mark chuckle, a deep sexy sound that filled the car and pricked her with jealousy. Shelley worked for several elite barns and had entry into the tight trainers' circle. No wonder; she was kind, always smiling and not prone to waspish mood swings.

Suddenly contrite, Jessica grabbed a pen and paper and jotted down notes while Mark talked on his car phone. Another round of hyaluronic acid for the claimer in stall thirty-two, a fifteen-minute media session at ten and the feed man agreed to remove the dusty alfalfa Mark insisted—quite forcefully, she thought—wasn't fit for horses.

"You working to keep the change?" He raised an eyebrow as he finished another call.

Flushing, she scribbled down the last details of his conversation. He had generously passed her one hundred dollars outside the department store, of which she'd only spent thirty, but the change had been shoved in her back pocket; she'd quite honestly forgotten about it.

"Sorry," she said, dropping the pencil and digging out the money. "I'll pay you back the thirty dollars next payday."

"Keep it," he said, reaching over and squeezing her hand. "Dino told me you cleaned all the spare tack. That's a hundred-dollar job, at least. You've been working hard."

She swallowed. His praise shouldn't make her heart leap. Casual sex and temporary relations were fine in theory but she'd never done either of them well, and she was beginning to care way too much. But impermanence was a way of life to Mark; he relished it, preferred it. Horses and people drifted in and out of his barn every month. While they were there he was attentive, kind, and caring. When they left, it was no big deal. Others simply took their place.

She swallowed, trying to clear her throat, glad it was dark so he couldn't see her struggle. A similar situation occurred with sports. When she was injured, there'd been a week of shared tears, but someone had quickly stepped up and filled her spot. Now it was as though she'd never existed.

Her grandfather also had an out-of-sight mentality. He and Mark talked regularly. She'd lingered during one of their conversations hoping Gramps would want a quick hello, especially since her phone had been stolen. Mark had been silent for a moment then just shrugged and gestured her back to work.

It was quite possible Gramps had forgotten she was at Belmont Park. Forgotten she was no longer living with her European ski host. That thought was so depressing, she was tempted to bolt across the seat and settle into Mark's comforting chest. Had to grip the seat to keep herself grounded.

She'd forgotten Mark was attuned to body language, conditioned to overseeing the welfare of his horses and staff. He reached out and tugged her to his side, and she was too needy to resist. He tucked her under his arm, expertly whipping through traffic as he steered with one hand.

"Don't worry, honey. You'll have what you want in three weeks. Not much longer to go." He spoke so sweetly, she turned her head into his chest so he wouldn't see her expression. A dog kennel. The idea seemed ludicrous now. She couldn't imagine not working with horses.

They drove the last miles in silence while she absorbed his quiet confidence, his rock-solid core. Gradually she felt much better, less alone. He did that with horses too, just placed a hand on their neck and soothed them with his touch.

Much too soon she spotted the glow of the backside and the looming security booth. Mark didn't move his arm, but his muscles tensed, so she slid to the passenger side, aware he didn't like public displays. Wouldn't want anyone to see them together, not at the track.

She stretched and pretended to yawn. "Oops, sort of fell asleep there."

"Jesus Christ," he said.

Two police cars blocked the road, their lights slashing red and blue lines across the dark sky. A security guard stepped up to Mark's window and studied his credentials. "You're okay if you hang left, but the apartments on the back section are restricted. I have to check your trunk too."

"What happened?" Mark asked after the guard scanned his trunk and returned to the driver's window.

"There's been a stabbing. Police cordoned off a section. Been investigating for the last couple hours. Ambulance left a while back."

"Aw, hell," Mark said, easing through the gate and veering left, away from the chain of vehicles. Pebbles rattled the bottom of his car as he circled, following a narrow horse track to the right and clearly not following the guard's directions.

A stabbing? Jessica leaned forward, peering into the shadows, her mouth dry as her thoughts churned around the boy.

"I have some employees living in that area," Mark said, squeezing her arm. "Want to make sure they're okay. But don't worry about Maria. Her apartment isn't in that section."

She nodded but couldn't unwrap her hands from the seat, haunted by visions of the man's deadly knife. *Please, God, let the little boy be safe.*

Mark drove with purpose, threading left and right until she was completely disoriented. He sped over one final hill and pulled over by a group of men. "That's Manuel," he said tersely. "Stay in the car."

She had no intention of getting out. Manuel and the Mexican Mafia. The name alone made her palms sweat. She leaned forward on the edge of her seat, watching as a man swaggered from the pack. The tip of his cigarette glowed bright red as he approached Mark.

A laugh, handshakes. She blew out a relieved breath. Friendly so far. Mark looked relaxed too, smiling, waving his hands like he did whenever he spoke Spanish. Manuel turned, made an impatient gesture and someone rushed over with two beer. Looked like Coronas, Mark's favorite.

Okay, this might be all right. The thumping in her chest steadied. Mark and Manuel seemed like old friends. But even Dino had looked a little pensive when he talked about Manuel, and nothing ever bothered Dino. Best to be ready.

She slid over to the driver's seat. Wiped her clammy hands on her jeans and cracked open the window. She could listen and then swoop up with the car if they turned mean.

Cool air gusted through the open window, carrying the murmur of male conversation and the smell of cigarettes. Someone was frying onions. But not too much seemed to be happening. She adjusted the seat, the mirror, then drummed her fingers on the leather wheel.

It didn't appear Mark would need rescuing any time soon. He'd casually hooked the bottle in his thumb and now spoke with another man in a stream of Spanish, broken only by his occasional question. Completely unexciting. Boring, even.

Mark gestured. Three heads suddenly swiveled to stare at her. She tried not to flinch. Manuel laughed, and Mark walked toward the car in his long relaxed stride, not hurrying at all. Her relief escaped in a whoosh.

"I said you were getting impatient and might drive off and leave," Mark said, pulling open the door. "Slide your butt over. This is my spot."

"Thought you might need rescuing." She peered over the dash, wanting a final peek at the infamous Manuel. "They don't act much like Mafia," she added, rather disappointed.

"Oh, Jess." He spoke so tenderly she almost forgot to ask what he'd learned, but obviously it wasn't one of his employees who'd been hurt. He was too relaxed, smiling at her in that intimate way that made her thoughts turn fuzzy.

"So? What did you find out?" she asked, once she could talk without any hint of breathlessness.

"Groom from barn eighty-nine. Stabbed outside the dorm and rushed to hospital. Manuel's cousin said Dick had been around a few days earlier asking questions."

"Dick? Tricky Dick? The man who has the clothes?"

"Yeah. Know him?"

She stared out the window, blinking furiously, trying to hold back a rush of tears. Not an innocent kid but a kind, generous man. "I know him," she finally managed. "He's a wonderful man. Raises a lot of money for Anna House. Is he going to be okay?"

"Sounds like he'll live. Luckily a neighbor was there." Mark eased his car into the lot close to his office. "Manuel said Dick was flashing a picture. Keen on finding out if anyone knew some guy."

"Oh no!" Horror jerked her forward. She gripped her hands so tightly they hurt. "Then it's my fault." Her voice quavered. "Dick took that picture when I was sorting clothes. He thought the man followed me…but I didn't know him. The first time I saw him was by the paddock, just before my phone was stolen."

"Whoa. Slow down." Mark frowned. "I saw that guy too. Kid ran right up to him. One of Manuel's guys told Dick the man in the picture has been around for a few months. Has a kid and qualified for a family apartment. The apartment's empty now though." He turned off the ignition and opened his door. "Tomorrow I'll ask the police to check Dick's apartment for the picture. They'll probably want to talk to you. Too bad they haven't found the kid. Might've helped Dick."

She squeezed her hands and averted her head, wishing the dome light wasn't so bright. "I did see the boy," she managed, afraid to look at Mark and see his condemnation. "Last night. But he ran away in the morning before I could tell you."

"You had all day to tell me."

"But I thought you'd call the authorities." She looked at him then, trying not to squirm beneath his incredulous stare. "And then he'd have to go back with his father, who might have been the man with the knife."

Mark said nothing, just stared as though she were a strange species he'd never seen before. She squeezed her eyes shut, feeling raw and exposed. "He was good at sorting betting tickets," she added, her throat thick with misery. "Maybe that had something to do with it."

Mark slammed his door shut and sat back in his seat. He reached over, his arm brushing her leg as he picked up her Walmart bag. Adjusted the powerful overhead light. Plastic rustled when he opened the bag and examined its contents.

"Kids' clothes?" Coldness filled his voice, chilling the car. "Clearly you expect him to return. You lied to me." He tossed the bag on her lap. "Go to your room. I'll be there in fifteen minutes."

She sucked in her cheeks, trying to hide her devastation. "I'm really tired. Can't we talk about this in the morning?" But when she scooped up the doggy bag of leftover cheese and crackers, his mouth flattened in understanding. *Oh shit*. And now a muscle ticked on the side of his jaw.

"We'll pursue this in your room. Tonight," he snapped.

Jessica curled on her bed, trying to block the relentless images of Dick and the brutal attack. But Mark's belief that the stabbing could've been prevented left her aching with guilt. Mark was fluent in Spanish, and it was possible the kid might have identified the man in time.

Possible, but maybe not. Maybe it wasn't the same guy. Maybe it was some jerk who didn't like Dick's lifestyle.

All the maybes made her feel better, and she almost convinced herself that telling Mark about the kid wouldn't have made the slightest difference. He was just huffy because she hadn't told him everything.

She heard voices as Mark spoke with the guard, the horses' soft nickers as he walked down the aisle. A stall guard opened, and she knew he'd stopped to visit Assets. A minute, then two of silence. He was probably checking the colt's legs now, maybe rewrapping if he thought the bandages were the slightest bit uneven. Or even if they weren't. Lately he'd been so fussy.

She jabbed her pillow, swept with regret. It was a busy season, and she didn't know how he managed all the horses, all the people, all the details. Certainly she hadn't made his life easier. The lesson on Ghost had taken more than an hour, and the extra time spent at his house, the slice of romance—

The hard rap on the door made her shiver. Definitely not a romantic visit now. He opened the door and stalked in, all broody, moody male.

Kato leaped from under the cot.

"Not now, Kato." She grabbed the cat before he attacked Mark's leg.

Mark's mouth curved just a bit but flattened when he spotted the boy's jeans drying on her bike. He shot her a look so full of reproach, shame filled her. He picked up the boy's black T-shirt, still damp from her washing, and scanned the label. Searched the jeans.

"Was anything in the pockets?" he asked.

"A couple of nails," she said. "Six pennies."

"So he knocks on your door? Asks for food? How does it work?" He pinned her with his hard-eyed stare.

"It was just one night," she said quickly. "And he followed me home. I don't think he'll come on his own." Her arms tightened around Kato. "So there's really no sense in hanging around trying to catch him."

"But we already know you lie, don't we, Jessica."

The bite in his voice made her flinch, but it was also rather annoying. "I didn't lie." Her voice rose. "I just didn't tell you."

"You certainly lied about buying tampons." He tossed the jeans back on the bike. "It's clear you expect the boy to come back. It's also clear you didn't intend to tell me."

She kneeled down and released Kato, not wanting to look at Mark's hard face. The chill radiating from him was daunting, and she could understand now why people scuttled away when he was in a foul mood.

"Turn out the light," he said. "Let's see if he shows."

"Fine." She rose, assuming her most aggrieved voice. "But I'm just going to put the cheese outside the door so if he does come and is hungry—"

"Get in the damn bed. Don't say another word." He shackled her arm, not rough but certainly not gentle, and this implacable side of him was so startling, she stopped talking and slid beneath the blanket.

The lights flicked out. The cot sagged as he lay down beside her.

"There's not enough room for you."

"Shut up." His hard hand covered her mouth.

No one had ever told her to shut up before, except in the most playful of ways, and she didn't like it. She tried to bite but his hand was way too big, blocking her nose, and she bucked in panic when she couldn't breathe.

He loosened his hand but when she tried to complain, clamped it back over her mouth. She lay still, afraid she wouldn't be able to get any air, not even speaking when his hand finally relaxed. His body was taut and wary as he listened for sounds in the aisle. She tried to assure him the boy wouldn't come, but his hand flattened over her face again, and he didn't seem at all concerned that she wasn't able to breathe.

The thought of being smothered in her own bedroom pissed her off, but she didn't speak again. Only concentrated on sucking in enough air.

It really wasn't that uncomfortable, the two of them crammed on the cot. His arms were around her, holding her, but his chest was warm. And if she was silent, the big hand over her mouth loosened. She knew the kid wouldn't come. He'd probably bolted the track, but she regretted he wouldn't get the cheese and crackers. Or the new clothes, especially the jeans with the fancy zipper pockets. She figured he'd really like those.

And she regretted Dick was stabbed. She really regretted that. *Oh, God, please make him okay.* Anguish banded her chest. She should have told Mark about the boy. Should have kept Dick safe. Shouldn't have been so selfish.

The stabbing *was* her fault—the admission sent warm tears trickling down her cheeks. She didn't often pray, but she knew it was the man at the paddock, knew deep in her gut it was the same man with the knife who'd stabbed Dick. For some reason he'd followed her, and Dick's concern for her safety had resulted in the brutal attack.

Her eyes tickled, and she sniffed. She tried to wipe her face, but he only adjusted his hand over her mouth even as his gentle thumb wiped away her flooding tears.

CHAPTER EIGHTEEN

Jessica woke with an ache in her neck and the nagging feeling something bad had happened. A horse kicked the wall, someone yelled a greeting and memories flooded.

She jerked up, sensing Mark was gone and the room empty. Turned the light on and checked her clock. Four twenty-five a.m. She didn't know when Mark had left, but if the boy had visited, she was certain she wouldn't have slept through the ruckus.

She stumbled to the bathroom, pulled her hair in a ponytail, grimaced at the puffy eyes staring back from the cracked mirror. It looked like she'd cried all night. Maybe she had. She hoped Mark's shirt was soaked. He'd almost suffocated her with his misguided attempt to quiet her and catch the boy.

Chewing on her indignation, she rushed back to the barn but shot a wary look at his office as she slipped past, hoping he wouldn't notice the time.

This probably wasn't a good day to be late.

Mark turned Ghost toward the gap. His first set already milled on the track, and his fatigue evaporated as he admired Assets. The mist lent all the horses an air of mystery, but it was clear from the colt's coiled silhouette that he was feeling particularly good.

The railbirds noticed it too. "That horse is the favorite for the Juvenile," a man in a baseball hat said.

"Looks good in the dark," someone else muttered. "Wish Russell would bring him out later so we could see him."

Mark trotted up beside Jonas, Assets' regular exercise rider. "Remember, easy gallop. Keep him contained. We're going to jog two laps again this afternoon on the training track."

"Sure, boss. He's feeling stronger since you started the extra jogging, and he's definitely more relaxed. Man, I ain't never been so impressed with a two-year-old."

Mark nodded, but Jonas' opinion gave his confidence a further boost. Jonas had galloped the Derby winner last year and knew the feel of a good horse. Every one of the colt's connections, from the hot walker to the groom and exercise rider, were working together to prime Assets for the ultimate goal.

Even Steve had shown up to jockey him in his works, the fast gallops necessary to keep a horse conditioned and on the muscle. Now Mark wanted to teach the colt to relax. His main concern was that Assets didn't always settle when pinned on the rail. A big field and a bad post would leave him vulnerable.

Still, the colt's race last month had been a breakthrough. Not only had he rated from an inside position, he'd dug in bravely when asked and beaten the sheikh's horse by four lengths.

"Slow gallop today," Mark called out, switching his attention to the other horses as Buddy trotted past. The gelding looked jaunty with his typical turnout of braids. Mark was still uncomfortable with the flamboyance, but as long as it kept Jessica and the horse happy, he'd decided to ignore it. And the color did deflect media attention from Assets. Buddy was much more accepting of the spotlight than the young colt. In fact, the old horse relished it.

As did Jessica.

He kept his gaze pinned on the horses but was acutely aware she stood by the gap, watching Buddy. Goddammit, he'd been mad last night. A kid who someone was trying to kill—a kid mixed up in God knows what—and she'd virtually adopted him. Most people would have been spooked after an encounter with a knife-wielding assailant, but she didn't seem to consider the danger.

The quicker that kid was caught, the faster police would track down the mystery man, and everyone would be safer. Manuel had also been a little tense, not happy that a stabbing had occurred in his backyard. A Middle Eastern man, they'd said. And he really didn't have time to worry about this. He had horses to train.

176

Shaking his head, he straightened his thoughts and swung Ghost to the outside, where Carlos hunched over the rail, trying to hide from two reporters and their huffing camera man. Breeders' Cup buzz had truly started, and soon there'd be no escape for his horses or beleaguered staff. Most of them, like Carlos and Maria, hated dealing with the media.

Mark leaned down over Ghost's muscled shoulder. "Pretend you don't speak English, Carlos," he said. "I'll ask Jessica to help."

Carlos nodded, and a relieved smile cracked his face.

Mark wheeled and stopped Ghost by Jessica. "Can you distract those reporters so Carlos can get Assets back to the barn?"

She nodded and instantly headed toward the reporters. Smart, competent, savvy. He liked how she could argue over the most trivial things but knew when time was critical. And then simply buckled down and did her job.

And did it well. As Assets walked toward the gap, Jessica flashed an animated smile at the reporters and gestured up the track. Probably spreading outrageous lies about Buddy. Whatever she said definitely drew their attention, or perhaps they were smitten by her looks. The photographer almost tripped in his haste to snap her picture.

Mark scowled as he trotted past the idiot photographer, not sure why he was so grumpy. Probably just tired. It had been a sleepless night waiting for the boy to come, holding Jessica while she cried. She felt responsible for Dick although she'd never admit it. Would never admit she was worried about the kid, the clothes or even the stupid cheese.

And Belmont was a big place. Maybe the kid couldn't find the barn again. Maybe he had to see Jessica, and then he'd pop out from his hiding place. Probably be a good idea to send her on some errands later this morning, use her to flush out the kid. The security guards had been alerted; it shouldn't be difficult to catch one little boy.

Carlos stepped up and slipped on Assets' lead, smiling now that he'd escaped the media rush. Mark shot a last scowl at the men still clumped around Jessica. He'd asked her to distract them, but they didn't have to fawn like she was some kind of princess. Christ, she wasn't even holding a horse.

He blew out a disbelieving sigh and mechanically continued his training routine.

"Egg McMuffins! You're a hero." Maria wrapped her arms around Dino in an exuberant hug. "Come late and bring breakfast every morning."

"Aw, shucks. It was nothing." Dino adjusted his cowboy hat then hugged Jessica and two more hot walkers, taking his time with each embrace. "And now, ladies," he gave his irreverent but handsome grin, "I gotta admit Mark told me to bring the food. He also told me to come late since I've been covering for him more than usual."

He glanced at Jessica. "Maybe you owe me another hug, sweetheart?"

"Maybe you should get over to the track with the last set," Mark said as he stuck his head in the door. "And Jessica, once you finish eating, run to the kitchen and bring back three coffees. Check with Tina first. See how she takes it."

Dino gave Jessica an unrepentant wink, turned and followed Mark.

"Anyone know who Tina is?" Jessica asked as she unwrapped her Egg McMuffin. Just the smell made her mouth water. She squeezed her eyes shut and took a big bite. It was delicious. They must have changed the recipe. She couldn't remember them ever tasting this good.

"Tina's a reporter, the one doing the article for *The New York Times*." Maria spoke between mouthfuls. "They were here last month taking pictures."

"I thought Mark wasn't letting the press in the barns," Jessica said, remembering how he'd asked her to distract the media earlier. He'd also asked her to run an irritating number of errands, sending her traipsing all over the backside, picking up a halter from barn thirty-three, some special vitamins from a guy way over in barn sixty-eight, a ring bit from a lady in barn twenty-four, and now coffee from the kitchen. Usually he was satisfied with the coffee in his office, but obviously he was trying to punish her for last night.

She popped the last of her Egg McMuffin in her mouth, pocketed another for lunch and wished she had her bike fixed. If she had her bike, the old blisters on her heels wouldn't have rubbed raw.

"Might as well take another one for supper, kid," Maria said. "They're good cold. And by the time you walk over to the kitchen and back, there won't be any left."

One of the hot walkers murmured in agreement and tossed Jessica another Egg McMuffin. She caught it and headed off to fetch the mysterious Tina a coffee.

"So, Mark, it's incredible you're cruising into your first Breeders' Cup with the overwhelming favorite." The reporter accompanied her question with such a fawning smile, it made Jessica cringe. "How does it feel knowing your horse is expected to beat the sheikh's runner, an animal that was purchased for three million dollars at the Keeneland sale?"

"Assets has to show up and run his race," Mark said, "but he's training well. I wouldn't trade places with anyone."

Tina flipped off her recorder, still showing two rows of pearly white teeth. "Thanks *so* much. I've got enough material now. We'll take a few more pictures, and hopefully you'll have time to join me for lunch. Just a couple more questions..."

Blah, blah, blah. Jessica sat cross-legged on the grass listening to the lengthy interview, waiting for a chance to deliver the coffee. Tina was pretty and hadn't stopped smiling, but her interest in horses seemed artificial. Clearly she was only after the human interest angle, with a specific interest in Mark.

Jessica sighed and took another sip of Mark's coffee, surprised to see it was almost empty. She hadn't intended to drink it all, had trudged back from the kitchen with three cups just as Mark had directed, but by that time the interview was in full swing. Rather than let the coffee chill, she'd pulled out an Egg McMuffin, sipped on the coffee and enjoyed a rare and relaxing picnic.

She tilted her face, enjoying the autumn sun. It had been a good morning despite the rocky start. Buddy and Missy had galloped perfectly, and, best of all, Dick was going to recover. He'd be allowed visitors by week's end, so she and Maria were already checking bus routes to the hospital.

Deep in her reverie, she didn't realize Mark was calling until he gave a rude whistle. She stuffed the empty food wrapping in her pocket, rose and picked up the cardboard coffee tray.

"Two cream for you," she said to Tina. "Black for you." She smiled at the camera man. He hadn't been a bit condescending—unlike Tina who hadn't even thanked her for making the trek to the kitchen.

"This is yours, boss. Sorry, it spilled." She handed over the depleted cup but couldn't meet his eyes, slightly intimidated by the memory of that relentless hand. Still with two media people around, she figured she was pretty safe.

"Get me another," he said.

Resentment flattened her mouth. Errand running wasn't exactly part of a groom's job and while she wanted to be agreeable, there was a limit to anyone's tolerance. Plus, her boot blisters still hurt from all the earlier walking.

"Get me another too. Mine is cold." Tina's lips curved in an aggrieved pout that magically disappeared when she turned to Mark. "Let's do some shots in your office and a final one with that gray horse, the one you and Dino roped on at Congress. If you wear your jacket pictured in my earlier feature, we can tie it in with career highlights."

Oh, shit. Jessica shoved her hands in her pocket and turned toward the kitchen, forgetting the painful blisters on her heels. "I'll get that coffee now," she said brightly, eager to be somewhere else when Mark stared hollering about his missing jacket.

When Jessica walked into the track kitchen, Maria and her friends were crammed in a large corner booth.

"Come sign Dick's card," Maria called as she waved a crude cutout of a horse. "And help us with the poem. We need a line that ends with throat."

Jessica winced. Dick had thirty-nine stitches. His carotid artery had been nicked, but a neighbor's quick response had saved his life. It was temporarily diverting trying to think of words that rhymed with Prada and Gucci but when the women switched to Spanish, she gave up and left.

Besides, Tina was no doubt thirsty.

She trudged back to Mark's office lugging the fresh coffee, including a third one for the nice camera man. Should be perfect timing. They'd almost finished so it would be quiet for her afternoon nap—one she definitely needed since Mark had kept her up almost all night, stubbornly waiting for the kid, although it was obvious he wasn't going to show.

She stepped into the office and placed the coffee tray on the corner table. "Saddle up Ghost and bring him out, Jessica," Mark said, his gaze not leaving Tina's face.

"But he's lying down," she said in dismay.

"Then you'll have to brush him first, won't you." Mark spoke as if she were a five-year-old. "And make sure the silver is spotless. Use metal cleaner."

Heat burned her cheeks as she turned away from the camera man's sympathetic smile, away from Tina's giggle. She limped into the barn, past the day security guard and into Ghost's stall.

The horse wasn't lying down, but he was definitely drowsy and not at all happy to be saddled for the second time in one morning. She thumped the heavy western saddle on his back, ignoring the stains on the silver, and pulled on a bridle, grumbling the entire time.

She left the saddle loose, knowing Ghost was cinchy and would resent abrupt tightening. Besides, a big-time trainer like Mark would always check his own cinch.

Ghost seemed to catch her mood. By the time she led him from the barn, they both bristled with ill-humor.

A panel van slowed, and a man with an ESPN cap stuck his head out the window. ""I saw *The Times* people were here," he called. " Is Mark Russell talking to the media?"

"He sure is. Stick around," she said. "He'll be here soon."

She and Ghost waited in front of the barn for another fifteen minutes and when Mark, Tina and the camera man finally emerged from Mark's office, a large ESPN crew had also assembled. Mark's eyes narrowed.

Tina complained she was supposed to have an exclusive, but Jessica fiddled innocently with Ghost's bridle.

"Thanks, Jess," Mark said quietly as he reached for the reins. The affectionate way he spoke her name blew away her resentment.

"The cinch is loose," she said, suddenly contrite.

But he'd already stepped into the stirrup. The saddle twisted, Ghost bucked and Mark hit the dirt.

She heard him curse but held on to Ghost who continued to buck, determined to rid himself of the saddle which now flapped like a giant monster beneath his belly. The horse's shoulder slammed her ribs, knocking the breath from her lungs, and a hoof flashed by her eye. Something hit her leg and pain seared. Bodies flailed as the media crew scrambled for safety.

Her arm burned from the yanks of the terrified horse, and she didn't know how much longer she could hang on. But then Mark was there. He shoved her aside, released the cinch and the saddle dropped harmlessly to the ground.

"You okay?" he asked as he calmed Ghost.

She nodded, unable to speak, ashamed his first concern was her safety. She'd had plenty of time to tighten the cinch too, knew he always wanted his barn to appear professional. But maybe he'd think she simply forgot. Maybe he'd think—

"You'll be a helluva woman when you grow up." He shook his head in disgust before turning and addressing the white-faced ring of watchers.

"So that's today's demonstration of why jockeying is one of the most dangerous careers in the world," he said. "Horses are unpredictable and accidents can happen, especially when you have inexperienced staff," he paused and gave Jessica a pointed stare, "on loan from another stable." He gestured at some ambiguous barn in the distance.

"Radcliff's barn," Jessica said. "I'm going back to Paul Radcliff's barn right now."

"Oh, man, this is great stuff," she heard the ESPN crew say as she walked away. "Did you see that horse buck? Be great if Mark could repeat the demo tomorrow."

She limped down the dusty road, not sure where she was going but vastly reassured by the weight of the Egg McMuffin in her pocket. She passed a couple dumpsters, but saw no sign of the boy, so she veered to the right, toward Dick's. Maybe she could find the picture. Do something useful.

Twenty minutes later, a horse pounded behind her. She glanced back, not surprised to see Mark and Ghost. Mark looked like an avenging cowboy and she sidled to the right, but there was really nowhere to hide.

"You shouldn't be walking down here alone, not with that unknown assailant around." He slowed beside her, his voice level.

She dared a quick glance upward, checking his face. "I'm sorry. Are you still mad?"

"About last night or this morning?"

"Last night?" Indignation replaced her regret and she jerked to a stop. "You almost strangled me."

"Hardly," he said.

She didn't like the way his mouth hardened and really didn't want to annoy him any more, so she changed the subject. "I'm heading to Dick's to see if I can find that picture."

"Good idea." He leaned over and extended his hand. "Climb on."

"Will he buck?" She stepped back, eyes narrowing as she stared at Ghost. Her feet ached but she'd never seen the horse ridden double before, and he'd certainly taken violent exception to the saddle dangling beneath his belly. He looked safe now though, head low, ears angled back, as if awaiting Mark's instruction. However, his earlier bucks had been scary and much more explosive than the playful antics of the racehorses. "I doubt I can stay on if he bucks like that," she added.

"No, I wouldn't expect one of Radcliff's employees to be able to do that." A hint of a smile pulled at the corners of his mouth and she stopped worrying, placed her hand in Mark's and let him pull her up behind him.

When Ghost resumed walking, she almost slid off and had to grab Mark's waist. It was strange, sitting on warm slippery hair. No saddle, no stirrups. Ghost's hindquarters pumped rhythmically but when she relaxed her grip, she was able to sway with his movement, and it was quite enjoyable to sit back and look around.

There was no racing today so the backside was virtually deserted, although several horses thrust their heads out, watching Ghost as he clopped along the road. A man whizzed past on a bicycle, his churning tires crackling the autumn leaves. Ghost flinched but Mark lifted his rein hand, and the horse steadied. After that, she watched Mark closely, noting how subtly he used his hands, his legs. The slightest shift made Ghost step sideways. She found it fascinating.

Much more fascinating than the rundown area they now approached. She stared in dismay at the older barns, devoid of flowers, picnic tables or any sign of life. "I've never been here before," she whispered, feeling like a foreigner in a strange land. "This isn't where Dick lives."

"We're circling from the back." Mark seemed to choose his words as he studied a tiny barn. "Ground is softer here, easier on Ghost's feet."

"Feels spooky."

He shrugged. "Sometimes when you have an injured horse and not enough stalls, you can stick them back here. Work with them, try to get them healthy, yet keep your race stalls full. My first year, I had three horses in that little barn over there."

Jessica stared at the crooked building. It was inconceivable Mark had started down here. Sometimes she forgot he wasn't always the successful trainer, and a reluctant respect filled her.

"Wouldn't it have been easier to stay in Texas? Where people knew you?"

"The easiest way isn't always the best," he said, walking Ghost toward the open door of his old barn.

She twisted, distracted by a bloodthirsty horsefly that stubbornly circled. Ghost swished his tail and she swiped at his rump, trying to discourage the persistent fly. A door creaked, and something shot from the barn, arms and legs flailing. Ghost leaped. She grasped for Mark but clutched only air.

Her gaze held the boy's in a startled second of recognition, and then her face smashed into the dirt.

Mark cursed, the boy yelped and Ghost's hooves pounded in pursuit but she was too shaken to do more than struggle to her knees. Red streaked the gravel in front of her, and she swiped at her nose, recognizing the metallic taste of blood.

She flinched as Ghost thundered back, afraid he'd run her over, but Mark leaped off and crouched beside her.

"Did you catch him?" she asked, keeping her head bent while she wiped her nose.

"I'm sorry, Jess. Sit still for a minute."

"I'm fine." She tried not to sniffle. "Go get the kid."

"Your nose is bleeding." He used his sleeve to wipe her face. "Everything else okay?"

184

"Just my face, I think." But her words were as ragged as her breath.

"Let's see, honey." He lifted her chin, studying her face, but his expression turned so pained, she twisted from his scrutiny. He pulled her into his arms, but the frantic thud of his heart scared her.

"Does it look that bad?" she squeaked.

"No, everything's good." But he spoke much too quickly. "Sit for a sec. We'll get the nosebleed stopped. Let the other blood dry. Then try to clean you up." But he looked so dubious, she permitted herself a tiny sniffle.

He wrapped her in his arms and pinched the bridge of her nose as he tilted her head downward. It wasn't uncomfortable. The sun heated her jeans, and of course Mark's body was always flaming hot. She closed her eyes, telling herself that at least she no longer noticed her blisters.

"Let's check it now." He finally broke the silence, shifted his arms and studied her sore nose. "Looks like the blood stopped. There's a tap by the barn."

He guided her past Ghost, who calmly munched grass, and turned the tap handle. *Squeak.* A brown spray bubbled out but quickly cleared. Mark wet his sleeve and gently wiped her face. "That's great. Doesn't look bad now." However, he sounded much too jovial, and he turned away before she could see his expression.

"Where are you going?"

"Just checking where the kid sleeps," he called over his shoulder before disappearing inside the dilapidated barn.

"Is this the extent of your first aid?" He didn't answer so she gingerly felt her face. Except for her right eye, it didn't hurt too much. Her hand came away with only a hint of red, so she guessed her forehead and left cheek were scraped but not deeply cut.

Mark abruptly strode from the barn with a dark scowl and a filthy AQHA jacket cradled in his arm.

"I feel a little dizzy," she mumbled. "Must have hit the ground harder than I thought." She clutched the sides of her head, peeking at his thunderous face, but he walked past and grabbed Ghost's reins. For a second, she thought he was going to ride off and leave.

"Come on," he said. "You ride. I'll walk."

His voice was a bit rough, but she gave him high marks for control. She hadn't realized the jacket was so special, and there was no way she was getting back on that devil horse. "No," she said. "I'll walk back."

Even ten feet away, she heard his impatient sigh. "It's okay. You won't fall off again. Ghost had a little spook, completely understandable. And if you'd been paying attention, you wouldn't have been dumped."

"It's not that. I just don't want to ride again."

"Come on, Jess. I've never known you to be a coward."

Both Ghost and Mark were staring at her as though disappointed, so she ignored the name-calling and let him boost her into the saddle. But her throat was dry, and she clutched the horn. It was hard to pretend she wasn't terrified.

"Dick's place is that way." She pried a hand off the horn long enough to gesture to the right.

"We're not going to Dick's," he said.

"Well then, this was a waste of time." Ghost's ears flattened as her voice rose. She turned silent and tightened her grip, wondering if the volatile horse intended to buck.

"No, it wasn't a waste," Mark said. "Now we know where the kid hides, that he's wearing a blue T-shirt, that he's three-and-a-half feet tall and about sixty-five pounds." He glanced up, his expression unreadable. "Plus I recovered my missing jacket which I value greatly."

"I'm really sorry about the jacket. I didn't mean for him to take it. But he was so cold." She swiveled in the saddle, absorbing Mark's statement, forgetting about Ghost's ill humor. "Sixty-five pounds? That's all? Wish I had a chance to give him my Egg McMuffin."

"If you have food in your pocket, hand it over. I'm starving."

So he wasn't lunching with Tina. That fact pleased her so much she passed over her cache of food with only minimal complaint. Besides, she already knew the boy preferred fish and chips.

CHAPTER NINETEEN

Jessica sealed another envelope and tossed it on the growing stack of outgoing mail. She hadn't realized horses and trainers received fan mail. Mark had told her to answer the kids' letters first and then work on the others. She adjusted her ice pack, stifled a yawn and glanced guiltily over her shoulder. Mark had agreed not to dock her pay if she helped in the office all afternoon but probably napping on the job was taboo.

He was on the phone, boots on his desk as he discussed a knee x-ray. He didn't look tired, but she guessed he must be exhausted. Dino had left a mound of paperwork; despite the number of calls Mark had made, though, the pile didn't appear dented.

She turned her attention back to her letter writing, deciding the best way to handle the ridiculous marriage proposal was to explain that Mark was happily gay.

"You better not be causing me any trouble," he warned as he closed the phone, his eyes narrowing on her mischievous smile. "And put the ice on the side of your eye. Tomorrow that's where the swelling will be." His phone chirped again, and he tucked it back under his ear.

A strange tightness did pull at her eyes. She adjusted the ice pack, guessing he was probably right. The swelling would be worse tomorrow. She sighed, but the changing timbre of his voice grabbed her attention—eager, excited, much different from his tone with the vet.

"Yeah, there's a few I like. Hip 641, 665 and 689," he said. "Three hundred should get us one of them."

She bent over the paper, doodling energetically and pretending not to listen.

A wariness crept into Mark's voice as he glanced in her direction. "Sure. I can meet you in Keeneland," he said.

She finished her row of hearts then began a sketch of Buddy's blazed head, careful to keep her head bent.

Mark's voice lowered. "I think she'd like to talk to you...too busy? Okay...see you later." His tone flattened as he swiveled his chair and cut the connection. Paper shuffled. She waited for him to say something, to announce he'd just talked with her grandfather, but that was the ticklish part about eavesdropping. You heard enough to make you curious, but could only ask questions in the most casual way.

Mark didn't give her a chance to do that. Just shoved his chair back and rose. "Keep that ice over your eye," was all he said when he strode from the office.

Mark turned away from the blood stain, preferring not to watch the gorging flies. Richard Maynard, or Tricky Dick as Jessica called him, had bled profusely, and darkened gravel now marked the spot.

The police officer continued removing yellow crime tape as he spoke. "We've made extensive inquiries, knocked on a lot of doors, but I'll add your information to the file."

And that file will be shelved, Mark guessed. He edged a few steps closer, trying to prick the cop's interest. "There might be a picture of this guy in Dick's apartment," he said. "And maybe the boy knows something. Word around the track is that the kid accompanied this fellow up until a few weeks ago."

"I'm sure someone will talk." The officer tossed the tape in the back of his Buick. "That's usually how we solve this type of mugging."

"Sounds more like an attempted murder." Mark's gaze drifted to the feasting flies. "Look, if you guys are finished here, I'm going to clean up that blood. Kids play here all the time."

"Go ahead. We're finished." The officer didn't look at the grisly splotch, just slid in his car and rolled away.

Mark walked to the barn closest to the apartment complex. A groom with curly blond hair and a matching earring stood by a rack of bridles, squeezing soap from an oversized sponge. "Shocking, isn't it?" The groom glanced past Mark at the receding police car. "Dick's a good guy—eccentric maybe, but a good guy. Doesn't sound like the cops have a clue."

"Or that they're looking for one," Mark said grimly. "Got a bucket I can borrow? I want to dump some water on that blood spot."

"Yeah, sure. Poor old Mary doesn't want to see that. The knife cut Dick's artery. Just missed the jugular. She clamped her hand over his neck and called 911."

"Who's Mary?" Mark asked as the groom filled four black rubber buckets and even topped them off with generous squirts of soap.

"Lives in the bottom apartment. Helps Dick with fundraising."

"Think she has a key to Dick's place?" Mark picked up two frothing buckets and walked back, accompanied by the helpful groom.

"I'm sure she does," the groom said.

They sloshed water on the ground and watched the liquid dissipate in loopy veins through the gravel. The protesting flies rose in a dark buzz. "Hey, Mary!" the groom yelled, setting down his empty bucket. "Come on out."

A curtain lifted. A moment later the door opened, and a small woman stepped outside. Short, broad shoulders, strong arms. Looked like an exercise rider.

"Got a key to Dick's place?" the blond man asked.

"Who wants to know?" she asked, staring at Mark with wary eyes.

Mark stepped forward and introduced himself, and the woman's thick shoulders relaxed. "Oh, okay. I've heard your name. Jessica works for you," she said. "Yeah, sure, I have a key."

"I'll take these buckets back," the groom said. "Good luck in the Juvenile." He hesitated, then gave a hopeful smile. "If you're ever hiring, I'm interested and experienced. Name's Jim."

"Grooms come and go," Mark said, "so keep checking." He turned to Mary. "Did the police borrow your key and check out the place?"

"Nope." She shrugged. "But I heard someone up there early this morning. Maybe the cops got a key from housing. If you want to take a look, fine by me. But I'm coming with you."

189

Mark followed her up the wooden steps. She turned the key to Dick's apartment and shoved open the door.

"You first," she said, stepping back. "I'm a little spooked about all this."

He entered slowly, absorbing the endless racks of clothes, the stacked boxes. If there was a picture in this mini-warehouse, it seemed impossible to find.

"Your groom sorted most of this stuff," Mary said. "Dick said she had the best eye for clothes he's ever seen."

"Really?" Mark jerked around. "Jessica did this?"

"Yeah, the clothes are up on the website two weeks early, thanks to her."

Mark shook his head and moved down the narrow hall, past a room stuffed with boxes and into another room, clearly the bedroom. "Does Dick usually keep his drawers upside down?" he asked.

"No." Mary scowled and pushed past him. "Must be those damn cops. They always leave a mess. I'll straighten it up before Dick returns in the spring. He spends winters upstate."

"Jessica will want to help," Mark said. "I'll send her by late tomorrow morning."

"Great." Mary's shoulders relaxed with relief. "She can pick the key up from me. As long as you don't think she'll mind?"

"She'll consider it a pleasure." And an opportunity, he thought wryly. After talking with Jessica's grandfather, it was clear she'd need a few more clothes.

He returned to his office, bone weary, unsure if he needed coffee or sleep. Opened the door and saw Jessica ensconced in his chair, boots propped on the desk and a telltale peppermint bulge in her left cheek. She dropped her feet to the floor with a thud.

"I was breaking down the vet bill for each horse," she said defensively, "and needed a bigger work space."

"It's okay, stay there. I'm going to have a nap." He scanned her work and couldn't resist giving her ponytail a playful tug. "Looks good."

A thirty-minute nap wouldn't hurt. He stretched out on the cot and closed his eyes, oddly enjoying her presence—the click of the calculator, the rustle of paper—and fleetingly wondered if he could persuade her to join him. But the moral dilemma that would involve, considering his no-sex rule, was far too weighty. He fell asleep before completely analyzing the thought.

When he woke, the blackened room felt empty, and it was obvious he'd overslept. Appalled, he leaped from the cot. Six-thirty! Christ. Carlos would be forever feeding supper and checking bandages. He rushed to the entrance of the shedrow, but Carlos looked relaxed, lounging by the front door, talking to the night guard.

"Hi, boss," he said. "We're all fed. Jessica said you'd want to wrap Assets. Everyone else is finished and looking good, though. Some heat in the gray filly, but her leg's a lot better."

"Good." Mark nodded, relieved, but still shocked he'd slept so long. "I'll wrap Assets now. Where's Jessica?"

"In her room, I think." Carlos frowned. "Her face is messed up. Heard she fell off Ghost. He's probably too much horse for a beginner."

His voice held a note of disapproval, but Mark let it go. He wasn't feeling very good about it either.

He slipped into Assets' stall and ran his hands down the colt's legs. Tight and cold. So far, the horse had never taken a lame step. He wrapped quickly, ensuring the bandages were firm and tendons evenly supported, then secured the door.

Further down the aisle, Buddy stuck his head out, watching with hopeful eyes. Mark slowed and gave the gelding a quick pat, wryly studying his curly mane. The horse was immaculate, but Jessica was forever experimenting with braids and colors, and Mark endured endless ribbing from other trainers. He impulsively slipped Buddy a peppermint, hoping the alert chestnut in the next stall wouldn't hear the crunching, then turned and headed to her room.

Knocked. No answer. Tried the door and was happy but slightly annoyed to discover it unlocked. She lay on the cot, breathing deep and even, dark lashes fanning her cheeks. He'd anticipated Kato's rush but still wasn't fast enough, and sharp claws pinched his leg.

He picked up the cat, cradling him until he settled and when Kato started to purr, put him down by his food dish. He turned and gently shook Jessica's shoulder.

"Mark?" she mumbled, not opening her eyes.

"Yes. Thanks for letting me sleep, sweetie. You hungry?"

"Yes, but I'm too tired to get up."

"Move over," he said. He edged in beside her, wrapping her in his arms as he sucked in her floral smell, the same smell Buddy had. "Do you use a horse shampoo," he whispered, "or does Buddy use people shampoo?" He freed her hair from the ponytail, stroking the silky strands, liking the way it cascaded over her shoulders.

"Neither. It's the conditioner."

She sounded more awake. Probably alert enough to hear her grandfather's request but hopefully not alert enough to realize the prick hadn't wanted to talk to her. Again. "I'm meeting your grandfather at Keeneland," he said, sliding his hand through her hair and rubbing her neck. "We're looking at some horses. He wants you to come."

Her eyes cracked open. "What's he up to?"

"I don't know," Mark admitted. It was strange Boone didn't ever talk to her on the phone but suddenly wanted her to attend a sale in Kentucky.

Her nose wrinkled. "I only have two weeks to go. Maybe he has some plan to make me quit. Or something he thinks will make you fire me. You did promise you wouldn't fire me though, right?"

"I did. And I won't," he said. "I promise."

She sighed and relaxed in his arms. "Guess I'm okay then. When do we leave?"

"Tomorrow afternoon. We'll be gone two nights. Friday is the sale. Dinner with your grandfather is that night."

"Oh, no." Her dismayed sigh fanned his throat. "I can't go. I don't have clothes for that."

"You can borrow something from Dick. I told Mary you'd be happy to come by his apartment and help clean up."

She laughed, a bubbling sound that was contagious, and he stopped worrying about the depressing hock X-ray, the unorthodox media interview and all the calls from whining owners. He stopped thinking about the fugitive kid and the strange events that seemed to be plaguing the track.

"And you promised that as further punishment," she asked, still laughing, "or because you knew I'd need some nice clothes?"

"A little bit of both," he said as he found her mouth in the gloom. He only intended an affectionate gesture, but her taste, her feel, the familiar way her lips parted were too arousing, and he shelved the list of things he had to finish before they flew to Keeneland.

He slipped his hand under her shirt, stroking her breast, molding her against him. She felt so right, so perfect. The urge to yank down her pants and lose himself in her was almost overwhelming.

No wonder his father had kept a double bed in his tack room for frequent fucking.

He jerked back as though drenched with cold water. "I have to stay away from you at the track," he said. "No one can know."

"Of course. We wouldn't want you acting like your dad."

He stiffened, surprised she could read him so well. She lay unmoving, but her voice was flippant, the way it always turned when she tried to hide her hurt. And he didn't want her hurt. "This is where I work," he said, choosing his words carefully, "and having sex here is too frivolous."

Apparently he didn't pick his words well enough. She jackknifed to a sitting position, her eyes stormy. "Frivolous? Our relationship is frivolous?"

"Of course not. That isn't what I meant. Want me order you a pizza?" He rose from the cot, suddenly eager to escape. "I have a meeting in Queens, but the guard can bring it down."

She was still glaring and there was really nothing to say, so he backed out the door, exhaling with relief when she remained mute on the cot. It was always best to escape before they started dissecting words and relationships. He'd always been careless with women. Training was too demanding a job to even consider a high-maintenance relationship. And Jessica was as high maintenance as they come.

She rose and slammed the door in his face, the lock clicking with a finality that made him smile. Yes, she left him drained but also thoroughly entertained, and it was great she was going to be around for another two weeks. He only wanted the best for her, and hopefully she'd find a suitable career, something that didn't hinge on her grandfather's approval.

After she left, he might hire that curly-haired guy, Jim. The barn needed a tougher groom, one who could handle colts, since Breeders' Cup exposure was already bringing more horses. Stakes horses. His staff would earn bigger bonuses, and lives would all get a little easier. Maybe he could even hire a fulltime office manager.

Maybe Jessica?

No. He shook his head as he walked down the aisle, automatically checking each stall. She'd master the job in a week and end up hating it. And him. She was too mercurial, the type who needed a challenge, needed to be her own boss.

The guard jerked to his feet, pretending he hadn't been sitting for the past twenty minutes.

"Can you see the back door from here?" Mark asked.

"No." The man shuffled sideways and crossed his arms. "I'd prefer to shut the back door for security reasons, but Jessica insists the horses need fresh air."

"She's absolutely right," Mark said. "So you'll have to make regular rounds. The horse I'm most concerned about is in stall twenty-four." He opened his wallet and flipped through his bills. "I'm going to order a pizza. When it comes, track security will call and send the driver through. Make sure Jessica gets it." He noticed the guard's empty cookie container and added, "You hungry? I was planning to order a medium but can make it a large."

The guard lowered his arms, relaxing enough to smile. "I appreciate that, Mr. Russell, but I always bring a lunch so a medium pizza is probably big enough. I doubt the little jockey eats much."

"What jockey is that?" Mark asked, scanning his phone for the pizza number.

"Jessica's boyfriend. The one who sleeps here."

"Oh, right. Jessica's boyfriend." He stared at his screen, his thumb pausing in midair before tapping in the phone number. "What's that guy's name again?"

"Didn't meet him, but I saw them coming from the shower together." The guard chuckled. "Good thing he rides. He'll never make a singer."

A jockey boyfriend? How the hell had he missed that? Mark felt as though he'd been kicked in the stomach but paused a moment, his mind scrambling as the lady on the phone repeated her request for his order. "Small pizza with the works," he finally said. Thought a moment. "And can you add anchovies and lots and lots of jalapenos."

CHAPTER TWENTY

Jessica finished dressing, bubbling with anticipation as she tugged on her boots. Keeneland Day! She didn't know anything about the place, other than it was a quality racetrack in Kentucky, but there was bound to be lots of good food. And a hotel with a big tub and a real bed.

She grabbed her water bottle and took another gulp, hoping to soothe her ragged throat. Mark had thoughtfully arranged for her supper last night, but the pizza he'd ordered had been horrible. It had smelled delicious though, and she'd been hungry. However, she hated anchovies and thought he knew that.

Unfortunately, fish juice had leaked all over the cheese. Plus, she hadn't found the jalapenos until it was too late—but by then her stomach was screaming for food, and she couldn't resist.

Big mistake. She hadn't put the leftovers outside for the boy, figuring he'd pull better food from the dumpster. The salt must have made her eyes swell, because her face felt tight and puffy. She grabbed her shampoo—she'd left her conditioner in Buddy's grooming kit—and rushed to the bathroom for her morning shower.

She glanced in the cracked mirror, saw her swollen face and yelped. Her eye was bluish black and scary, the ugliest shiner she'd ever seen, uglier than the bruised boxers on television. Groaning, she jerked away from the mirror and into the shower, trying not to cry as water sluiced over her face. She looked so ugly, so battered, so utterly repulsive.

She yanked her clothes on, hair still dripping, and bolted to Mark's office. Irritation darkened his face when the door burst open, but she was gratified when his expression turned to horror.

"See. I knew it," she wailed "I can't go to Keeneland like this."

He just stared, his upper lip twitching.

"Don't you dare laugh." She crossed the room and smacked his shoulder. "I'm going to miss out seeing all those beautiful horses. The hotel. And my grandfather. All because of that crazy horse you made me ride." Her words trailed off to a miserable choke.

"Hey." He rose from the chair. "It's not that bad."

She squeezed her eyes shut, wishing she could crawl into a hole, but he tilted her chin and gently traced her face. "We'll put a little poultice here and draw out the swelling. Doc just dropped off some new stuff. And if that doesn't work, sunglasses." His voice tapered off. "Really big sunglasses."

She choked on a hysterical sob.

"Makeup too," he added quickly. "A lot can be accomplished with makeup."

"I don't know." She opened her eyes and groaned. "Finally seeing Gramps and pretending I'm doing well when I look so...ugly."

"You'll never be ugly, and you're doing very well. I've told him that many times."

"Do you talk to him much? I know he's really busy." She hated the wistful note that crept into her voice. She'd always been good at pretending indifference when her mom sent her away, but sympathy flashed in Mark's face and she knew he wasn't as easily fooled.

Rap, rap. They both turned and looked at the door as Carlos stuck his head in. "First set is almost ready, boss. Just need your opinion on some legs." He flinched when he saw Jessica's face. "*Dios mio!*"

"Switch Assets to the second set," Mark said. "I'll be a bit longer here."

"Don't think you should do that, boss," Carlos said, still staring at her with such a look of dismay it would have been comical if it wasn't such a disaster. He tossed a section of *The New York Times* on the desk. "I expect there'll be lots of media around later. One of the trainers brought you a bouquet of dandelions. Another left chocolates. They're all laughing."

Mark scanned the paper then cursed. "Jess, we'll put the poultice on after the first set." He dropped the paper and rushed out with Carlos, leaving her alone to read the article:

At six feet three inches and two hundred and twenty-six pounds, Mark Russell doesn't gallop many horses, preferring to oversee his stable of forty runners from the back of a Texas-bred quarter horse. With both a racing and rodeo background, as well as an astounding win rate of twenty-seven percent, Mark heads into the Breeders' Cup with the unquestionable Juvenile favorite.

Ambling Assets, a two-year-old colt by Barkeeper out of an Asset Man mare, is not fashionably bred but is undefeated in five lifetime starts and has an affinity for the Belmont strip, attested by his recent half-mile bullet. Capable of stalking, this speedy colt has been pointed to the Breeders Cup and is one of only three contenders coming off a six-week layoff.

"I don't want him to do too much," Mark explained when interviewed outside his barn yesterday. "He's learning to relax and tuck in behind horses. He's a good-looking fellow who always tries, the kind of horse who's easy to have around."

Easy to have around, indeed. "Who do you like?" is a common expression at the track. But with a dynamic trainer and an upstart colt leading the Breeders' Cup charge, it has also revived interest in the human element. At the track kitchen, Mark Russell's name topped the vote for "Bachelor of the Backstretch," and if his deft touch with horses reflects his popularity with the ladies, Markomania is just beginning.

Good grief. Jessica dumped the paper back on the desk. She'd been right about that reporter. Tina was incapable of writing a sensible piece. She hadn't included a picture of Assets; instead she'd used the one of Ghost, along with a completely inaccurate caption, 'Russell Rescues Inattentive Groom.'

Tina didn't mention that Jessica had hung on to Ghost for almost a minute while the horse threw his freak-out fit. The picture only showed Mark pushing her back as he grabbed the reins.

Jessica bent closer, tracing a finger over his ripped arm. Awesome muscles, nice flex. Not a bad picture really.

She squeezed her eyes in misery. Going away for a two-day trip with the Bachelor of the Backstretch, and she looked like a Cyclops. She peered out the window. It was still dark, but figures bustled amidst giggles and gruff laughter. Everyone was having a good time teasing Mark. He'd worked hard for his success and had earned their respect.

He was the most decent man she knew.

Sighing, she squared her shoulders, resolving to table her vanity and join the festivities. Her boss had hit the big time, and it was only fair she step outside and cheer him on.

Jessica slipped Buddy a carrot, feeling the soft velvet of his muzzle as he gently lifted it from her hand. Never pushy, always a gentleman. She loved gazing into his liquid eyes, so kind and accepting, a reflection of his kind nature.

She stepped closer and ran a hand over his sleek neck, across his muscled shoulder, down his forearm. His knee was flat and clean. The swelling she'd reported to Mark last week had disappeared, and she inspected each leg, knowing them as well now as she did her own.

One old splint on his right cannon bone, a wind puff on his right fetlock, some scar tissue on his front heels. Inconsequential blemishes, Mark had said. Nothing to worry about.

She edged around Buddy's hindquarters and ran a hand through his silky tail, ostensibly checking for tangles but really just enjoying his company. He sounded so content when he chewed his hay, when he dunked it in his water and sloshed it around, the way it stuck out of his mouth when he turned and looked at her with those dark, soulful eyes.

He never worried about anything but the present, and it was refreshing sharing his stall. In another week she'd own him.

"Last set. Let's go," Carlos called to the riders in the aisle.

Mark stopped by Buddy's stall, holding goggles, a can of gooey yellow stuff and a bottle of something that smelled like turpentine. "Come on. I'll put this on your face now. You can stay in my office until it's time to wash it off." He turned and watched the line of horses as they filed out. "Don't be too tight on her face, Aaron," he called. "You're pissing her off." He turned back to Jessica. "This will bring the swelling down."

"It doesn't matter," she said. "Go watch your horses. They need you, especially since you'll be gone for a few days."

"So you're not going to the sale?" His voice and face were expressionless, and she couldn't tell if he was disappointed or relieved.

"Oh, I'm going," she said. "But you have more important things to do than rub goop on my face. Especially now that you're a big hero," she gave a teasing smile, "saving my life yesterday and all that."

"We heroes do tend to be busy." He spoke so solemnly she tossed a wet clump of Buddy's hay at his chest. But then he chuckled and she felt his relief, knew his time was already spread much too thin. "Okay, Jess," he said. "I'll finish up and see you at noon. Don't go to Dick's without me."

Two hours later, Mark finished with his last horse, and they drove to Dick's apartment.

"How long will the teasing last?" Jessica twisted in the car seat, watching Mark's face as the bearded trainer in barn fifty-three gave a sardonic wolf whistle.

"Probably be over by the time we return. When there'll be an article about someone else."

She nodded but was unconvinced. Mark was attractive, accessible and articulate. She guessed he was a beacon for the media and much more interesting than men like Radcliff. Personally she'd like to know more about Sheikh Khalif. His horses were here, along with his trainer, but she hadn't seen anyone who looked remotely sheikh-like. He owned some of the best horses in the world but even so, his top two-year-old was only the second favorite. The news that experts considered her grandfather's horse faster than the sheikh's was somewhat staggering.

Curious, she turned toward Mark, forgetting about keeping her face straight so he couldn't see her ugly eye. "You must be nervous about the Breeders' Cup?"

"I just want to get Assets to the gate, healthy and happy," he said. "And hope we're lucky."

She raised an eyebrow. "I've seen your preparation. And how you train. I don't think it has much to do with luck."

"It always comes down to luck. And since you're handing out compliments, you must be gunning for a raise." He punched in a number, already distracted with his phone calls.

He didn't think much of her, she realized with an ache. Her grandfather had saddled him with a novice, and Mark was simply making the best of it. Of course, Assets was his top horse so she was, in a way, a fringe owner. He had to be nice to her. And he'd never made any secret about the fact that he liked sex.

She tucked her knees against the seat, feeling small but determined to hide it.

"No, Dino," Mark said, adjusting the speaker. "We'll stay with the afternoon jog on the training track. Good for him mentally too. Is your knee sore?"

She looked over, realized he'd cut the phone connection and was talking to her again. "No, my knee's great," she said. "I was just thinking."

"I know you're worried about that kid, but it'll be better for him once he's found. The night guard thought he heard something but didn't see him when he checked outside."

"It's hard for the guard to watch both entrances," she said.

"Guess you'd know that." His voice sharpened, and he accelerated so abruptly her shoulders pressed against the seat. "Remember, it's cause for dismissal if you have anyone overnight. Anyone."

"I'm sorry. He only slept with me once, and I won't let him stay again." She craned her neck and gestured over her shoulder. "You just passed Dick's place."

Mark swore, jammed on the brakes and made an aggressive U-turn. The mini vacation would be good for him too, she decided. He must be distracted about something since he wasn't the type to miss turnoffs.

"Want me to call when I'm finished?" she asked as he pulled his vehicle in front of Dick's apartment.

"No, I'll wait here. Figure out my entries. Be in later though. Maybe we can find the picture Dick snapped."

She nodded and stepped from the car. Mark thought the picture was so important, but she didn't see why it would make any difference. Dick had already shown it to everyone on the backside and, although a few people had seen the man around, no one knew his name or where he worked. Still, if Mark wanted it…

She stuck her head back in the car. "You know that Mary has the camera?"

"And?" He was already flipping through his worn condition book and didn't look up.

"And, the picture of that man should be on her memory card," she said.

He did look up then, smiling with such approval, her pulse jumped. "Clever girl," he said. He snapped his briefcase shut and joined her as they climbed the steps to Mary's apartment.

Mary flung the door open before they knocked. "Lord, what happened?" she asked, staring at Jessica's face. "Horse?"

"Yes."

She nodded in total understanding and passed Jessica a key. "I've had lots of wrecks. Expect to have lots more. That's horses."

"Yes. That's horses." Jessica's shoulders squared with fraternal pride. Maybe it wasn't so bad to have a messed-up face. "Have you talked to Dick?" she added.

"Sure have. Every day on the phone. And soon he'll be allowed visitors." Mary launched into an account of how Dick hadn't seen his attacker, how grateful he was Mary had called 911, and how mortified he was to be stuck in an ugly green hospital gown.

Mark shuffled his feet, and Jessica gently interrupted. "Mary, we were wondering if you have your pictures from the last four weeks."

"Honey, I have them for the last two years."

"We're looking for one taken three weeks ago," Jessica said. "Same time as all the clothes were catalogued. Dick took a picture of a dark-haired man leaning against that wall." She pointed at the apartment across the road.

"Should be able to dig it up," Mary said. "Think he's the psycho who cut Dick?"

"Don't know," Mark said, stepping forward. "Might be a coincidence but Dick was flashing the picture, asking questions. Maybe he stirred up something." Jessica flinched with guilt, and Mark gave her elbow a reassuring squeeze. "But it may have nothing to do with the picture," he added.

"Give me your e-mail," Mary said, "and I'll send the picture soon as I can find it. Poor Dick. He's such a generous man too. Loves horses and people."

"I'll be upstairs." Jessica blinked rapidly, trying to control the tightness behind her eyes. Palming the key, she trudged up the steps to Dick's door. She entered the silent apartment, lonely and depressing now that Dick no longer filled it with his unique energy. The racks of clothes were still there but shoved rudely against the wall, and many of the dresses had slipped from the metal hangers.

She rehung them, desperately trying to work the lump from her throat. However, the picture of Dick, stuck in a sterile hospital bed, was much too vivid. He was all alone in an ugly green gown, with no visitors, isolated from the charity work he loved. God, he must have been terrified when that blade cut into his neck.

She dropped her head in her hands, overwhelmed with guilt.

She didn't hear Mark enter, but his familiar arms slipped around her. He didn't try to stop her tears or even speak, only held her as she turned and cried into his shirt.

"You really are the most patient person," she finally muttered, lifting her head and swiping her face. "Sorry. Now your shirt is all wet." She turned away, still knuckling her cheeks, but desperate to force some gaiety into her voice. "This place isn't too messy. It looks about the same as last time."

"Check Dick's bedroom," Mark said. "I think someone else was looking for that picture."

She hurried down the hall, slowed to a stop at the sight of the overturned drawers, the flipped mattress, the carnage of strewn paper. "I can't believe the police would do this."

"Probably they didn't." Mark's jaw flexed. "Don't think they're looking."

She drew in a shaky breath. It would take time to clean and choose her Keeneland wardrobe, and the plane was leaving in less than five hours. Yet this room wasn't just messy, it had been ransacked—and if not by the police, it had been the work of a scarily determined intruder.

Jessica tightened her seatbelt as the plane taxied along the runway. She'd forgotten to nab the seat on the left, but it didn't seem as though Mark noticed her ugly eye. And if he didn't care, she wouldn't either.

Not that he was paying any attention to her. By the time the plane leveled in the air, he'd already pulled out the Keeneland catalogue and was focused on pedigrees. A stewardess brought him a coffee but rushed off before Jessica could ask for a juice.

She twisted in the seat, trying to attract someone's attention, but the attendants had already moved down the narrow aisle.

"Need something?" Mark asked, circling numbers with his pen.

"A cold drink. I've been thirsty since that pizza last night."

The corner of his mouth twitched, but he didn't look up. "What would you like?"

"Orange juice. A big one. But it looks like I'll have to wait. They've passed our row."

"I can get it," he said with utter confidence. She didn't hear him speak but somehow he snagged the stewardess's eye, and she bustled back. A smile, a murmur, and she brought Mark two glasses of orange juice and four bags of peanuts.

"I think she likes you," Jessica whispered.

Mark just smiled, somewhat smugly she thought, and continued flipping pages.

She peered out the tiny window and checked the scenery, but a shroud of white clouds extended in every direction. Sighing, she slipped on the headphones, but the music was boring no matter how many channels she checked. She'd always used an iPod when she skied, the perfect tool for staying relaxed, but today she was restless and couldn't find any decent songs.

She glanced at Mark's catalogue, saw he'd circled a Barkeeper colt and perked up. "That colt is by the same stud as Assets. You interested in him?"

"Maybe, but Barkeeper is best at siring precocious two-year-olds. And not so good for the three-year-old races like the Derby. A lot depends on what your grandfather wants."

"Seems like everyone wants to win the Kentucky Derby," she said. "What does black type winner mean?"

"Graded stakes. The best horses run in those."

"Did Buddy ever win a stakes race?"

"No, honey," he said with a smile. "But when he was younger, he won a few allowance races. And he always tries his best. Can't ask a horse for more than that."

Honey? She fumbled for the headsets she'd dropped in shock. He was calling her 'honey' in public. Of course they weren't at the track, but it did feel rather nice, and her cheeks flushed with pleasure. Fortunately he was too engrossed in the catalogue to notice.

"Do you have another of those auction listings?" she asked.

He glanced at her then rummaged through his briefcase, producing a shiny new catalogue with gold print. "It's a mixed sale so circle what you like," he said. "But we're only buying a two-year-old. We can compare horses tonight."

Ah, yes. Her grandfather wasn't arriving until tomorrow. Her gaze flickered over Mark's chiseled mouth, his lean hands as he snapped his briefcase shut. When his muscular thigh grazed her hip, her entire body tingled. This was going to be so much fun. An entire night away from the track. Just the two of them, no sneaking required.

Maybe he shared her anticipation—and they'd do much more than compare horses. His warm fingers suddenly brushed hers and her breathing stuttered, escaping in a disappointed sigh when she saw he'd merely pressed a pen into her hand.

CHAPTER TWENTY-ONE

The hotel receptionist slid Mark two room cards. "Elevators are to the right," she said. "Rooms are on the third and sixth floor. Enjoy your stay."

"Do you have a preference?" he asked Jessica as they waited for the elevator.

"No, as long as my room has a tub. I plan to soak forever."

The image of that bare skin made his throat go dry. He grabbed their luggage and shoved it onto the elevator. "You take third then," he said gruffly. "I'll meet you at nine in the lobby. The restaurant is pretty good here."

"Okay." She swept from the elevator, almost forgetting her bag, obviously preoccupied with her upcoming bath. He passed it to her before the elevator doors closed. Not surprising she was in a rush to reach her room. She'd endured the primitive track bathrooms for over a month but, even so, her total lack of interest in him was rather deflating.

Probably for the best though. Her grandfather was his most important owner, and Boone wouldn't be happy if he discovered they'd slept together. From past conversations, it was clear Boone had plans for Jessica, and they didn't include a Texas horse trainer. Being a day away from seeing Assets' owner made Mark realize they needed to be cautious.

He unlocked his door, tossed his bag on the luggage rack and paced. Of course, there wasn't much to his relationship with Jessica. Nothing Boone needed to know. She'd asked for help forgetting an old boyfriend, and he'd obliged. Simple. Only he hadn't anticipated enjoying her company quite so much.

At least Boone would be pleased with how much she'd learned. She'd turned into a dedicated groom, a little slow maybe, but that was because she spent so much time dawdling with

Buddy. And though she wasn't ready yet to handle a rambunctious colt, she had loads of courage. She hadn't dropped Ghost's reins when he pitched a fit. It took lots of guts to hang onto a twelve-hundred pound freak-out. And she'd done it earlier with Assets. There were probably many things she'd excel at, so long as it was something she liked, something that didn't choke her creativity. She just didn't realize she was so capable.

He checked his watch—another hour before dinner. It would have been a much better start to the evening if she'd invited him to join her in that hotel tub. She must really like her jockey friend.

He scowled, pulled out a Belmont program and scanned the jock list. He'd already checked it twice, trying to figure out which guy she was seeing, but the guard's description had been vague. He could probably find out from Emma Rae or Steve—jockeys were notorious gossips—but he doubted Jessica would appreciate his snooping. She'd made it clear their sex was casual and temporary. Exactly what he wanted.

He tossed aside the program and rechecked his watch. Eight o'clock. Maybe he'd have a quick shower in case she invited him to her room later. Neither Boone nor the singing jockey were around tonight. Hopefully after a few drinks, she'd relax and they could enjoy each other's company. Or maybe she needed some consolation. It was clear she was eaten up with guilt over Dick's stabbing.

Didn't matter what they did. He was suddenly very impatient to see her.

"Thanks," Jessica said as Mark expertly refilled her wine glass. "You're an attentive host. Is this how trainers always treat their owners before a big sale?"

He raised an amused eyebrow. "So you're an owner now, not my groom?"

"Two weeks left," she said with a flippant smile, a smile that took so much effort it hurt. "Two more weeks, and I'll be gone. But you can bet I'll keep an eye on you, making sure you treat Gramps' horses well."

"Good. I hope you visit often."

"Only if you promise not to make me muck a stall." Her voice was bright even as her chest constricted. He spoke so casually about her leaving, didn't guess the thought of not seeing him made something jab against her ribs.

"Feel like dessert?" he asked, blue eyes watchful over his glass.

"Wish I could, but I'm too full." Her dismay was genuine. She'd been planning to order the chocolate cheesecake but not now, not with her stomach flipping. "I can't even finish this wine."

"Okay. Want to go somewhere and compare horses?"

She sucked at her bottom lip, trying to control its quiver. He was trying hard to look after her, but the pedigree information was too new, too confusing. She preferred to see horses in the flesh, had always finalized her bets that way and didn't want to admit she hadn't circled a single animal.

Didn't want to admit she'd been hoping for a more romantic type of evening.

Even the clothes she'd borrowed from Dick's apartment had been chosen for a lover's tryst. Snazzy black pants and metallic sweater tonight, form-fitting jacket for the sale, and a strapless cocktail dress for tomorrow's dinner. She could have worn her comfortable boots and jeans for all that Mark noticed.

"Think I'll just go to my room." She struggled to keep her voice level. "I probably ate too much. Do you know what time Gramps is coming tomorrow?"

"Around noon. I'm going to the pavilion in the morning, but we won't be bidding until the afternoon. If you want to come with me, that would be fine. Just let me know." He dropped his napkin on the table.

The perky waitress materialized at his side. "Tea, coffee?"

He raised a questioning eyebrow at Jessica, but she shook her head, too miserable to speak. Fine if she accompanied Mark in the morning, fine if she didn't. The lovely meal she'd eaten felt like a brick.

"Just the bill then." He nodded at the waitress, his face inscrutable.

"How does this work?" Jessica asked. "Do you bill this trip to my grandfather? Because I don't have any money, and the hotel and food—"

"You're always fretting about money. Don't worry. Sales are fun. If you change your mind and want to study some horses, I'll be in the bar."

Jessica pointed the remote and flicked through an assortment of TV channels. A feature on heli-skiing in the Rockies looked mildly interesting, and she raised the volume. Now this was promising; she'd always loved adventure skiing, and it was a treat to watch TV again.

She fluffed her pillows and stretched on the huge bed, watching as three skiers with tanned faces and sparkling white teeth climbed into a helicopter. It rose in a crescendo of noise and swirling white. The snow cover wasn't too deep, about to Buddy's knees, although horses would definitely struggle to get through the higher banks. It was probably fun to ride in the snow. Wouldn't hurt a bit if you fell off.

She rose and wandered into the bathroom. Leaned close to the mirror so she could inspect her eye. Still blackly bruised, but Mark had said it would turn yellow soon. She reapplied her makeup, stood back and studied her face. Marginal improvement. She flicked off the bathroom switch and stared at the mirror. In the dim light, the bruise was almost indistinguishable.

She returned to the TV. The skiers grinned with anticipation as they adjusted their packs and stepped into their bindings. A few more minutes and they'd be ready to tackle the mountain.

She picked up the sales catalogue and flipped through the sire list, surprised when she recognized several names. Buddy's sire wasn't listed, nor was his grandsire or his dam sire.

But Barkeeper, Assets' sire, was on the list. He had five weanlings and two yearlings offered for sale, and it was thrilling to read that Assets was his first black type winner. Interest pricked, she grabbed a pen.

Some colts didn't have names yet. Mark said owners often liked to name their own horses and that it was a selling feature, but it made her sad thinking the babies had gone six months without a real name. Sometimes the business side of horse racing was depressing.

The horses she found most appealing were ones with the same sires or broodmare sires as runners she'd watched at

Belmont. She remembered betting on a bay gelding that hadn't won a race until he was four—certainly a late bloomer—but his delighted connections had enjoyed a raucous time in the winner's circle. Maybe it was preferable to have an older gelding who wasn't a superstar, a horse with no pressure to retire and exploit his breeding value.

There'd be no need to rush the training either. Despite studies that proved horses raced as two-year-olds lasted longer, she knew Mark worried about Assets' fragile bones. He was always trying various poultices, checking and rechecking legs.

She flipped to the front of the catalogue and reviewed pedigrees. The skiers were irritating now, so she clicked the TV off and focused on the reams of information, circling any horse she found interesting and adding asterisks to the most appealing.

Tomorrow might be fun after all. They'd be able to inspect the horses too. Mark was fussy about legs, always noticing tiny things, whereas she tended to focus on the look in the eye. Sometimes she couldn't get past a pretty head.

She glanced at the clock. Eleven-thirty. He might still be in the lounge, and it was obvious now she'd done her homework. She didn't check her makeup, just grabbed her catalogue and hurried to the elevator.

A hubbub of noise spilled into the hotel lobby—droning voices, music, the clink of glass. She circled through the foyer, past people sprawled on oversized chairs and speaking in earnest whispers. Clearly this was a popular hotel for the horse crowd, as several had sales catalogues spread on their laps.

She slipped into the bar, pausing to let her vision adjust to the muted light. Seemed an odd place to study a catalogue: busy, hard to see, no privacy. On the plane, she'd noticed how Mark had turned the page when anyone ventured too close, always making sure his notations remained private.

A plump blonde with reddened eyes and tight white pants barged past. Jessica stepped sideways and spotted Mark. His back anyway. His hip was propped against the bar, no sign of his catalogue, and he was in deep discussion with a beautiful lady who looked vaguely familiar. Definitely not a track worker—too much of a power suit, too much assurance.

Mark, however, didn't seem at all intimidated. He leaned down with a lazy smile and whatever he said made her laugh, a tinkling laugh that drew the attention of several envious men. A flirtatious laugh that cut Jessica's heart and froze her feet in the doorway. Her hand drifted to her wounded eye, and she stared for another agonizing moment before backing away and retreating to the sanctuary of her room.

CHAPTER TWENTY-TWO

Jessica woke at four a.m., flipped the pillow and tried to fall back to sleep, but new habits were hard to break. At six-thirty she finally dozed off, and at the next check it was after eight.

She scrambled out of bed and rushed into the pristine bathroom. Studied her eye. More yellow today. Not so bad. Turned on the shower and stood beneath a reviving spray of warm water while she considered her options.

There weren't many. Hide in her room and wait for her grandfather, or call Mark and insist he take her with him. And she really wanted to see those beautiful Thoroughbreds.

She'd have to call him before he left. He might still be in his room, but if the woman from the bar answered his phone, Jessica didn't know if she'd have the aplomb to handle it. Safer to call his cell, even though it was long distance.

"Mark Russell," he answered, so cool and crisp she waited a beat before she was able to speak.

"Hi, it's Jessica."

"Good morning." His voice seemed to warm. "Rested up?"

"Yes, I'd like to come with you this morning...if that's okay." She strained to hear the background noise, to hear if the woman was in his room.

"Good. Come to the lobby," he said. "I'm in the parking lot. Pick you up at the door."

She gulped, staring in dismay at her bare feet, at the fluffy bath towel wrapped like a sarong. "But I just got out of the shower. How long can you wait?"

He chuckled as though she'd made a joke. "As long as you want," he said.

*

"Oh, wow!" Jessica stared in awe as Mark guided the rental car past the Keeneland sign and cruised along a smooth drive lined with white fences, lush grass and spacious stables. "This is gorgeous, like a private farm. And Kentucky grass really does have a bluish tinge."

She lowered her window to absorb the atmosphere and watched as impeccably-dressed handlers led gleaming horses along a pathway. White hip numbers were apparent even from this distance, and her eager fingers grabbed the door handle. This was going to be so much fun, especially as it was just the two of them, and Mark seemed genuinely happy to have her company.

He parked in a treed lot, flush with yellow and red leaves. "Let's look at the two-year-olds first." He gestured at some barns on their right.

She hurried after him, trying to keep pace with his purposeful stride. Several people called out greetings. He replied but didn't stop, not until they reached the rail beyond which horses paraded along a walkway.

"Oh, my. The horses are turned out so nicely." She stared in appreciation at their shiny coats, their perfect manes and flowing tails. Even the leather halters glistened.

"Prepped by professionals," Mark said. "Makes a difference in their sale price."

She noted not a single horse was braided and guessed he was making a little dig but was too enthralled to care.

"Watch that colt walk," he said. "What do you see?"

"Big stride, long, kind of flowing. His hind legs land way past his front."

"Good girl." Mark smiled at her. "A nice walk usually means a big gallop. If you can get an extra inch or two, it can make a difference. Now look at that bay filly walking toward us," he added. "Notice how the left leg wings slightly."

"But she looked straight standing still," Jessica said. "And she has a beautiful head. What a shame."

"Doesn't mean she isn't fast. Just might be a problem keeping her sound. But I've run horses that looked worse and stayed sound, and I've had correct horses break down. A lot of luck is involved."

"I like that bay colt over there." She pointed to her left. "He's gorgeous and so full of himself. Struts like he owns the place."

Mark chuckled. "Good-looking guy but way out of our price range. That's a Dynaformer baby. Same breeding as Barbaro. In May, we'll come early to the Derby and visit Three Chimneys. See their studs...if you want."

"I'd *love* that," she said quickly, praying he meant it. Prayed Assets would make the Derby. At least then they'd have Gramps' horse as a link.

"We need to avoid the fashionable bloodlines," Mark went on. "I think your grandfather prefers to buy yearlings. But I've only been to one sale with him, last fall when we bought Assets."

"So you found Assets for him? He must be deliriously happy about how that worked out."

Mark shrugged. "Think so but it's hard to tell. He doesn't throw away much praise."

"Yes, I know," she said ruefully.

Their gazes locked. They both grinned and she felt light with shared understanding. Didn't feel the necessity to hide her feelings behind a flippant comment.

Around them, horses were walked, circled and pivoted. Whinnies, murmurs and jovial greetings filled her with a heightened sense of buoyancy. This was much better than any shopping she'd ever experienced, and with Mark beside her, sharing his knowledge, she became more discerning.

Occasionally he would check his catalogue and request a horse be led out, and people would linger and watch his inspection, clearly respecting his opinion. And always he was attentive, listening to her opinion. Sometimes even agreeing.

After watching the tapes of several two-year-olds and their works, Mark squeezed her shoulder. "Want to take a break? Stop at the kitchen? Your grandfather's plane has arrived. We're meeting him in the pavilion at one."

"I see." She hid her hurt behind a quick nod but had expected Gramps to call her directly at the hotel. He'd never paid her much attention until her mom died. Had never been impressed with her skiing, no matter how hard she tried. For a brief period they'd consoled each other, but her life had been crammed with skiing, training and travel, and his with work.

When he'd pressured her to quit and work for Boone, she'd suspected he really wanted a replacement for her mother. It had been easier to concentrate on skiing—until her knee blew.

She must have sighed because Mark slid his arm around her waist and gave a comforting squeeze. "He'll be glad to see you. He's pleased at how well you've done."

"I've done well?" She looked up, studying Mark's face.

"More than well. You've surprised me every day." His approving smile made her heart kick, and she stopped worrying about her grandfather's opinion.

A man in a blue ball cap hailed Mark, holding the glass door open as they entered the spotless kitchen. Jessica studied the overhead menu while the two men talked; the smell of sizzling bacon made her mouth water.

"What would you like?" Mark asked as he joined her. "The pizza's good here."

"No." She gave her head an emphatic shake. "That last one filled me for a while. I really don't like anchovies."

"I don't like them either." He gave a wry smile before stepping up to the counter.

"Why'd you order them then?" She frowned, following him and ordering an egg sandwich with extra crisp bacon on the side.

"We can talk about that tonight. In my room, after dinner. Okay?"

"Okay." She pretended rapt attention as the cook flipped the bacon, afraid Mark would hear the thud of her heart and guess that in his room tonight was exactly where she wanted to be. And clearly he hadn't hooked up with any blonde.

Excitement spilled from the sales pavilion, and a crowd thronged the outer paddock as horses circled, awaiting their turn to enter. Cell phones rang, beeped and played songs and all around them, people whispered and pointed.

"Did you hear the news, Mark?" a man in a Barbour jacket called. "Sheikh Khalif paid five million for a Smart Strike colt."

"Number 621?"

"Yeah, they're interviewing Bobby now. Consignors are ecstatic with the prices."

People clustered around a lady in a beautiful coral suit, the same lady who'd been with Mark at the bar, and the ESPN microphone pricked Jessica's memory. Cathy Wright: the sports reporter who covered horse racing. Jessica had seen her on television in the rec room, had even admired her. The reporter was always insightful, gracious and professional.

Cathy asked something, and the stern man she was interviewing nodded. He didn't look like a sheikh, just an average man in western clothes, but he'd shelled out five million for a colt—definitely cause for excitement.

Mark watched the interview with an amused smile.

Jessica edged closer. "Is that Sheikh Khalif?" she whispered.

"No, that's his agent. I've never seen the sheikh, just his bodyguards. They're an elusive bunch to nail down. Cathy will be delighted to land this interview."

"You know her?"

"Yes." He turned and guided Jessica to the other side, clearly uninterested in the media scrum. "Did you have hip 621 circled?"

"Sure did." She waved her program. "Three asterisks. How much will my grandfather spend?"

Mark laughed. "Not that much. Three hundred thousand maybe."

He seemed content to lean on the rail and watch the horses as they waited to enter the pavilion, and didn't look at Cathy Wright again. Someone called Dutch, wearing a huge cowboy hat, joined them and made an obscure joke about a horse called The Green Monkey. She tilted her watch. Twelve-thirty.

"I'm going to check out the gift shop," she murmured to Mark, who was absorbed in Dutch's animated monologue about folks and horses they both knew back in Texas, a monologue that included an obvious jab at Dino's ex-wife.

She slipped into a boutique crammed with horse ornaments, Christmas decorations and unique clothing. Sweaters, jackets, stunning hats. Dick would have been proud to offer these designs on his website. She fingered a gorgeous scarf, lovingly sliding the silk through her fingers, but the price was way out of her range, and she reluctantly put it back.

"Jessica."

She turned toward Mark's voice.

"Your grandfather has arrived," he said.

Mark watched as hip number 665 was led onto the stage, a wide-eyed bay colt with straight legs and a powerful hip and shoulder.

A Hard Spun colt. Could be a good horse. Boone had said he'd pay up to three hundred thousand; hopefully that would be enough. The dam was bred for stamina but had never made it to the races. Mark had contacted the breeder, who assured him it was no fault of the mare's. She'd been kicked in the knee her first week at the track and promptly retired.

He glanced sideways at Boone, who studied the stage with his usual reserve. Jessica and a man called Ian, apparently a Boone employee, sat on the right side of Boone. Jessica was affectionate with her grandfather, but Mark noticed Boone had stiffened when Jessica hugged him, as though unsure how to handle her affection.

Mark blew out a sigh and stretched in his seat. Be nice to get a hug like that. It had been tough not to put his arm around her this morning, tough trying to figure out what she wanted. It seemed when she didn't need him for a bath or food, she preferred to sleep alone. Or maybe she'd blown him off last night because of her mysterious jockey friend.

Her grandfather's presence was also a damper. There hadn't been time for much conversation before rushing to their reserved seats. But Boone's reaction to her bruised eye had been one of obvious displeasure.

The Hard Spun colt nickered from the stage, reclaiming Mark's attention. An attendant closed the door, and the auctioneer began his spiel. Bidding began at fifty thousand but escalated as the handler, well-dressed in a crisp black suit, showed the horse. Spotters gestured, noting each bid as the numbers on the display climbed.

Mark lifted his finger at two hundred, but there was a flurry of bidding and at the third lull, high bid sat at three hundred thousand and belonged to someone in a wool cap who sat two rows in front.

Boone leaned forward. "If you really like this one," he murmured, "I can go a little higher. Maybe fifty more."

Mark nodded at the spotter. Silence. He waited, taut with anticipation, not daring to breathe. Finally, the auctioneer shouted, "Sold for three hundred and twenty thousand!"

Jessica leaped in her seat, giving him such an enthusiastic thumbs up, he grinned and wished she sat closer. Purchasing this colt was the icing on the cake. He'd attended many sales but had

216

never enjoyed one so much—and it was because of her. She was savvy, fun and genuinely loved the horses. In contrast, Boone had already whipped out his cell phone and was urging an employee to finalize a stock report.

Jessica's eyes glowed as she leaned past her grandfather. "This is so much fun. I really liked that colt too." She smiled and held up her catalogue, showing Mark the two asterisks she'd drawn by his number.

"You're just like your mother." Boone lowered his phone, and his lip curled. "She loved to spend my money too. Not good at making it though."

Jessica's smile flattened. She leaned back and stared woodenly at the next horse on the stage. Boone seemed oblivious he'd just sucked away her pleasure, although it had been like that for the last hour with his never-ending barbs at Jessica and her mother. The pen felt awkward in Mark's hand as he signed for the colt. It was going to be a long afternoon.

Three horses later, someone slipped in beside him. "Our group can go to sixty," Cathy Wright whispered. "If you have a stall available, we want you to buy something. We're looking for a horse that will give us some fun."

"How many people?"

"Eight, all from ESPN."

"Sounds like trouble." But he smiled. "Okay, there are some horses here, ready to race, and I'll have an empty stall next week. You around later?"

"Yes, but I'm working so I'll find you. Thanks, Mark." She brushed his cheek with a kiss and left.

He flipped through his catalogue, scanning the older horses. There were several three-year-olds that looked promising and two of those he'd checked outside their stalls, mainly because Jessica had been interested. They'd even watched some race video. She had made extensive notes; he hadn't. At the time he'd been concentrating on finding something young for Boone.

"Let's get out of here," Boone suddenly said. "I have some important calls to make."

Ian leaped from his seat, but Jessica rose with a mutinous expression. It was clear Boone liked to be in control and equally clear she resented it. Maybe one of Boone's calls would require urgent attention, and he'd have to fly out tonight, Mark hoped as he trailed them up the steps of the amphitheatre.

"We have dinner reservations at Dudley's for seven," Boone said, looking up from his phone to Jessica. "What are you going to do now? I assume you need money for a dress?"

"I'm fine, Gramps," she said, but despair thickened her voice, and a wave of protectiveness propelled Mark forward.

"I have to buy a horse for another client," he said, "so I'll meet you at the restaurant. I would appreciate seeing your notes though, Jessica, so I can remember which ones we liked."

"Then you'll take care of her?" Boone asked. "Get her to the restaurant on time?"

"Jessica can take care of herself. I'm the one who needs help with the horses." Mark tried to keep his tone light. Boone didn't realize he treated Jessica like a rebellious child, and Mark understood now why she hated the idea of working for him. It would be torture.

Boone pushed open the glass doors. Mark's shoulders relaxed as the man vanished in the crowd, trailed by the fawning Ian.

"Are you really buying another horse or do I owe you a thanks?" Jessica asked, her voice subdued.

He didn't insult her intelligence by pretending he didn't understand. "Your grandfather loves you, Jess."

She shook her head in resignation. "He was like that with Mom too. When I was nine, Dad was killed in a car crash, so we moved in with Gramps. Said he'd lost his only son and didn't want to lose his granddaughter as well. Made Mom feel guilty if she ever mentioned moving. It's no problem. I'm used to it." Her face brightened as she glanced at her catalogue. "Are you really buying another horse?"

"Yes. For new owners who want a horse ready to run. But sixty thousand is their limit."

"That's the type of horse I'd want," she said wistfully. "They're just as much fun and a lot less pressure."

"We have plenty of time to find one." He checked the hip numbers circling outside the pavilion. "Let's go back and check the horses you liked. That'll be a good start."

She poked his ribs, her teasing smile back now that her grandfather was gone. "I bet you want me to waive my usual finder's fee."

"Heck, no." He looped his arm around her slim waist and propelled her toward the barns. "I'll pay double what you charged your last client."

"Oh, goodie," she said.

CHAPTER TWENTY-THREE

"And the oysters on a half shell are for you," the waitress said, sliding a square, white plate in front of Boone.

"The papers say the colt looks good," Boone said, ignoring the waitress as he spoke to Mark. "Two more weeks until Breeders' Cup. What are our chance of beating the sheikh?"

"Your colt has faster times and has already won at Belmont. Assets seems to have a good shot. Of course anything can happen."

"You trainers always expect the worst." Boone scooped out a glistening oyster. "What's the harm in saying he's going to win? Sounds like he has to fall on his face to lose."

Mark flinched. His recurring nightmare was that Assets stumbled coming from the gate. "Your Afleet Alex filly, Belle, is running on Friday," he said, switching the subject. "She has a good chance too."

"Maria is very excited about that." Jessica smiled across the table at Mark.

"Who's Maria?" Boone asked.

"A groom, like me."

"You're much more than a groom, Jessica." Boone set down his fork and wiped his wet mouth. "In fact, Ian here is heading up a development in New Hampshire. It'll have some of the best skiing anywhere in the east and is the perfect entry point for you."

"Entry? Entry into Boone?" Her voice rose. "But I only have two weeks to go."

"Surely you won't be foolish and squander this opportunity." Boone frowned. "I thought a ski project would interest you much more than a dog business. That's one of the reasons I'm investing."

Boone looked so puzzled, Mark felt a spike of pity for the man.

"Sorry, Gramps." Jessica raised her chin in a stubborn gesture Mark had seen before. "I'm holding you to our deal."

Boone's mouth tightened. "You'll never make anything of your life if you waste time on manual labor, be it dogs or horses. It's the people at the top who always benefit. You tell her." He glanced at Mark. "What percentage of trainers are rich?"

"Not many," Mark said. "Of course it depends on your definition of 'rich.' But we all love our work—"

"Not many. Exactly." Boone turned back to Jessica. "And I want much better for you."

As though on cue, Ian extracted a glossy brochure from a briefcase. "The condos will be here." He tapped the page with an eager finger. "The mountain has two faces we'll develop with beginner and advanced terrain. I'm the project manager and it will truly be an honor to work with you, Jessica." He gave her a smarmy smile.

The entrees appeared on beautifully garnished plates, so Ian reluctantly folded his brochure.

"Salmon. Lamb. Another lamb. And steak for you, sir," the waiter said placing the last plate in front of Mark.

Silverware clinked; otherwise the table was blessedly silent. Mark glanced at Jessica, but she was too busy eating her salmon—no, not busy, just toying with it, and his irritation with Boone grew. She loved salmon and needed a good meal. Had enjoyed her fish so much with Sophie and Devin, and the food here was superb. Much too good to waste.

He paused to sip his wine, noting Boone's expression. The man had thick white eyebrows that almost touched when he was unhappy. Or when he was thinking. And right now the man seemed to be doing both. It was a shame he couldn't stop his manipulating and let Jessica find her own way.

Mark ate fast, desperate to escape. The downside of horses was that owners came with them. Even Ian looked uncomfortable, cutting pieces of his lamb and checking Boone's expression before every bite.

"Sorry for interrupting, Mark," Cathy said, materializing by their table. "But we're all eager to hear how you made out today." With unerring instinct, she zoomed in on Boone. "I'm Cathy Wright," she said. "It's a pleasure to meet you, sir."

Boone leaped to his feet and shook her hand. "Please join us," he said graciously. "I'm Edward Boone, and this is Jessica and Ian."

Jessica and Ian didn't rate last names, Mark noticed as he sank back in his chair. It was a relief Cathy had stopped. She was always a pleasant diversion and could eat men like Boone for breakfast.

"Did you buy a horse today too?" she asked Boone. "Mark is absolutely one of the best trainers. We're so lucky to have him."

Boone nodded, but it was clear from his blank expression that he thought all trainers were basically the same.

"We're sitting at that corner table," Cathy added, "and wanted to know our horse's name so we could proceed with a proper toast." She gestured at a throng of waving hands and raised glasses. Clearly celebratory. Mark wished he and Jessica were seated with them.

He glanced at Jessica. "Why don't you tell her the name of the horse we bought for them?"

"TV Trooper," Jessica said with a big smile. Cathy's eyes widened with delight.

"The name was pure coincidence," Mark said. "He was the best of the bunch. Got him for fifty-five. Pretty nice fellow."

"With a name like that, it doesn't matter if he can run a lick." Cathy's grin widened. "It'll be a blast. The guys are already talking about doing a documentary on the pros of shared ownership." She flashed her table a thumbs up, and they cheered, ignoring the headwaiter's disapproving frown.

"Okay, party's on," Cathy said. "Thanks, Mark. And good luck to you, Edward. Maybe I can interview you during the Breeders' Cup?"

"It would be a pleasure," Boone said.

She nodded politely at Jessica and Ian and turned to Mark. "Give me a call next week and let me know when Trooper arrives. Trooper, I like the sound of that. Rugged, tough." She gave him a wicked smile and left.

"Nice lady." Boone watched Cathy rejoin her table.

"Yes," Mark said, turning his attention back to his steak. They'd dated sporadically, but he couldn't remember the last time they'd slept together. Sometime in the spring, maybe before she went to Dubai. His gaze drifted back to Jessica. She wasn't eating, hadn't touched her vegetables which she damn sure needed, and his irritation with Boone swelled.

The man needed to back off. Women were like horses. You couldn't rush them. Best to wait them out. They'd let you know when it was time to step it up a notch.

"Finished with your meal?" he heard the waiter ask Jessica. "Maybe you have room for dessert? The Chocolate Bliss is very popular."

Jessica cocked her head in thought, but Ian whipped out his stupid brochure, and she leaned back. "No, thank you," she said to the waiter with an apologetic smile.

Ian looked over at Boone who gave a negligible head shake, and the brochure disappeared.

Mark leaned forward. "So your new horse will be shipped to the track. We'll bring him in and start galloping. See what we got."

"Fine," Boone said, glancing up at someone behind Mark.

"Good evening," a coolly familiar voice said. "Good to see you again, Edward."

Paul Radcliff. Mark turned and nodded a reluctant greeting, but Jessica made no pretensions and simply glared.

Didn't matter. The rude son of a bitch concentrated on Boone, not acknowledging anyone else. Radcliff had once trained for Boone. Mark didn't know all the history, although the two men were obviously still on speaking terms.

"We're just leaving," Radcliff was saying. "I have a limo picking up my party."

"You better hurry then," Mark said, unable to resist a jab. "Think I see the car now." He probably should have booked a limo for Boone too. No doubt the man enjoyed that type of display, although Mark rarely bothered with such indulgences. Of course, when owners had a horse running in the Breeders' Cup, they deserved anything they wanted.

"Another time, Edward," Radcliff said with an exaggerated plumy accent before weaving through tables, nodding and bestowing greetings like royalty.

Jessica watched him go, then looked at Mark and rolled her eyes, clearly sharing Mark's opinion. Ian looked horrified at her breach of etiquette, but her grandfather was oblivious, more concerned about his buzzing phone. He reached in his jacket pocket and checked the display.

Just turn the sucker off, Mark thought, glancing at Jessica. She wanted time to chat now that Ian had put away the company brochure. Probably wanted to tell her grandfather about Buddy's win, her pet cat and even the second mare she now rubbed.

Whenever Mark mentioned how hard she was working—how much she was learning— Boone had brushed it off, predicting she wouldn't last much longer. But he must be proud of her. Jessica had been dumped into the bottom of a foreign, class-conscious society, slept in a tack room with mice, ate cold beans from a can and rose every morning at four. And she hadn't only coped, she'd flourished.

Hell, *he* was proud of her, and he wasn't even her grandfather; he was only... He didn't know what he was. Displaced lover? Soon-to-be ex employer? But maybe she'd drop by the track occasionally. Better yet, dump the jockey and drop by his house.

Boone now tapped messages on his fancy phone, so Mark signaled for the bill. He had no desire to prolong this agony with dessert and coffee. It was already clear Jessica had finished eating; she and Boone could take their meeting elsewhere.

"Jessica, you'll ride back to the hotel with me," Boone said. "Mark, I'll call you next week. Ian, get the car."

Ian scurried away. Jessica rose, the expression on her face mirroring his own relief.

He dipped his head and murmured close to her ear, "Dino called with a funny story about Buddy. Come by my room when you're finished with your grandfather, and I'll fill you in."

Her eyes widened with alarm. "Is Buddy okay?"

"He's fine. I'll tell you later." Perfect. That would bring her to his room yet still give him time to meet his new owners, the lively ESPN group, and he'd also be able to see Dutch and catch up on news from home. Finally the evening was looking up.

CHAPTER TWENTY-FOUR

"We had a deal, Gramps, and I expect you to keep it." Jessica crossed the room and splashed more scotch in her glass. "I appreciate the ski venture, but I'm just not interested. I've been doing a lot of thinking though and instead of the dog business, I want to set up a Thoroughbred retirement farm."

She lifted her head and held his stare. The retirement idea had been brewing for weeks, but this was the first time she'd acknowledged it, even to herself. Yet it made perfect sense. She loved caring for horses, and if she could place them in good homes, it would be the most rewarding work she could imagine. She could help nice horses like Buddy. Maybe if she had her own farm, she could even keep him.

Her grandfather snorted, clinking the ice in his glass. "And who would pay you to do this *charitable* thing?"

The dismissive way he spoke made her stiffen. "Well, start-up money will come from you." He raised an eyebrow, but she forged on. "Of course, only the equivalent of what a dog place would be. And I'll repay every cent. The rest I'll raise from horse lovers, and anyone who admires the animals. Most of the owners I've met are very conscientious."

His mouth thinned at her veiled barb, but she was running on passion now and the vision bloomed. "I have a friend who raises money simply by knowing who to call, and I'm sure Dick will be happy to share his fundraising list." Especially true if Dick were in the hospital and she could check his files, she thought wryly.

Gramps poured himself another drink, but she waved off his offer of ice, too excited to sit. "So, what do you think?" she asked.

"I think," he spoke through thin lips, "that next month you'll have a different plan and what you really need is firm direction."

"What?" Heat flamed her cheeks. "You think so little of me? Even though I lasted at the track?"

"You still have two weeks to go. And if you do manage not to be fired, I'll finance the dog care, as agreed, but definitely not the horses. However, the most responsible decision is for you to drop this foolishness now. Join the company. Don't be like your mother. Let me show you how to make some real money."

He paused, studying her face, his eyebrows leveled in caterpillar lines of disapproval. "You look like a grubby street brawler with that black eye." His phone chirped, and he checked the display. "I have to join this conference call. But trust me. In a year, you'll be grateful for my guidance. Glad I showed a firm hand." He picked up his briefcase and strode toward the desk.

"Good night," she said. Anger muddled her thinking, but she still had the presence of mind to grab his bottle of Glenfiddich before stalking from the room.

"No more for me, Dutch." Mark drained the last of his beer and edged away from the bar. "I'll let Dino know his old ranch might be for sale. And I'll have a stall ready. Let me know when you're shipping."

"Appreciate it," Dutch said. "They're not giving my little guy much of a chance, but he's a true sprinter, and he's won some tough races. I haven't slept a wink since qualifying for the Breeders' Cup. Seems like it's changed my life, you know."

"I know." Mark shook his friend's hand. "See you in a week."

He headed back to his hotel room with thoughts of Breeders' Cup ping-ponging in his head. Eight championship races were crammed into the main day, with purses ranging from a million to four million. Dutch's horse was running in the Sprint, which was two races after the Juvenile. So Assets would be finished and cooled out, and Dutch would still be chewing his knuckles.

He opened his door, walked to the mini fridge and grabbed a beer. Kicked off his boots and sat back, staring at the dark television. It was incredible to think Assets was the favorite entering the race. Talk about an overachieving horse. But Dino, Carlos and his hard-working staff had done an excellent job. In fact, his entire stable clipped along at an impressive win percentage.

Even Buddy had stepped up for a win, mostly due to Jessica's dedication. Yet when Mark had told Boone about her success with the horse, the man hadn't seemed very interested. He was like a pit bull, so focused on dragging her onboard with Boone Investments that he dismissed her achievements—and anything else standing in the way.

Mark checked his watch, trying to control his growing disappointment. He'd hoped she would stop by after visiting with her grandfather, but it didn't seem as though she wanted his company.

He took a thoughtful sip of beer. It had to be that new jockey from Canada; the guy was single, good looking, cocky as hell, and he'd ridden a few of Mark's horses. She would have had plenty of time to meet him—and of course, the jock would have honed in on her like radar.

Rap, rap.

He leaped from the chair and yanked open the door. Jessica stood there with teary eyes and a great bottle of Scotch.

"Oh, honey." He pulled her into his arms and pushed the door shut with his foot.

"He's just so stubborn." Her voice muffled against his chest. "How do you stand to work for him?"

"We get along best over the phone," he admitted, stroking her hair. He eyed the precariously tipped bottle with concern; it would be a shame to spill the scotch but holding her was far too enjoyable. She was in his arms now and after thinking she wasn't coming, he didn't intend to let go.

Much too soon, she swung away and waved her arm. "Well? Would you like a drink of Gramps' finest?"

"Absolutely. Water, or just ice?" he asked as he set out two glasses.

"I don't need a glass." She swigged from the bottle.

"That bad, was it?" he asked wryly.

"He doesn't hold me in very high regard." Pain twisted her face. "Thinks the breeding on my dam's side is rather weak." She tried to force her usual flippant smile, but her mouth wobbled. She looked so forlorn, so uncertain, he crossed the room and pulled her back into his arms.

"Well." He kissed her on the forehead. "I think you're wonderful."

"Really?" She tilted her head, her nose wrinkling. "Then why has your boyfriend-forgetting service been so spotty lately?"

"I thought I was replaced."

She looked confused. Probably the Scotch.

"The guy you're showering with," he added.

"But I had to get that poor kid clean. And that's ridiculous, Mark. He's only about nine." She looked so disgusted, he knew he'd been wrong. And then he understood. The boy. The fucking security guard had screwed up.

He dipped his head in her hair, hiding his relief as he sucked in her familiar smell. "How did you get the boy past the guard?" he asked, his voice husky.

"Back door and some loud singing. Maybe I did pretend he was a jockey. I can't remember. But how did you know? Was it Terry who squealed? That weasel."

"I pay the guards. They'd better tell me everything." He tried to scowl but couldn't stop his grin. "So you're still having that same trouble? Forgetting the old boyfriend?"

"Oh,...yes. He's constantly on my mind."

"Poor baby. That must be so hard." His hand shifted an inch, and he thumbed the bottom of her breast.

"It's terrible. He was so nice." She gave a dramatic sniff.

"Did he touch you like this?" He traced her nipple beneath the thin fabric of her dress. It pebbled beneath his finger, and the sharp intake of her breath sent blood rushing to his groin. "Or maybe more like this?" He slipped her dress down and cradled her breast, watching her eyes as they darkened. Her bra was black and frilly; the lace contrasted with her light skin, and he couldn't look away. He hooked his finger around the top, inching it down until her breasts spilled out.

The bottle was still clutched in her hand. He pried it from her fingers and trickled the liquid over the swell of her breasts. Then dipped his head, running his tongue over her warm skin spiced with Scotch. He wanted to linger, take his time, taste every inch of her, but just the sight of those enticing curves created a pulsing need.

He slipped a hand under her dress, stroked the smooth skin on her thigh, then moved between her legs. She gasped and arched against him, and he sought her mouth, tasting her, sharing her passion. A few flicks, and the dress clumped around her ankles.

He abruptly scooped her up and laid her on the bed. Stared down, drinking in her body, the full breasts and hips, those gorgeous long legs, the sexy black shoes. He kicked off his pants. Rolled on a condom, watching her watch him. Her lips were full and parted, eyes brimming with such emotion, he feared she was thinking of someone else.

He angled her legs wider and guided himself in. Cupped her chin, forcing her to look into his eyes as he drove deeper into her tight, velvety warmth. "Don't pretend I'm him, Jessica." He enunciated each word with a possessive thrust. "Not—any—more."

Jessica woke the next morning in a cocoon of muscled male, soothed by the rhythmic beat of Mark's heart. She loved the feel of his chest, the way his hair tickled her cheek. Loved running her fingers over his hard body. She tilted her head, studying his face. His dark eyelashes spiked and flickered but he didn't wake, his jaw softer in sleep although the dark stubble gave him a rakish appearance.

She impulsively leaned over and kissed his mouth, tasting scotch and salt and passion. And her happiness turned to fear. She was falling in love with this man. Last night he'd stripped her defenses. She'd shown him with her body how much she cared, yet love was the last thing he wanted. He'd run a hundred miles if he suspected.

However, she could no longer pretend to be hooked on an old boyfriend. Mark had made certain of that. She fought a hysterical squeak of laughter. She couldn't remember Anton's face let alone his kiss or touch. He'd been a prop she used so Mark would feel safe.

She stared at his head, resisting the urge to caress his beautiful mouth. Little wonder his old girlfriends drooled. Even the ultra-composed TV chick was still smitten. Jessica could usually sense the signs, the way a woman talked or moved, and it was clear Ms. ESPN had shared Mark's bed. And would be happy to do so again.

And that was the problem with Mark. Even if he wanted to keep seeing Jessica after her work stint was over—and she guessed he might, at least for a while—she cared too much to be satisfied with a weekly sleepover. It would drive her crazy wondering if he'd been with anyone. At least it wouldn't be one of his own employees. Thank God for his Three-F rule.

But there were some attractive jockeys, so many other exercise riders, grooms, hot walkers and media—all susceptible to Markomania. Oh God, he would smile and be nice as he always was and even if nothing was going on, she'd suspect and be miserable.

Unless she was close by. Her thoughts churned. She loved being around horses, although she'd always be a little intimidated by the aggressive colts. Buddy would be gone, enjoying his retirement somewhere, but there must be other quiet horses that needed a groom. Surely Mark could hire her to do something, even answer mail, and then she'd be around to monitor him. Make sure he didn't stray.

She jerked sideways, her thoughts skittering—

"Morning, honey," Mark mumbled, giving her a drowsy squeeze. "Plane isn't until ten." His eyes flicked shut.

She checked the bedside clock. Not much time left but she had him here, beside her right now, and luckily he was groggy with sleep. Trailing her tongue over his chest, she reached down and cupped his heavy balls.

He stiffened immediately, and she played her fingers along his growing length. "I was thinking maybe I should stay and work for you. After the Breeders' Cup."

His breath shortened, and she lowered her head and dragged her mouth over his chest. "Let's make a deal," she murmured, circling a flat brown nipple with her tongue.

He was stiff as a flagpole now, which was rather surprising considering what they'd done last night, but this was perfect. Once Mark made a promise, it was rock solid.

"What?" he mumbled, moving his hand to her breast.

She twisted away, needing to keep her wits, knew if his hands were on her for over thirty seconds, her mind would turn to mush.

"I'll apply for an apartment on the backside and stay on as your groom. Okay?" She felt a twinge of guilt, realizing she'd turned into an unscrupulous dealmaker, just like Gramps, but pushed away that unwelcome thought. All was fair in love and war.

"We'll talk about that later." He pulled her on top of him. She tried to wiggle away, but his hand edged between her legs. Stroking her. Not even thirty seconds, she thought in dismay as she let him position her over his swollen cock.

She climaxed in a volatile mixture of rapture and regret. Couldn't do this one little thing right. When he finished, she fled into the bathroom and turned on the shower, hoping the hot water would rinse away her frustration. And fear.

A moment later, Mark slipped in behind her. "What's this all about?" He spoke so gently she was ashamed she'd tried to take advantage. "Isn't your grandfather helping you with that dog business?"

"He doesn't want to," she said, "and I know now I'd rather work with horses."

"Then do it."

She turned beneath the pulsing water and hugged him. "So you'll keep me on?"

He stiffened, and her heart dropped as she felt his arm muscles tighten. "Please, Mark," she said. "I'll do all the things everyone else hates. Paperwork, buckets, rake, clean leather, anything."

He seemed to pull away even though he didn't move. "You need to do what you want, Jessica. Not what your grandfather or I want." He spoke in that infuriatingly reasonable trainer's voice, and her shoulders slumped.

She choked back the agonizing lump in her throat and forced a flippant laugh. "Just checking to see what I was worth. Wondered if my performance last night was inspired enough."

His expression turned stony and she grabbed the shampoo, hating her words even as she spoke them. "Turn around, big guy, and I'll wash your back. I love muscles in my men, and you have a few more than the last ones." He stood completely still, arms at his side, so she reached up and soaped his chest, ignoring the taut cords visible in his neck. "I sure don't want any of my lovers to ever say Jessica Boone left a job unfinished," she added gaily.

"Enough." He pushed her hand away, so forcefully the shampoo container tumbled to their feet, careening for a moment around the side of the slippery tub. Somehow she managed to paste a brittle smile on her face while suds sluiced down his ridged stomach and dripped on their bare toes.

"Time to get to the airport anyway." He slid the door open and grabbed a towel, leaving her alone in the shower.

Where there was no longer any need to hide her pain.

CHAPTER TWENTY-FIVE

"The game's up, girl. Mark knows everything."

Jessica froze, her grip on the molasses slipping as she stared at Maria. She didn't think Mark knew about her feelings. How could he? "What do you mean?" she squeaked.

"While you were away, Buddy wouldn't eat his grain, so I had to tell Dino he needed triple the brown sugar and molasses. I'm sure Mark knows by now."

"Oh," Jessica managed. "Yes, he does know." She remembered how Mark had chuckled when he told her. Not mad at all. But that had been last night in the hotel room, when everything had been perfect. Things weren't so perfect today. They'd been back for seven hours, and she hadn't seen him since he'd dropped her off at the barn.

"How were those owners Mark wanted you to entertain?" Maria shuddered with revulsion. "What an awful job."

Jessica stared at the brown container of molasses, silent for a moment. Maria had an aversion to all owners except for her recent acceptance of the New Jersey ladies, and Jessica didn't want to admit that the uncaring owner was really her grandfather.

Maria didn't know Jessica's last name was Boone. On the backside, names didn't matter. Worth was measured by how you performed—and clearly both Mark and her grandfather found her wanting.

"They were all pricks." She spoke with such feeling even Maria gaped.

"Jessica." Mark's crisp voice sounded from the doorway. "See me in my office."

Maria blanched as he turned away. "Maybe he didn't hear you," she whispered. "Maybe it's about the molasses. Just tell him I told you the wrong amount."

"Oh, Maria." Jessica's lower lip quivered. "You're the best friend I ever had, but I don't think this is about molasses."

She fed Buddy his regular grain and defiantly added the extra molasses and three carrots before trudging to Mark's office. He hadn't spoken much on the flight home, and she knew she'd hurt him, but all she had left was her pride. Which she intended to keep.

Setting her shoulders, she opened the door and walked in.

He leaned over his desk, studying the screen on his laptop. "Mary e-mailed three pictures." He motioned her over. "Recognize any of them?"

She glanced at the screen, and a chill attached to the back of her neck. "That's him." She pointed. "The man with the mean eyes."

"All right. I'll e-mail it to a friend at the police station. Find out if he has a name." He reached in his top drawer and slapped a thick envelope in her hand. "Here's the two grand for Buddy. He'll race in nine days."

She stared at the kiss-off money, even considered tossing it back, but Buddy shouldn't be a pawn. Somehow she'd pay Mark back. She raised her head and forced a cool smile, ignoring the fact that her insides were shriveling. It wasn't even necessary to pretend. He was still engrossed in his computer. She left with her head held unnaturally high, and Buddy's precious purchase money clutched in her hand.

"More coffee?" the guard asked as he reached for his steel thermos.

"Better not," Jessica said. "I probably shouldn't have had that first cup. But how about another cookie?" She hadn't quite forgiven Terry for telling Mark about her visitor in the shower, but he was pleasant company and his chocolate chip cookies were delicious.

"Here." Terry passed her the container of cookies. "And do whatever you want at night. Nothing will go in my report. Take one for your boyfriend too."

"Thanks, Terry." She pulled out two cookies loaded with chocolate chips. "I'll buy some muffins for us tomorrow night."

Buddy stuck his head over the stall, ears pricked, seeming to suspect she carried something tasty. She slipped the cookies in her jacket pocket and waggled her empty hands. "Go eat your hay, Buddy. Look, no treats."

She checked over her shoulder. Already Terry was just a large shadow by the front door, and she guessed she'd be indistinguishable at the far end of the aisle. She eased out the back entrance, grabbed the bucket hanging on a bridle hook and added the precious cookies to her food cache.

The kid had to be getting it; the food was always gone in the morning. But she never saw the boy, no matter how long she lingered. It was apparent she'd destroyed his trust ever since Mark had flushed the boy from his hiding place, the day she'd fallen off Ghost.

She tried to quell her concern, but October nights were chilly and soon, she wouldn't be here to help rustle food. She leaned against the doorway, staring at the gloomy sky as her thoughts circled back to Mark. Two thousand dollars. Buddy would be hers in just over a week.

She jumped, banging her elbow against the rough wall as something slipped from the darkness—the kid—moving so easily she'd mistaken him for a shadow. His wary eyes stared past her, searching for the guard, nervous as any feral animal. She nodded a welcome, slipped the bucket off the hook, turned and walked to her room. Didn't let herself look back. Acted as though his presence was unimportant.

She left the door open. A second later the boy edged in and dropped cross-legged by the bucket. He gobbled the cookies first then a chicken sandwich, dribbling crumbs down the front of his dirty shirt.

A horse blanket was stuffed under her cot, and she pulled it out and spread it by the bike. His teeth flashed in a trusting smile. Her gut wrenched because she had to call the guard—had to betray this boy. It was clear he needed much more than she could provide.

He pointed at her old stooping bag, still filled with unsorted betting tickets, then thumbed his chest in a clear offer to help.

"No, it's okay," she said, aching inside. So young, and already he knew nothing was free.

But he scrambled to his feet and spread some tickets on the cot, clearly determined to work for his food. She watched him for a moment, hating the thought of turning him over to Terry. Surely Maria could talk to him. Figure out the best way to help.

She pointed at her watch and motioned she'd be back. He nodded, barely looking up as his nimble fingers stacked the stubs according to race, obviously remembering her previous instructions.

The barn phone was at the end of the aisle, close to the guard, so close she was afraid he'd hear. But she hurried down and punched Maria's number, guessing from the huskiness of her voice that she'd been sleeping.

"Can you come?" Jessica whispered. "He's in my room now." She hung up and glanced at Terry who shuffled his feet and studied the floor, as though suspecting a *ménage et trois*. She gave him a mischievous grin. "I wonder if I could have a third cookie?"

Maria shook her head. "You're wrong. This boy doesn't speak Spanish. I don't know a word he's saying, but he sure is cute. Maybe he can draw something." She picked up a pencil and paper and sketched her apartment. Tapped her chest and held it up.

The boy's wide eyes locked on Maria, and he nodded, seeming to find her gentle face reassuring. He took the pencil, held it awkwardly in his fist, and began to draw.

Jessica leaned forward, watching as a picture slowly took shape.

"A playground," Maria said.

"No, look. There are little heads. It's a plane." Jessica gave the boy an encouraging pat on the back. "Good drawing."

Maria frowned. "I still think it looks like a playground."

Jessica pushed the paper back in front of him. "Draw something else." But his attention had jumped to Maria, and he reached up and shyly touched her cheek, distracted by something he saw in her face. Jessica sighed and pulled out the third cookie, waved it in the air and pointed at the paper.

"You're not supposed to use bribes," Maria scolded but they both leaned forward, craning to see as the boy eyed the cookie and started sketching again.

"It's just a horse shoe and a bunch of flowers," Maria said. "With a skinny tree," she added as he finished with two lines. "He's definitely not an artist."

"One more picture," Jessica said.

She hid her disappointment as a crude horse emerged. The picture wasn't detailed enough to identify the animal. In fact, it was hardly recognizable as a horse with an ugly head, knobby knees and a big hump. "Oh, it's a camel," she said. "Someone said the man was from the Middle East. Obviously this kid is too."

They both stared at the boy.

"Definitely not many camels around here," Maria finally said. "Better give him the cookie."

The boy snuggled into Maria's lap and stuffed the cookie into his mouth. He definitely liked Maria. Of course, if he was from the Middle East, her coloring would be more familiar. That had to be the reason, Jessica decided with a pang.

She flipped through Mark's magazines, searching for an old article, then dropped the page on the floor in front of the boy. His eyes widened, and he shrank against Maria's chest.

"What did you show him?" Maria snapped as she stroked the boy's head with a protective hand. Jessica passed her the picture—a line of colorful camels with tiny figures crouched on their backs, surging through the desert sand. "I read about this last month," she said. "Camel racing is popular in the Emirates, where they use little boys as jockeys. Some of the bigger tracks switched to robots, but apparently kids are still recruited."

"What do you mean, recruited?" Maria puffed like a mother hen and tightened her arms around the boy, making soothing noises deep in her throat.

"Sold, kidnapped or otherwise persuaded," Jessica said dryly. "Unless you think maybe he's the sheikh's son and got mixed up with his horses."

They both looked at the boy's dirty face.

"He doesn't look much like royalty," Maria said.

Jessica flipped through another issue of *Thoroughbred Times* and found a picture of a sheikh in traditional dress. "Here's something. See what he does when he sees that." She passed over the magazine. The kid had really attached himself to Maria, she noted with another twinge. Young as he was, he must have sensed Jessica could barely look after herself. She brushed away her sense of loss and focused on his reaction.

He glanced at the sheikh but nothing. Not a flicker of recognition.

"I don't think we should tell anyone. Not yet." Maria shoved a strand of lank hair off his forehead. "I could keep him in my apartment for a while. Clean him up, feed him. Teach him some English."

Jessica sighed. "We have to tell Mark. He'll be furious if we don't. He thinks the boy can help find the guy who stabbed Dick."

"But how can he do that?" Maria asked. "He doesn't speak English. Or Spanish. He's just a little boy who'll be lost in the system. I already know it doesn't work well for this type of kid." Her voice heated. "They might send him back to race camels."

Jessica's head hurt, and she rubbed the throbbing ache in her temple.

"There's a guy from Pakistan who does acupuncture for horses, barn eighty-nine." Maria's voice turned persuasive. "I'll get him to talk to the kid. And you'd be helping Mark too. He doesn't have time for all this extra stuff. But we gotta figure out his name." She turned to the boy and thumped her chest. "Maria." Then pointed at Jessica and said her name. After a few repetitions, she pointed to the boy.

"Abdul," he said.

"Abdul? That's your name?" Maria grinned. "He's so smart," she said over her shoulder to Jessica. "Come on. This isn't like you. You're usually the last one to worry about rules."

Jessica's head pounded with increased pain, and she tugged on her lower lip. "That was before I saw Mark mad," she said.

Mark's first set of horses filed from the barn with exercise riders up, most led by their grooms. Predawn was his preferred hour. The track was smoothly harrowed. It was too dark to worry about reporters and what they would or wouldn't write, and the horses looked elegant, almost mysterious. It seemed he gained a better sense of them, that he was more attuned to their feel rather than relying on sight alone.

Buddy definitely felt good and gave an exuberant buck as soon as he exited the shedrow.

"Jessica!" he called. "Lead Buddy today."

She appeared with a lead line, said something to Slim that made the rider laugh, and slipped on the line. Buddy lowered his head in cooperation. Probably the horse had bucked so Jessica would walk beside him. Slim had also brightened. The jaunty exercise rider was always happiest when a pretty girl was around.

Mark stopped Ghost by Dino. "From now until Breeders Cup, make sure all grooms lead the horses to the gap. No exceptions. There's too much traffic, too much excitement, even for horses like Buddy."

Dino nodded, and Mark turned Ghost and led the line of horses to the gap. He watched as they broke off, following his instructions. The little chestnut filly moved into a jog; she was excitable and needed to get right to work. The seasoned bay mare was to walk half a mile then jog. Two-minute lick for her today.

He softened as he looked at Assets. The colt gleamed under the track lights and exuded vitality. Too bad the race wasn't today. He nodded at Steve, confirming a four-furlong work, and turned to check Buddy.

Slim puffed out his chest as he rode Buddy past a rapt brunette who watched from the rail. "I braided him just for you, babe," he called, and the girl giggled as Slim and Buddy strutted past.

"Four furlongs, but keep him contained," Mark said to Slim. "He's in a claimer in three days."

"Sure thing, boss." He cast a backward glance at the girl by the rail, looked at Mark and lowered his voice. "Gotta tell you, Buddy is a my pickup horse. Chicks love his braids."

"That's not how you felt last month," Mark said, adjusting his stopwatch.

"I'm not afraid to admit when I'm wrong." Slim gave the brunette a cocky wink before moving Buddy into a lively trot.

Mark stiffened as his last horse, a chestnut colt, jogged off, lame in the right hind. He pushed Ghost into a lope and caught the rider. "Damn, Tommy, can't you feel that?" he said to the bleary-eyed man. "Horse only has three wheels. Take him back to the barn. Don't ride him back either." His scowl deepened when he caught a whiff of Tommy's potent breath. He reached down and grabbed the colt's reins. "Thought you stopped drinking," he snapped.

"Wife left me, boss. Couldn't take the gambling."

"Go to the chaplaincy and get some help," Mark said. "We'll find someone to fill in."

Tommy nodded, shoulders slumped with despair.

Mark led the horse back to the gap and handed him over to the waiting groom. His gaze drifted to Jessica who stood at the rail on the right side of the gap. She gave a guilty start and averted her head, and he automatically glanced up the track to check Buddy. Horse was moving fine, gaudy purple braids glinting under the light, and Slim showing off for all the women. Situation normal.

But Jessica rarely displayed guilt, so there had to be something major.

Ghost felt his tension and started to prance; his irritation mushroomed. He slapped the horse on the neck then immediately regretted it. "Sorry, fellow," he said, and let the horse lope on the outside rail to the finish line, trying to compensate for his impatience. Ghost always loved an excuse to stretch out.

"Morning, Mark. Who you working today?" one of the clockers called.

"Ambling Assets is going four furlongs. So is My Best Buddy."

"That's Sheikh Khalif's horse coming now," a man behind him said.

Mark edged Ghost closer to the watchers on the outside rail. A big bay thundered down the stretch. Nice, even stride. Switched leads when asked. Carried his head low. Blinkers. Rundown bandages. Galloped out impressively.

"That's your main competition in the Juvenile, Mark. What do you think?"

"Wasn't really watching," he said without turning around. He sat on Ghost, keeping his face impassive as he waited for his horse.

"Is this Assets' last work before the race?" the same voice asked.

Mark saw his colt break away at the quarter pole and was preoccupied with his stopwatch.

Assets was a smooth blur as he covered the ground. Steve sat chilly, not asking for more but not holding him back either, exactly as Mark had instructed. So far, so good. Assets seemed to be moving slower than the sheikh's horse but definitely effortlessly.

"Wow," someone said.

Mark pressed his watch as Assets blazed across the finish line. A shade over forty-six seconds. Perfect. He softened with relief. Ghost lowered his head and rested a hind leg, ever in tune to his rider's mood, and Mark scratched his shoulder while he waited for Buddy. Didn't bother with his stopwatch. He'd leave this one to the track clockers. Besides, it was just a freshener. He'd told Slim to keep Buddy under wraps; didn't want the old gelding going into a claiming race with too impressive a work.

A dark shape sizzled down the track, and Ghost's ears pricked as though aware it was one of his barn mates. Purple sparkled under the main lights. Was Jessica using fluorescent colors now?

"Is that a Breeders' Cup horse?" someone asked.

Dammit. Slow him down, Slim, Mark willed.

Slim's arms and legs were braced as Buddy blasted across the finish line. Mark swore under his breath, turned Ghost and galloped after him. Slim stood in the stirrups, wrestling with Buddy, trying to slow him to a canter.

Mark charged up beside him. "What the hell were you thinking?" Mark yelled as he snagged the horse.

"Horse got away from me, boss. Ducked his head, pretending he was scared of some pigeons, grabbed some rein and bolted."

"Christ, Slim. You're riding like shit. This is the easiest horse in the barn."

"Used to be easy," Slim said, unabashed. "He's a tiger now."

"A very old tiger," Mark said, hearing Buddy's labored breathing. "Make sure you dismount by the gap and grab his front leg. Look upset. Get the groom to look after him, and everyone will notice."

Slim nodded and pasted on a bleak look but wrecked the impression by singing the words to "Pickup Truck" as he diligently scanned the rail for pretty girls. Mark shook his head but waited until the old mare finished before heading back to the gap to meet his second set.

And there they came. He always felt a stir of pride when his horses walked onto the track, wearing saddle pads in his distinguished brown colors. Every groom now led a horse; Dino had passed the word quickly. Jessica accompanied her new mare, My Silent Miss, but her face was strained and her eyes—

Damn. Something was wrong. Maybe she thought Buddy was really hurt. He trotted Ghost to the gap, called out his directions, then wheeled to the side and dismounted. "Can you help me over here, Jessica?" he asked, hooking his stirrup over the horn.

Her cheeks glistened with tear tracks, but she hurried over to help.

"Buddy's in a claiming race in two days," he whispered, hating to see her upset. "He's not really hurt. Whatever Slim did or said was for show."

Another huge tear rolled from the corner of her eye.

"Aw shit, Jess, I wasn't thinking. I just wanted Slim to pretend Buddy was hurt. Look," he added, "I heard you and Maria were planning to bus it to the hospital. Once the office work is cleared up, I can drive you two over."

She nodded with obvious appreciation, but he wanted more than gratitude. At least she had Buddy's purchase money now. He needed her with him because she wanted to be—not because of a horse, a job or an old boyfriend.

She was definitely more complicated then he preferred. Before, if a woman had a snit, he didn't stop to analyze. Just labeled her as difficult and moved on. But Jessica was like a promising green filly that was worth some extra effort.

A lot of extra effort, he thought wryly.

"It'll be great to see Dick," she said, "now that he's finally allowed visitors." But another plump tear rolled down her cheek, and something twisted his gut.

"Then stop crying. Please." He yanked his cinch tighter, needing something to occupy his hands, anything to keep him from touching her. There was no way he could console her here, not at the gap, not where everyone watched.

He stepped back on Ghost, feeling off balance and frustrated. "Please don't cry," he repeated, leaning over his horse's shoulder, conscious of the curious press but reluctant to leave. "I gotta go, but you're killing me here."

She gave a watery smile. "Don't be silly. I'm just happy."

Silly? Hardly the trainer's image he wished to portray. But he lingered, ignoring the clicking cameras, and even reached down and grazed his thumb over her cheeks before riding away.

"Just a sec, Dino," Mark paused by the barn door and glanced at Jessica. "Did you ice Buddy where everyone could see?"

"Twenty minutes," she said, "plus Doc stopped to talk so his truck was outside for a while."

Mark nodded and turned back to Dino. "So Assets worked in forty-six and change and they got Buddy going almost as fast? Dammit."

"No one's going to claim an old gelding like Buddy," Dino said with a grin. "Especially one with obvious leg problems."

"Just the same, bump him up to eighteen thousand. Be the fourth race on the card."

"Tough competition, though," Dino said. "And you always run to win. He won't have a chance in that company. It'll screw up our win percentage."

"Doesn't matter." Mark scowled. "Emma Rae is riding. She'll take care of him. I just want the horse to go out sound. Understand?"

"Oh, I understand. I definitely understand." Dino's gaze shot to Jessica, and he clutched at his heart.

Mark scowled and wheeled away from Dino's smirk. Stomped into his office and checked his messages. Nothing from the police. Obviously Bruce hadn't seen the picture yet. His cop friend has been impossible to reach lately. He sent another message: 'Please check pic asap. Two more Breeders Cup seats.'

He called Sophie and Devin. It was a relief when they didn't answer, and he left a message that Buddy would run on Friday. Dino had pinned up a note that the starter wanted extra gate work on the Storm Cat filly, and the race stewards insisted on a meeting tomorrow at eleven. He called the chaplain to see if his exercise rider had dropped by for a chat. Breathed easier when he was told Tommy had registered in the addictions program. Dutch's horse was arriving on Sunday and was allergic to straw, and the Breeders' Cup committee wanted him to host a fan fest breakfast on Wednesday.

Damn, maybe he shouldn't have told the girls he'd drive them to the hospital. It would take hours, since traffic always snarled in that area. He dropped his head in his hands and blew out a sigh. Heard the light footsteps.

"Anything I can do to help?" Jessica asked quietly.

"Sex would make me feel better," he said. Her laugh energized him, but he didn't know why she thought it was a joke. "A lot of stuff piled up while we were in Kentucky," he added, "and Dino deserves an afternoon off. You and Maria need to give me another hour."

"Maria can't come." Jessica turned her back and studied a picture on the wall. "She's busy with an acupuncturist from Pakistan."

"That reminds me," he said, not really listening as he scrawled another note, "I need to double the chiro sessions on the chestnut in stall six."

"I can help with some of this. If I can't handle it, I'll write it up. Especially the Breeders' Cup stuff. That makes so much extra work."

"Yeah. A shame we're in it." He regretted his comment as soon as the words slipped out, as though somehow it might draw bad luck.

But she knew when to ignore him and merely slapped a coffee in his hand, slid a mound of paper to her side of the desk, and he was finally able to make the calls he'd postponed.

At some point she confiscated his phone and arranged for deluxe bales of dust-free shavings for Dutch's sprinter. She was good at detail stuff and excellent with people on the phone. Much better than him. He wandered over to the cot and stretched out, feeling pretty good now that the office work was getting done. Dino would be impressed.

It was also relaxing hearing her confident voice in the background. The only time she hesitated was when Cathy called, wanting to know when he'd have an available stall for TV Trooper.

"I'll call her in a few days," he mouthed, then listened while Jessica distracted Cathy by talking about the excitement of owning Thoroughbreds. He didn't know what qualified Jessica as an expert, but she was a damn good talker.

It probably wasn't good policy to have an old and new girlfriend getting chummy, but he shut his eyes anyway and fell asleep.

"Your snoring is interfering with my phone calls," Jessica whispered in his ear, prodding him awake.

"I know a way to stop it." He tugged her on top of him. She was still talking, and he took advantage of it, slipping his tongue in and exploring her sweet mouth. "Tastes like you found my private peppermints," he said, keeping his eyes shut, too content to risk opening them.

"Feels like you found something private too." Her voice was husky. She didn't make any effort to pull away; this was the way he enjoyed her best, all sweet and soft and cuddly. No prickly moods.

"Think you're safe here, don't you?" he said, moving his thumb to her nipple.

"I've heard about your no sex rule," she said, "from many sources."

"True. So there's no need to move." He slipped his hand under her shirt, loving the feel of her smooth skin, the curve of her hip, the way she smelled. She had sensitive breasts, and he knew what she liked. A perfect time to extract some answers.

"What was wrong yesterday? In the hotel?" he asked as her nipple pebbled beneath his fingers.

She wiggled in reaction, almost kneeing him in the groin and he rolled sideways, clamping her against him.

She pushed against his chest, but he had her pinned, and she knew it. "First you wouldn't give me a job." Her voice was so low he had to strain to hear. "Then you paid me off with Buddy's money. It...hurts that you don't want me."

"Oh, Jess." He laughed at the absurdity. "I want you." He slid his fingers behind her silky hair, tipping her head so she could see his eyes. "You're feeling a little adrift right now. And no wonder. Your grandfather is a hard man. But you need to take control of your life. Not just move from his house to mine."

"Do you mean that in a literal sense?" she asked.

He paused. He hadn't really considered her moving in with him, but the idea wasn't exactly repugnant. However, her grandfather wouldn't like it, and he certainly wasn't going to risk losing Assets before Breeders' Cup—not even for Jessica.

She felt his hesitation and gave a flippant smile. "The apartments here are more convenient anyway. You know, muck and fuck."

The hurt in her voice put him on the defensive, and he immediately stiffened. "Whether you're living in a tack room, an apartment or at my house if you're working as my groom, there's a control element that isn't healthy. I don't want to think you're with me for any reason other than that you want to be."

"Ah, yes, I keep forgetting about your little hangups. A father's mistakes and all that."

She was turning into a sour old mare again, and he wished they were home so he could fuck some sense into her. That was usually the best way to communicate with a woman. A good diversion was always second best.

"Thanks for helping me with the office work," he said, holding her, despite her little wiggles that showed she wanted to leave.

"You're welcome," she muttered.

"Want to go for dinner tonight?" Usually when he was with someone for two days in a row, he was relieved to return to his solitary lifestyle. But last night he'd missed her. Had even considered driving back to the track to see if she'd come home with him.

"Sorry, but I'm already invited to Maria's."

"Maybe tomorrow then." He hid his disappointment with a quick kiss. "Guess we should get you to the hospital." He opened up his arms. "Run along, then."

She leaped up, smiling impishly when she spotted the telltale bulge in his jeans. "Poor baby." She stretched, and her shirt rose, exposing her flat belly, the curve of her hip. His hot gaze met hers, and she must have seen something in his expression because she took a prudent step backwards. "Come on, remember your rules," she said. "And I really want to see Dick."

"We could drive to my apartment instead," he said, but she'd already moved to the door. He gave a resigned shrug, rose and walked to the desk. He scanned the impressive amount of work she'd completed then opened his briefcase. "I meant to give you this yesterday, but you were sulking on the plane. And since we're going to the hospital…"

He passed her the silk scarf she'd admired at the Keeneland gift shop. At first he'd been surprised because she didn't seem the type to wear scarves, but later he'd guessed why she had eyed it with such longing. "Perfect for covering knife scars," he added.

"Oh, thank you, Mark! Dick will love it."

And her beautiful smile made him happy he'd taken the time to circle back to the shop.

CHAPTER TWENTY-SIX

Jessica watched as a squealing Abdul twisted on the floor while Maria tickled his narrow feet. He was clean, happy and already had gained three pounds. Her satisfaction clashed with trepidation when she spotted three bags of boy's clothing beside the ancient television.

"Looks like you're planning to keep him," she said.

"He reminds me of my nephews in Tijuana." Maria stopped tickling Abdul's foot and looked at Jessica. "He loves my cooking. He's happy."

"But it's been four days. We have to tell Mark soon. And what if that man discovers Abdul is here and pays a visit?"

Maria gestured toward the kitchen. Pedro looked up and gave Maria such a tender smile, Jessica's heart ached. If only Mark looked at her like that. He was certainly demonstrative in private but very reserved when people were around. It was hard to be confident with a man like Mark.

"Pedro will keep us safe." Maria spoke with absolute certainty as she returned to the toe tickling.

Jessica tried not to flinch at Abdul's high-pitched squeals but now understood why camels ran faster with screaming boys. "So what else did your acupuncture friend find out?" She had to raise her voice so Maria could hear.

"He was sold by his parents when he was four but doesn't remember the village he came from," Maria said. "Somewhere in Pakistan. He raced camels and was shuffled around. Then he was put on a plane and told to pretend he was someone's son. Nothing hard. He just had to steal a few things."

"He was pretty good at stealing," Jessica said dryly, remembering how Abdul had swiped her phone. The boy was now absorbed with his crayons, and Jessica admitted she was a bit hurt he'd transferred his affections to Maria and Pedro so quickly. After all, she was the first one to feed and clothe him. She was the one who'd suffered Mark's wrath. Which she would suffer again if Mark discovered the boy was here.

Sighing, she crossed her legs and leaned back on the worn carpet. "I think we should tell Mark today," she said. "He already sent the picture to the police. With the right questions, maybe they can figure out why that man stabbed Dick."

"But Abdul doesn't know anything about it. All he saw was the man dig under the flowers. Then Abdul was supposed to get a bike, but the man was really cross so he ran away." Maria beamed with pride. "He's such a smart boy."

Abdul put down his crayon and passed Jessica a folded paper. She opened it and saw a bright drawing of a heart and a heaping plate of food, and his smile was so grateful, her heart flopped.

She clasped the precious gift close to her chest, moved he hadn't forgotten her after all. "Yes, he definitely is a smart boy." Her smile wobbled. "That's why we should tell Mark."

"But we can't." Maria crossed her arms. "Not yet. The authorities will take him from me. We have to wait. Once Belle wins on Breeders' Cup weekend, my bonus will pay for a lawyer."

"I didn't know Mark had another horse in the Cup," Jessica said.

"Not on Saturday. She runs on Friday," Maria said. "Belle is the filly Trish didn't cool out. Same owner as Assets." She rolled her eyes. "The kind of owner who doesn't know his horse's barn name."

Jessica dipped her head and nervously folded a corner of the drawing. She didn't want to tell Mark about Abdul and disappoint Maria, and she prayed Maria would accept her if she found out she was a Boone. But the way Maria's lip curled whenever she discussed owners showed a deep-rooted bias.

Racing was a class-conscious society, and Jessica had experienced it firsthand. When she was dressed up at the sale, escorted by Mark, she'd had a lovely conversation with two owners; they'd even handed her their business card. Yet this morning, in dirty jeans and pushing a muck cart, those same owners had glanced the other way, as though afraid she might stop and try to talk.

Abdul yawned. Jessica rose and pulled on her jacket, conscious of Maria's imploring brown eyes. Maybe it wouldn't hurt to hide the boy a bit longer. Abdul had already told the acupuncturist everything he knew. It probably wouldn't matter if they waited a few more weeks.

"Thanks for supper," Jessica said. "Looks like everything is working out for this rascal." She tousled Abdul's hair then dropped a stack of bills on the TV. "Abdul and I sorted through most of the betting tickets. That's what we made so far, almost a hundred and fifty dollars."

"Keep it," Maria said. "We have everything we need. Use it to buy your horse."

"Mark loaned me money for Buddy." Jessica turned away, hiding her expression, not sure if her discomfort was due to the puzzled look on Maria's face or because, once again, she was relying on a man for support. "Did I tell you Dick has a single room. He's doing great!" Jessica added, eager to change the subject. "But he hates the hospital food. Doesn't remember anything about the attack. If Mary hadn't looked out the window…" She shuddered and reflexively rubbed her neck.

"Horse people are good to have around," Maria said. "They think fast and know first aid. Brave and loyal too." She squeezed Jessica's arm as they walked to the door. "*Gracias.*" Maria often reverted to Spanish when emotion tangled her thoughts, and now her words raced.

Jessica smiled, understanding the sentiment if not the words, and shoved aside any lingering reluctance to hide the boy. Abdul was doing great. In fact, Maria, Abdul and Pedro already acted like a family. And when Pedro left the kitchen and shook her hand, Jessica felt pretty good about herself.

Yet when she left their cozy apartment to trudge back to the barn, her loneliness returned. It'd be nice to have a place close to them. An apartment was bound to become available once the Belmont meet ended and workers moved to Aqueduct. If Mark gave her a reference, she'd be able to get another job, even if it were only as a hot walker.

However, Mark's operation was so professional. She sighed, knowing she'd always wish she worked for him. She'd find excuses to drop by—just like Trish. She'd ache to be part of his team and resent him dropping in for afternoon sex. Anything good they enjoyed would quickly sour.

She simply needed more reassurance than he was able to give, and the knowledge that she was so needy left her hollow and disheartened.

She kicked a rock, listening as it bounced into a shallow ditch. Sometimes it was creepy walking along the backside, but she could see the lights of her barn now, and in a few minutes she'd be home. Home, but only for nine more days. Everything would be much simpler if Mark just relented and hired her.

A light flickered in the tow ring next to Mark's barn. Someone shone a powerful flashlight on her face, and she flinched, squeezing her eyes shut.

"Oh hi, Jessica." The guard shifted the light. "Just had a tip that the boy Mark wants to find was hanging out back here."

"That's great. Good luck, Terry." She smiled, glad the dark hid her expression. "Mark will be so pleased if you can catch him."

Humming, she slipped into the back of the shedrow and padded down the aisle. Jerked to a stop, surprised by the strange man in a ball cap standing in front of Assets' stall. He fumbled in his pocket, and the irritated colt stretched over the stall guard, impatient for a treat.

"Hey, stop," she called. "Only the groom can feed that horse."

The man ignored her. He simply glanced toward Terry's absent post and held out a carrot. Rude fellow. And feeding by strangers was totally against Mark's rules.

She rushed forward and snatched the carrot from his hand.

The man wheeled. Her heart slammed against her ribs. The ball cap was different, but the eyes were horribly familiar. Flat, expressionless, cruel. Adrenaline spiked, and she froze. Couldn't move. Opened her mouth to yell, but her shout surfaced as a squeak.

He reached in his pocket. Her mind suddenly connected with her muscles, and she whirled and ducked into her room. Slammed the door shut. Fumbled with the lock but her hand was too numb, too awkward. The force of his kick whipped the door open and knocked her against the wall.

She rose on wobbly knees. Her mouth was bone dry, her panicked call for Terry barely a gasp. She stared, horrified by the knife in the man's hand. He edged forward, his face carved with intent. She whimpered but couldn't force her legs to move. Somehow when she needed them most, her legs were unresponsive.

Movement blurred, and Kato launched his little body from underneath the cot. His claws attached to the stranger's right leg; the man jerked sideways. Fear galvanized her, and she bolted past him, through the door and down the aisle, screaming like a banshee until every horse in the barn churned with shared fear.

Terry rushed wide-eyed from the dark, a flashlight in one hand, the other on his holster.

"Man with a knife," she yelled, sinking to her knees and gesturing behind her.

Terry spoke crisply into the radio on his hip then edged down the aisle. Her knees buckled, and she peered outside, terrified the man would circle and reappear through the front door. But tires crunched and yellow lights banded the dark as two more security guards rushed in. A warm arm circled her back.

"I don't feel very good," she muttered.

Someone wrapped her in a blanket and led her outside. Lights strobed. Terry's concerned face flashed in front of her, and other faces appeared. Strange arms tucked her in a warm car, but she couldn't talk, and her shivers wouldn't stop.

"Is my neck bleeding?" she finally managed.

"No, you're okay," Mark said.

"Oh, hi. When did you come?" But her words were thick and clumsy, and her mind scrabbled. "Did you see Kato?" she asked.

Mark stared at her, his eyes filled with regret, and she knew.

"Oh, no," she groaned. "He saved me. When I came back from Maria's, a man was feeding Assets a carrot. He chased me to my room. Kato jumped out, and I got away."

"Same man as in the picture?"

She nodded, and Mark's arms tightened.

"I'll be back soon. Wait here." He murmured something to the man in the driver's seat then adjusted the blanket around her shoulders. "What's in your hand?"

He pried the carrot from her fingers and held it under the dome light. "Damn. Look at this. The carrot's hollowed out."

Jessica watched as the man in the front seat dropped it into a plastic bag, but her mind remained sluggish. Disinterested even.

Someone with a blue notepad came and asked a lot of questions but talking was hard work, and she was glad when Mark said something and the man left. Terry's head leaned in the window, and he squeezed her shoulder. She was moved to another car and fell asleep.

She woke in a cold sweat, panicky with fear. Didn't know what bed she was in except that her head was pressed against Mark's chest, and she was cradled in his strong arms. Her breathing steadied as she sucked in his familiar smell. She sensed he was awake, and then the unbearable knowledge rocked her.

"Kato?" Her words clogged in a painful whisper.

"Didn't suffer." His hand soothed along her spine. "We can bury him behind the barn, if you'd like."

She choked into his dampening chest. "Be a g-good spot." Her voice was scratchy and it hurt to talk, but she tilted her head, straining to see his face. "He...was my first pet. I'm still gl-glad you gave him to me."

"So am I, Jess. God, so am I." And he stroked her hair until she fell back to sleep.

"Want to sleep any longer?" Mark murmured in the darkness.

"No, I really want to get back." She stared at his bedside clock, watching as the fluorescent numbers changed to four-thirty a.m. "Where's Kato now?"

"In my office."

"What was in the carrot?"

"They suspect arsenic, but we won't know until tests are run."

"Why?"

"Guess someone doesn't want Assets running in the Cup."

Anger jerked her upright, and she swept the sheets aside. "That man was definitely an Arab. And that means the sheikh killed my cat!"

"Whoa!" His arms banded around her. "I doubt the sheikh was involved."

She struggled to get loose. "Your horse is the favorite. His is the second favorite. It's so obvious. With Assets out of the way, he'll win."

"Sheikh Khalif wins races all over the world, and it's not because he feeds the competition poisoned carrots."

"You don't know that." She chopped her hand against his arm and tried to wrench away, but Mark's biceps were as hard as his head and he didn't notice.

"You had a scare, and Kato was killed," he continued in an infuriatingly calm tone, "but you can't return to the track unless you can say 'no comment' and remain composed."

Fine for him. He just worried about his barn, she thought, pinching his arm, getting more and more frustrated when he didn't seem to feel it. "You can't tell me what to do, and I can think what I want." Her voice quavered. "And I have to bury my cat today."

He squeezed her with such compassion her anger collapsed, replaced with an aching grief. "I'm okay," she mumbled after a moment. "I won't say anything. I just need someone to blame." She sniffed. "Kato wanted to go out when I left for Maria's but I made him stay. He'd still be alive—"

"And you wouldn't." Mark's voice was harsh. "Baby, I am so glad you left him in."

He did sound glad, she decided, swallowing a hard lump. "He was the best cat in the world, and I'm fine, and I'm glad your horse is fine, and I promise not to say anything bad about the sheikh." She wiggled in his arms, trying to see his expression in the dark. "Now can I get up?"

"No. And the next time you see thugs around the horses, just call the guard. Goddammit, Jessica. I was so scared you were hurt." He gave her a little shake.

"The guard wasn't there," she said. "He was off on a false alarm about the kid."

"How do you know it was false?"

She stiffened, couldn't think of an answer, so she dipped her head and kissed his chest, hoping to distract him.

"How did you know it was a false alarm?" he repeated, his voice crisp.

Clearly he wasn't as easily distracted as she. When his mouth was on her chest, it made her melt. The fact that he was immune always miffed her, and she was able to summon up some genuine indignation. "Well, quite obviously it was a ploy to get rid of Terry."

"There was a second man," Mark admitted, "who told Terry the kid was out back. But he was taller and older than the guy in Dick's picture. Terry said he spoke with a Mideast accent."

"See!" she said. "I knew it was the sheikh. Just wait until I see that man." Mark chuckled, and she figured she was close to getting him off the tricky subject of Abdul.

"It only means there are two men." But his voice softened and he began kneading the stiff muscles in the back of her neck. "The security company is sending over a second guard, but I want you to sleep here until this is over."

"Gosh, I don't know." She sighed and tilted her head, giving him better access. "Let me think. A bed, food, sex."

"And bubble baths, foot rubs and intact horse magazines," he added.

"You had me with the bed," she said.

CHAPTER TWENTY-SEVEN

"Who do you think is behind it?" Dino asked. "Radcliff is a jealous prick, but even he wouldn't poison a horse."

Mark dragged a hand over his jaw. "Guess there's a Middle East connection that wants Sheikh Khalif's horse in the winner's circle. I just can't believe the sheikh is involved."

"We wouldn't know about that connection if not for Jessica," Dino said. "Assets would have been sick. Or dead."

For the twentieth time, Mark glanced out the door to where Jessica was icing Buddy's front legs. He paced the office, still punchy with fear. "Jessica might have been dead too. The police haven't matched a name with that picture. Dick didn't see his attacker, and no one can find the kid. But we've got two guards on now and only a week to go. They can't get to the horse. Only person left is the jockey." He swung around, fists clenching. "Better call Steve and warn him. Don't think they'll go after the jock, but…"

He shrugged and stared out the door. Jessica had finished with Buddy and was leading the horse inside. Horror still chilled him when he thought of what had happened last night, what would have happened if Kato hadn't leaped.

His gaze shifted to the pitiful bag behind the desk. He'd have to find something better to wrap around the cat. He owed Kato, and Jessica wouldn't want her beloved pet buried in a feed bag. Impulsively he grabbed his roping jacket. It would hide the stiffness and was the proper sendoff for a hero cat.

Dino groaned. "I don't believe it. American Quarter Horse Roping jacket. For a cat?"

Mark ignored Dino's incredulity. Just arranged Kato's tiny body in the jacket, tied the sleeves and headed for the door. "Don't forget to make those calls."

Dino rose from his chair, his voice solemn. "Sure, boss. But first, I think there's a funeral I want to attend."

Mark entered the shedrow and stopped in front of Buddy's stall. Jessica glanced up, her smile slipping when she saw what was in his arms. But her mouth braced and she carefully accepted the precious bundle. "Thank you," she said. "I just need a minute."

His throat thickened as she disappeared into her room. Goddamn. He helplessly rubbed his knuckles, wishing he'd been the one to meet the man last night. He jammed his fists in his pockets and joined Carlos at the end of the shedrow.

"Hole is ready, boss." Carlos gestured. "Maria had some boys move the big flower basket, the one with the concrete, and I'll make sure it covers the spot once we're done." He shook his head. "Never thought a cat would save my horse."

Technically, Jessica had saved Assets and Kato had saved Jessica, but Mark only nodded. It was clear Carlos was grateful. As Assets' groom, Carlos would make a lot of money if the horse won.

Mark was damn grateful too. He propped his hip on the edge of the door and stared at the dark hole. He hadn't really thought of the horse, was still grappling with the fact that Jessica almost had her throat slit. He'd relish five minutes alone with the creep.

He sensed her presence and straightened as she appeared with Kato's body cradled in her arms. He couldn't bear to look at her anguished face, so he stalked from the wall and walked directly to the tiny hole. Maria, Dino and Carlos appeared with a few other workers trickling behind them.

Jessica walked up and passed him the bundle, clearly expecting he wanted the jacket back. His chest tightened at her resolute expression, so sad but so brave, and he tucked the leather collar over Kato's head and arranged him in the hole. Someone had lined it with a purple cooler—he guessed Maria, and he thought it was one of the nicest graves he'd ever seen.

"Thank you, Kato," he said. "You were a good cat."

He punched the shovel into the brown dirt and began refilling the hole, conscious that Dino had wrapped his arm around Jessica. He didn't like the familiar way Dino hugged her so he sped up, so fast a sweat broke out on the back of his neck.

He continued dumping the moist earth back into the hole, simultaneously trying to keep an eye on Dino.

Jessica looked numb, and Dino had turned her against his chest, holding her much too close. Mark dropped the shovel and stalked over to Dino. "I'll take over here." He rammed the shovel in Dino's hand, guided Jessica back to his office and slammed the door.

"That was nice of you to give Kato your jacket," she said. "Maria said she'd make sure there were flowers when I'm gone."

Mark just stared as she spoke about plastic flowers in the winter, but he couldn't focus on her words. He'd never realized he had such a possessive streak. Possessive with horses, sure, but not with women. Never with women. She was leaving in a week, was extremely high maintenance, not to mention Boone's granddaughter. And he hated those gaudy purple braids.

But life would be so gray when she left. She didn't just color his horse, she colored his world.

Unable to speak, he stepped forward, pulled her into his thumping chest and simply held her.

Jessica chewed on the tip of her pen as she deciphered Mark's scribble. Usually she liked office work but after the funeral Mark had assigned her such boring tasks, she suspected he was really looking for an excuse to keep her inside.

She rose and edged to the door, but he raised an eyebrow and motioned her back to the desk. My God, he was a tyrant. She'd liked the work for the first couple hours; in fact it had made her feel useful. But now she was bored and keen to slip over to Maria's.

Abdul knew ninety-six words of English now, and Maria and Pedro were eager for her to hear every one. Plus, Maria had a funky roll of purple wool that Jessica intended to braid Buddy with tomorrow. His last race—Buddy would definitely go out in style.

Mark uncoiled from his chair, still talking on the phone, and tossed some brochures in front of her. Retirement homes for off-track Thoroughbreds. Now that was more appealing. She sat back, her interest caught as she flipped the pages. Two of them weren't homes, just adoption facilities, but the third was an actual center.

No grass though. She chewed thoughtfully on the end of the pen. She wanted Buddy to have pasture turnout and maybe another sweet gelding or two for company. Or maybe he'd prefer a pretty mare. Mares tended to be bitches though, and she didn't want him bossed around. Mark said geldings liked to be told what to do, but she didn't believe that. No one liked to be told what to do.

She jotted down a list of questions for the center and waited for him to finish his phone call. Sometimes he let her use his cell, but usually she had to pry it from his hands. He'd been on this call a long time, and she could tell by his laugh that he liked the person on the other end.

He laughed again, not a chuckle but a real laugh. It was good to hear that; he'd been quiet all day. Almost brooding. She knew he was worried about Assets but with two guards, no one could harm the colt now. She glanced out the window, reassured by the stern man standing by the shedrow entrance, arms at his side, alert to any intrusion. He'd even made her show credentials, and his clone watched the back door.

"Okay, Cathy. I'll meet you at seven. And I'll have a stall ready on Sunday."

Her fingers tightened around the pen as she realized he was laughing with the beautiful and successful Cathy Wright. Jessica had checked *Tattler* back issues searching for snippets of gossip. Mark and Cathy had been romantically linked in spring and summer issues, but there had been no mention of them in the fall.

Mark was still smiling as he passed her the phone. Yes, indeed, dear Cathy made him very happy. "Want to grab something to eat after you call those places?" he asked.

She glanced at her watch, almost five o'clock. "I don't know," she said, swept with an odd contrariness. "I'd rather eat in a couple of hours. Maybe around seven. I need to get Buddy's mane conditioned for tomorrow, give him a little massage, put that new poultice on."

"Okay. Seven then." He pulled the phone back. "I just have to reschedule a meeting with Cathy."

"But I need to use the phone now," she said, "so I can call this retirement place before they close for the day."

"Which one do you like?" he asked, passing her back the phone.

"I'm not really sure." She stared blankly at the phone, hating her moodiness, her despondency, her desperation. But in a few days Buddy would be on a trailer heading to his retirement home. And in another week she'd be gone too.

Her breathing jammed at the thought. Mark was so focused on Breeders' Cup, catching the kid, finding the knife man, keeping his clients happy, talking to the police, looking after forty horses, he probably wouldn't even notice when she left.

She slapped the phone back in his hand. "It's too late to call now. I think I'll just eat at Maria's. That will give you time to see Cathy and look after your…business."

His eyes narrowed on her face. "Jessica, it's only payment for Trooper. I'll be an hour with Cathy, no more."

She rose and shoved her chair back, hating her insecurity but unable to shut up. "Sure. I know. It's your job."

A muscle ticked in his jaw. "It *is* my job. It's what I do. You're going to have to work this out for yourself."

She bit her lip, chewing on despair. All she needed was a little reassurance, something to hold on to when he was off in the evenings. But he'd already turned away. She heard the slam of his briefcase, the jingle of keys as he shoved them in his pocket.

"Come on. I'll drive you to Maria's," he said, heading for the door. "And don't walk back. I'll pick you up at eight."

"Will you let me know when Trooper arrives at the track?" Cathy asked, passing Mark a silver-embossed check. "We're going to shoot some 'before' footage."

"Before what?" He folded the check and placed it in his wallet.

"Before you turn him into a famous race horse."

"Ah," he said, "the crushing weight of owner expectations." But he smiled, confident he'd be able to get the horse into winning form. "We'll run him at Aqueduct a few times. Maybe look for some races at Gulfstream. He's done well in New York though and doesn't appear to mind cold weather."

"It's going to be so much fun." Cathy's smile turned mischievous. "Some of our owners have horse-crazy kids. They're hoping to bring them along for a visit."

"Okay. We'll schedule a day, and I'll put Trooper in the last set. The kids can come to the barn afterwards and pat the horsey."

"Horsey?" She laughed so hard, she spilled her wine and had to grab a napkin. "I was joking, although they'll be thrilled if they can bring their kids. But what happened to the man who liked his barn silent as a tomb? No running or laughing, restricted visitors and all those other rules?"

She still smirked. He didn't want to encourage her but couldn't hide his smile. "There's been a lot of disruption over the past six weeks but the horses have coped. Flourished, in fact," he admitted. "Guess they find life more interesting."

"And I think you find life more interesting too. Is that the reason you pretended to turn off your ringer but were really checking the time?" She reached across the table and grabbed his hand. "Come on, I'm a trained reporter so I'll figure it out. Does it have anything to do with that stunning girl you were with at Keeneland? The owner of Ambling Assets?"

"Jess isn't the owner."

Cathy released his hand and leaned back, oozing satisfaction. "So it is her. She did look a bit fiery. Not one to follow rules."

"She's damn difficult." His mouth clamped.

"Well, you prefer difficult horses too. When we filmed Assets, I thought he was a jerk, trying to bite everyone. But he was already your favorite, and that was before you turned him into a stakes winner."

"That spirit makes him a better fighter down the lane," Mark said. "Did I tell you his last work was perfect?"

Cathy waved off his effort to change the subject. "Is Jessica the reason we had our last sleepover six months ago?"

"No, I believe it had something to do with your trip to Dubai."

Her face turned dreamy. "Oh, yes. That's right."

He leaned forward. "Maybe you can help, Cath. You know their culture. But this has to be off the record." He waited until he extracted her reluctant promise before telling her about the poisoned carrot.

"Sheikh Khalif isn't behind it," she said flatly. "His enemies are more likely to poison his horse, not Assets. They resent his close relationship with the West. Al-Qaeda thinks Dubai's ruling

261

family is hurting the economy with their lifestyle. That they've turned the UAE into a whorehouse. So even if it was some sort of terror attack, it doesn't explain why extremists would go after your horse."

Her phone buzzed. She gave him an apologetic smile and took the call. He flipped open his own cell and checked his messages. Nothing from the barn, and Boone hadn't called back. Apparently he was somewhere in Europe and, according to his tight-lipped assistant, much too busy to worry about horses.

They both flipped their phones shut at the same time, looked at each other and laughed.

Traffic was sparse, and Mark was well on schedule. Seven-thirty. Jessica would have no reason or excuse to leave Maria's early. At least she was safe. Still, Cathy's mention of terror attacks left him chilled; he reached for the controls and turned up the heat.

He didn't know who Jessica's attacker was or why he'd tried to poison Assets, but surely the man would be caught soon. Every security guard carried the picture Dick had snapped, and even Jessica seemed shaken, so it was unlikely she'd wander off alone.

But if this man was a trained extremist, he'd know how to blend in. What they really needed was a larger data base. His cop friend hadn't come through at all. In fact, Mark hadn't heard from Bruce since he e-mailed the picture, even with the offer of two more Cup tickets. Of course, Bruce hadn't been very happy during their last conversation—when Mark had complained bitterly about Jessica's treatment by the police.

He punched in Bruce's number, talked to his secretary and was dismayed to learn the man was on vacation. No wonder he hadn't answered. Mark blew out a sigh as he racked his memory for other cop connections. Couldn't think of any, not ones he trusted. His association with Bruce had developed because bailout of employees was occasionally required.

He and a rowdy friend had even spent a few hours in Bruce's jail, although his buddy had managed to get them released quickly enough. Something about Canadian police and international privilege.

262

He slowed his car as he considered Kurt MacKinnon. He hadn't seen him in a while, not since their boisterous celebration following an upset win. But he remembered Kurt admitting he had something to do with the RCMP. Something secretive.

He scanned his directory for the number. Kurt was probably running at Gulfstream but maybe had moved to Woodbine. He found a cell number and punched it in, praying it worked.

"MacKinnon."

The laconic answer made him smile with relief. "You're in a bar, aren't you?" he asked.

"Yeah, my girl just won another race. Can't lose with a hot jock." Kurt's chuckle was slightly wicked. "And no training tips. You'll have to win the Juvenile on your own."

Mark turned down his whirring heater, straining to hear Kurt's voice over the country music in the background. "I have a police question," he said. "Need your help."

"Just a sec."

Muffled conversation. He heard Kurt talking to someone called Julie. A lilting, feminine voice. A door slammed. "What's up?" Kurt asked, his voice distinct in the sudden quiet.

"Guy tried to poison my big horse. I have a picture, but police here can't match it with local mug shots, and the track can't ID him. He might be foreign. I'm hoping some database somewhere—"

"Horse okay?"

"Fine."

"Send me the picture," Kurt said. "Can't do much over the weekend but should have something by Monday."

Mark's shoulders relaxed as he recorded Kurt's e-mail address. If there was anything on record, Kurt would dig it up. The man was coolly capable and a helluva guy to have beside you in a fight. "Coming for the Cup?" he asked.

"No, not until I have my own entry," Kurt said. "Be cheering on your horse though. Good luck."

Mark closed his phone, then considered calling Maria's house and telling Jessica he'd be early. However, he was still annoyed at her innuendos. Training involved meetings, phone calls and dinners; it was impossible to hold her hand and reassure her before each one.

He parked as close as he could to Maria's apartment. Checked his watch. Seven forty-five. He'd been here a couple times before, but Maria had never invited him in and probably never would. Ironic that she'd befriended Jessica; Maria slotted owners and trainers in the do-not-mingle category. Of course, she probably didn't know Jessica was a Boone.

He climbed the steps, smiling at the boisterous laughter leaking through the thin door. Sounded like a neighborhood party. Maybe Maria would let him in after all. He had a hankering to sit back in a homey living room and relax. Watch some kids play. Despite Cathy's teasing, he didn't mind children. Jessica clearly liked them too.

He recognized Maria's voice and heard a high-pitched squeal. Must be a neighbor's kid or someone she brought home from Anna House. A truck backfired and he spun, relaxing as taillights flashed red then vanished around the corner. Just a noisy truck. Normally he'd be irritated if traffic scared horses. Now he was only relieved.

He raised his hand to knock then stiffened, rooted by the blend of languages—including one he didn't know, spoken by a child. He squeezed his eyes shut, frozen with anger. For a second he couldn't breathe.

The kid is here. All this time, all the worry, and the kid had been right here. He wheeled and gripped the wooden railing, staring blankly at the rows of illuminated barns.

Fuck.

He forced his stiff legs back down the steps to his car. He'd have to fire Maria if he saw the kid, and he didn't want to do that. Not until he thought about it. She'd be devastated, and no doubt it was Jessica who'd talked her into this.

Jessica, who he'd promised not to fire.

His phone rang, but he ignored it. Probably Jessica. She was smart. No doubt calling to make sure he didn't come early, probably wanted to meet him outside Maria's apartment.

He squeezed the bridge of his nose as the phone buzzed, again and again. Finally he couldn't stand the noise and checked the display. 'Long distance.'

He snapped it open. "Russell," he said, in a voice that sounded strange.

264

"Received your message," Boone said. "Glad my horse is okay. What was in the carrot?"

"Arsenic." Mark straightened.

"Is Breeders' Cup the last day of the meet?"

"No. Sunday, the day after the Cup is the last day."

"Okay," Boone said. "Then sometime over the next seven days, I want you to fire Jessica."

Mark's knee jerked so hard it smashed into the steering wheel. "What! What grounds?"

"You decide. Just make it real. She can't know."

"But she's working so hard," Mark said. "Doing a great job—"

"Yes, I know," Boone said impatiently. "You've said that before. But I want her working for me. Been waiting a long time for this." Muted conversation sounded in the background. "I'll call you tomorrow," Boone added, his voice distracted. "Probably best to fire her on Tuesday. I'll be back in New York then, and the timing would work better for me."

Mark heard the click but continued to hold the dead phone, staggered by Boone's ruthlessness. Her efforts, her sacrifice, all in vain. And his staff. They'd spent so much time teaching her. She'd been a sponge too, eager to learn, never complaining about the work, not even during her inevitable loneliness.

Yet Boone had planned her failure from the very first day. No wonder she had security issues; he'd probably jerked an invisible chain her entire life. It was clear her knee was fine. She hadn't limped in weeks, other than from boot blisters, and he'd even seen her jogging around the backside in cute little shorts, healthy as any stakes horse.

Mark's phone rang again—another long distance number, but he didn't answer. Might be Boone again and he was too disgusted to talk.

He stared over his steering wheel, watching as a lone figure plodded down the road and into a shedrow. Night check. Jessica's job for six weeks. And on pauper's wages. What a prick. Boone shouldn't have bothered putting her through the grind. Mark didn't know how long he sat, but the watchman reappeared and plodded back down the road again.

His phone rang, and he checked the display. Maria's number. He opened it with a weary flip.

"Hi Mark," Jessica said. "Just let me know when you're coming, and I'll meet you at the bottom of Maria's steps, okay?"

He squeezed his eyes shut and grunted.

CHAPTER TWENTY-EIGHT

Jessica shifted in the passenger seat and peered again at Mark. His jaw was so rigid, she feared it might crack. "Maria sent along some cookies she baked. Would you like one?"

"No," he said, not looking at her.

"I'll have one then. They're still warm." She bit into a cookie, hoping it would stop her babbling. She'd thought Mark liked cookies, but now he wouldn't even try one. Maybe his reserve was related to the meeting with Cathy—maybe they'd had a very intimate meeting and he wanted to invite her home but couldn't because Jessica was staying there. The cookie lodged in her dry throat, and it was hard to swallow.

Or maybe there was something wrong with a horse somewhere. Not Assets or Buddy. She'd been with Mark when he stopped at the shedrow. Assets was as nippy as ever, and Buddy gleamed, all spic and span for his race tomorrow. Must be a problem with the ESPN people or maybe the deal had fallen through. Too bad—the media exposure they'd bring would have been good for Mark and his staff.

Concern tangled in her throat. "Is everything okay with Cath—" she coughed as the cookie blocked her words.

"What?"

Her throat convulsed and she choked. Tried to cough but couldn't make a sound. Tears trickled down her cheeks.

"Cough it up," he said, slowing the car.

The cookie container tumbled to the floor, and she fumbled for the window switch. If she could only get some fresh air, she'd be fine. Cold air blasted her face as Mark lowered the window, but it didn't help.

Her panic swelled. She had to get out of the car. Eyes watering, she yanked off her seatbelt, groping for the door handle, desperate to escape. If only she could stand. She'd be able to breathe if she could stand.

"Wait!" He grabbed her wrist as the car bounced over the rutted shoulder.

She tried to break his grip, consumed with terror. He didn't understand. The car lurched to a stop, and the pressure on her arm lifted. She stumbled out, gasping for breath. Cars whizzed by, spotty blurs of color, and she sagged against the door. Something jerked her upright, a jolt of pressure in her chest and she was finally able to suck in a breath of sweet, beautiful, painful air.

Mark turned her, gripping her shoulders, one hand still on her chest, his eyes a slash of blue. Her ribs hurt, but she forced a shaky smile. Sputtered for a moment until she realized she could breathe again.

"Thank you. Guess I shouldn't talk with my mouth full," she managed, her voice wispy.

"Dammit, Jess." But he smiled and hugged her with such relief, the scare was almost worth it. "You'll have to talk to Maria about her cooking," he added, helping her back into the car.

She wiped her wet eyes, too shaken to hide the truth. "Actually it's not Maria's fault. I traded some stalls tomorrow for the ingredients and made those cookies. Just didn't want to admit I was baking for you."

"Feeling guilty, were you?" His sharp tone made her squirm.

"I don't know what you mean." She adjusted her seatbelt, avoiding his gaze. Did he mean guilty because she was jealous earlier? Or guilty because she'd taken extra carrots for Buddy? Or maybe guilty because a fan had written after she'd been so wildly creative with his mail?

"When we get home," he said, "you're going to answer a few questions."

She peeked sideways, straining to see his face through the gloom. His jaw wasn't as rigid as before, but it definitely wasn't relaxed. "What kind of questions?" she asked.

"And let you prepare?" He snorted. "I don't think so."

"Then why did you tell me? Now I'll worry all the way home." She flinched a second after she said 'home,' but he didn't seem to notice her mistake, so it was okay.

He gave a humorless smile but said nothing.

The drive was much too short. He parked in the driveway, and she trailed him up the steps to the door. Climbing made her chest ache; she wheezed, and that was the only time he really looked at her.

"I pushed pretty hard. Ribs okay?"

"Yes, no need for the hospital," she said. "Thanks again, by the way. That's never happened to me before."

He unlocked the door, dropped his briefcase on the floor and stalked into the kitchen. She pulled her boots and jacket off, then hesitated. She wasn't at all hungry so there was no reason to join him. Especially since he was in a foul mood despite just saving her life.

No, it was probably best to duck into the Jacuzzi—he'd understand her chest would be tender and with any luck, he'd either be asleep or in an improved mood when she stepped out.

She eased down the hall. Saw him sprawled in a chair at the kitchen table, glass in his hand, bottle of rum and phone beside him. His eyes locked with hers, and he kicked out a chair with his foot. "Sit."

She swallowed, walked into the kitchen and sat. He didn't offer a drink, just swirled the ice in his glass, his blue eyes glittering with resentment. "Where is the kid now?" he asked.

She squared her shoulders and stared back, determined not to look guilty. But he was much better at this, and she was the first to look away. "With Maria and Pedro."

"Whose idea?"

Oh, God. She gulped. Mark had such strict rules. Even if he didn't want to, he'd be obligated to fire Maria. And the job meant everything to her.

Her gaze darted to the left and clung to a fridge magnet. She was leaving in a week. It seemed a small lie to protect a loyal friend. But it wasn't small. Especially when Mark was sitting there, staring at her, acting like the truth was so important.

The kitchen clock ticked in the sticky silence. She tore her gaze from the magnet and back to Mark. "My idea," she whispered but her heart pounded with such intensity she could no longer hear the clock.

"May I see your knee?"

She scanned his face for a flicker of a smile, but he didn't seem to be joking. She rose and unzipped her jeans, pulled her leg out and extended her knee.

He kneeled, watching her face while he manipulated her knee. "Any pain?"

"No. It feels great." She leaned forward, eager at the chance. "I know you don't want me as a groom, but I could walk hots. I never get tired anymore...I can walk all day."

He ignored her. Continued poking and prodding. A wrinkle of concentration appeared between his eyes. "Not a bit of swelling now, but you had some when you came." He spoke so thoughtfully he appeared to be talking to himself.

"Yes. Every two weeks, one of Gramps' doctors would inject a needle and drain the fluid."

"How did that work?"

"Hurt for a few days, but after a week it always felt better." His hair was rumpled, as though he'd been running his hands through his hair, and she resisted the urge to straighten it. If this was a job interview, she didn't want to screw up. "I haven't limped for weeks, well, except for a few blisters. But I'm good now. And I wouldn't braid or do anything you don't like," she added eagerly. "Really, I'd be no trouble."

He smiled then, but it was almost sad. Not reassuring at all. "You need to take charge of your own life, not have me or your grandfather telling you what to do."

"But I love working with the horses. And I like it when you tell me what to do."

He raised an eyebrow.

"I'm getting much better at listening," she said, trying not to plead. "I just need a bit more time to get it right."

"Tell me about the boy."

"His name is Abdul. He's from Pakistan and rode camels, and he doesn't know anything about that man. That's why we—that's why I—didn't think it was so important to tell you. Maria wants to keep him."

"The kid isn't a stray pup," Mark said, and she clamped her mouth shut at his curt tone. He pressed some numbers and she heard him order a security guard be posted outside Maria's apartment. It's a good thing he was likely to win the Juvenile, she thought bleakly. He was spending a fortune on security.

His next call was in Spanish, very brief, and she could only pick up a few words but heard Maria's name.

He closed his phone with obvious regret, and she bit her lip so hard she tasted blood. "Please, don't fire her, Mark. She loves children so much. You just have to see them together. Abdul is like her little nephews, and she'd be a wonderful mother."

He ignored her and pressed more numbers on his phone. "Dino, do we know anyone from Pakistan? A woman, not a man. Someone good with kids."

He glanced at Jessica and switched to Spanish, and she winced. He didn't trust her. The knowledge hurt almost as much as the fact that he was going to fire Maria.

She rose and walked numbly down the hall, past the main bathroom with the Jacuzzi and into the little shower in the spare bathroom. She stood under the pulsing water, chewing her fingernails and worrying about Maria. It might be possible to find a job without a reference from Mark, especially with a less prominent barn, but the chance for Maria to earn big bonuses was gone. She'd never be able to afford a lawyer, and Abdul might be sent back to the desert with nothing to eat and no one to love him.

She squeezed her eyes shut, letting the water spray her hot face. She wished Mark wasn't so rigid, so focused that he couldn't bend some rules. Probably the only reason he hadn't fired her yet was because her grandfather owned Assets—Mark would never jeopardize his chance to win a Breeders' Cup.

She stepped from the shower and pulled on a change of clothes. It was going to be an uncomfortable evening. No way would she sleep with a man who'd just fired her best friend. Indignation made her feel more in control, and she stalked down the hall, pausing outside his exercise room.

Thump, thump.

She peered in. Mark pounded a leather bag, his muscles bunching. His bare chest gleamed, and sweat dampened his hair. Gray sweatpants hung low on his hips, and his ragged grunts made her think of sex.

She licked her lips and tried not to drool. If he were a horse, she'd buy him in spite of his occasional surliness and strict rules. She must have made some sort of sound, or maybe she really did groan. He looked at the door and swiped his forehead with his

271

upper arm. She thought she knew his body well, had seen and felt him without clothes, but she'd never stood back and watched all those muscles work before.

"I didn't fire Maria," he said, his eyes dark with emotion.

"Oh, g-good. That is so good." Relieved, she turned and hurried to the bed. The thumping noise continued so she laid back on the pillow and studied the room. The noise stopped, replaced with a whirring. He must be on the exercise bike now.

She laid back on the pillow and studied the room. She'd never had much leisure time here. It was pretty bare, just a big bed, a clock and a night table full of condoms. Clothes shoved into an open closet and a collection of cowboy hats placed upside down on a shelf.

The whirring noise stopped, and she fluffed up the pillow, waiting for him to finish. Her heart was pounding, and she couldn't understand why her throat was so dry. It was much simpler when he just picked her up and carried her to bed. Waiting was nerve-wracking.

The punching started again.

She sighed and turned out the light. If she didn't agonize about Mark and Abdul and what she was going to do in seven days, she might be able to relax enough to nap before Mark came in. And tomorrow wouldn't be all bad. Tomorrow Buddy would be her horse. Only a race away.

She felt a swell of guilt that she had to use Mark's money. But she'd pay him back. She kept a detailed ledger of every cent she'd borrowed, right down to the scarf from Keeneland.

And she'd make Mark and the entire barn proud of Buddy. He might not win, but he was going to look magnificent. She'd braid in two shades of purple. She even had a purple jacket on loan from Dick's apartment.

"Take anything you want, dear," Dick had said. "You know the rules. Just return it washed." He truly was a dear friend. And he loved his new scarf.

She woke up groggy and disoriented. Buddy's braids had fallen out. Clearly, she couldn't braid right, and Mark said she had to get up. The shadow by the bed moved. It really was Mark, and she realized it wasn't all a dream.

"Time to get up," he repeated before vanishing from the room.

She sat up, rubbing her eyes. Checked his side of the bed. Even in the dark, she could see it was immaculate. Untouched. She scrambled onto the cold floor and quickly made the bed, her chest painfully tight. Probably sore because of the Heimlich maneuver. She absolutely was not going to feel rejected because Mark had anger issues.

The shower in the small bathroom was running, so she slipped down the hall and checked the spare bedroom. No mystery now. The bed was unmade, and the pillow still carried the imprint of his head.

She returned to the main bathroom and stumbled into the shower. The water didn't wash away her humiliation though, and the tightness in her throat made her cough. She had blithely crawled into his bed, and he was too cowardly to say he no longer wanted her there. Talk about embarrassing. A sob leaked from her throat.

She showered and towel dried, splashed cold water on her face and yanked on her change of clothes. He probably wouldn't wait if she wasn't in the passenger seat exactly on time. She jammed her toothbrush and spare clothes in a plastic bag—no way was she coming back here. Cathy could have him.

She set her face in a tight smile and walked down the hall, determined to hide her pain.

He was in the kitchen making noise with a blender. Poured a frothy white drink in a glass and passed it to her, his eyes inscrutable.

She stretched, pretending utter insouciance. "I slept so well. What a comfortable bed you have. Thank you." She accepted the glass, took a big sip and gagged. It was thick, gooey and disgusting, and she rushed to spit in the sink. "What was that?" she finally gasped.

"Egg and milk," he said.

She bent over the sink again, still gagging, forgetting about trying to look happy and carefree.

"Protein powder too," he said.

"If that's what you have to drink to get muscles," she reached for a tissue and wiped her mouth, "I'd rather be skinny."

"You're not skinny, honey. Come on."

She stared at his retreating back. The affection in his voice shocked her, and relief smoothed the jagged edges of her pain. "Do I have time to brush my teeth again?" she managed.

"No," he said.

CHAPTER TWENTY-NINE

"For immigration? So Abdul pretended he was the man's son?" Mark asked. "Thanks." He closed his phone and stared across the desk at Dino.

"Sounds like we need more coffee." Dino rose and refilled their cups.

"The Pakistani lady you found did a good job. Abdul relaxed. Talked willingly." Mark glanced at his notes. "He came on a plane with a man called Haddad. Was told his throat would be cut if he didn't do exactly what they said."

Dino shook his head. "And we thought spanking was bad."

"Abdul said it was warmer but some of the leaves were already red," Mark went on. "He thinks he was with Haddad about twenty nights before he overheard them planning to kill him. Apparently they didn't need a boy anymore. He'd become a liability, so he bolted."

"And Jessica helped him get away," Dino said. "That couldn't have made our man, Haddad, very happy."

Mark wheeled and glanced out the window.

"She's okay," Dino said, his voice solemn. "Still in Buddy's stall. Guards at each end."

Mark sank back in his chair, studying the blackness of his coffee. "It doesn't seem like the carrot incident was related to the boy. Abdul said there's another man called Karif who talked about a noble mission. Punishment for Muslims who violate Islamic law."

"Something to do with racing then," Dino said. "Anything odd happen to other Breeders' Cup favorites?"

"Spud's horse coliced last night."

"Jesus, no! His Smart Strike colt?" Dino's hand jerked, spilling his coffee. "Horse going to make it?"

"Doesn't look good," Mark said. "And the second favorite in the Classic belongs to the sheikh."

"So either the sheikh is playing dirty, or someone's trying to make him look bad."

"My guess is that Haddad and Karif don't like the sheikh." Too edgy to remain seated, Mark rose, returned to the window and stared at his barn.

"Think the media will pick it up?" Dino asked.

"Not from us. And Spud's too devastated to talk."

"Understandable. Imagine having a favorite in a Breeders' Cup race—the Classic, no less—and then, splat." Dino smashed his hand in his palm. "You got nothing. Hard to recover from something like that. Spud might never have a big horse again."

A muscle twitched in Mark's jaw, and he didn't dare turn around. "Yeah," he said softly, "it would tear out a man's heart."

"We owe Jessica," Dino went on. "Could have been our horse in that clinic." He gave a low chuckle. "I forgot, you *have* been thanking her every afternoon. Wish I could give her my personal thanks too, you know, as assistant trainer. Maybe I could cover for you sometime—

Mark whipped around. "That's enough, Dino."

Dino stepped back and raised his palms, but his eyes narrowed. "Just checking the lay of the land. So this is a little more serious than I thought? Think that's wise? Better be careful, buddy."

"I said that's enough."

"Whoa, relax. Your woman. Hands off. I get it. And between now and Saturday, I won't take my eyes off Assets or Jessica. Carlos and I can give the guards piss breaks. We've too much riding on this to let some feud fuck it up. What the hell are the police doing?"

"They're coming back for more interviews," Mark said. "And they went to the hospital again and talked to Dick Snow. Maria wants to keep the boy, but it has to go through the legal process. I have a couple psychologists lined up who'll say he shouldn't be removed from someone he trusts. The big knock is that Maria and Pedro live at the track." He paused. "Now where is she going?" he muttered, forgetting about Abdul as Jessica sauntered from the barn. Her hips rolled in a graceful walk, and even the stoic day guard craned for a better look.

Dino joined him at the window. "Easy on the eye, isn't she?"

"Doesn't listen well though." Mark spun toward the door.

"Wait." Dino grabbed his arm. "Don't yell at her. She's had a tough time. Besides, she isn't going anywhere. Only picking grass."

Mark returned to the window and rolled his aching shoulders. Last night, he'd worked out until he was exhausted, trying to think, trying to come up with a solution, and now every muscle protested.

"Jesus. Now the guard is helping her." Dino chuckled as the guard walked over and began pulling handfuls of grass from beside the wall of the barn. "Technically he hasn't left his post, but I can see where his attention is, and it's not on Assets."

Jessica said something, and the guard smiled. She bent back down, her jeans outlining her shapely rear.

Dino set his full mug on the desk and adjusted his cowboy hat. "Sorry, Mark, but the scenery is much better out there. Think I'll mosey over and help with Buddy's grass picking. You're the big trainer. You can stay and problem-solve."

"Keep your hands in your pockets," Mark said but Dino only gave him a cocky salute. Mark sighed and continued to flex his aching shoulders. Grabbed his phone and checked his messages, but there was nothing from Boone. Maybe he could avoid the man for six more days. Then he wouldn't have to tell Boone he couldn't fire Jessica. Damn, it wasn't right. She'd worked so hard, had saved Assets twice. She deserved a raise, not a kick in the ass.

He was already fucked though. No way would he be able to keep training Boone's horses after he told Jessica his suspicions—that her knee injury wasn't as serious as she'd been led to believe. He stared out the window, watching as she pirouetted and tossed grass at Dino, all easy grace and elegance. When she'd arrived, the limp and swelling were pronounced, right after an appointment with her doctor.

He blew out a ragged breath. She wanted to hide out at the track, but that was because her grandfather had been systematically knocking her down. God only knew how far Boone's power extended. However, skiing seemed to be her lifelong ambition, and she deserved another shot. He knew what it was like to have a dream, and the least he could do was give her the push to pursue it.

But the Breeders' Cup was *his* ambition. And Carlos needed the money to help his family immigrate, and Maria needed the money from Boone's filly for the lawyers, and Dino wanted to buy back his ranch. Goddammit, he needed to keep Boone's horses.

He raised a hand to his head and massaged the persistent pain in his left temple.

His phone buzzed, but the number showed a different owner than Boone. Normally he didn't welcome calls from Sophie and Devin, but Boone was the only one he was desperate to avoid today. He opened his phone.

"Hello, Mark," Sophie said, her tone too crisp for a happy call. "I see you moved our Bobby horse up to eighteen thousand claiming. Isn't that a steep jump?"

Mark took a patient breath. "Buddy won at twelve, and this new race is shaping up easy. A third at this level will make you more money than a win at a lower level."

"Oh, I see." Her voice softened. "I assumed you moved him to a higher claimer because you didn't care about winning. Thought you just wanted that girl to buy him. I do apologize."

"No need." Because your assumption is absolutely correct, he thought grimly. "You coming this afternoon?"

"Yes. And we don't accept checks from her sort of people." Sophie gave a disdainful sniff. "So tell that girl she needs two thousand in cash."

That girl. Mark didn't try to smooth the bite in his voice. "Of course," he said. "And we'll have your final bill as well. Since I won't be seeing you again, I also prefer cash."

He snapped the phone shut, deciding he better not take any further calls. It wouldn't be wise to piss off any more owners or there'd be no horses left to train. And unfortunately Boone was shaping up to be a very unhappy owner.

The security guard stiffened, swallowed a bite of cookie and abruptly rushed back to his post. The big dog must be coming, Jessica thought, glancing over her shoulder. Sure enough, Mark had emerged from his office, looking more relaxed than he'd been all morning. His smile slipped though when he saw the cookie in the guard's hand.

"You have grass stains on your uniform," he said to the red-faced guard before lowering himself on the ground beside her and Dino. "Thought you made those cookies for me?"

"You didn't want them," she said, studying Mark's face, trying to gauge his mood, "but these discerning gentlemen certainly did."

"That was last night. Today is different."

Today is different? What exactly did that mean. He'd ordered her to stay close to the barn, had seemed genuinely worried about her safety, but she knew he'd been making calls about Abdul. He definitely hadn't wanted her beside him last night. He was probably still annoyed, and rightly so. "I can make you another batch if you want," she said.

"You can make me some cookies too," Dino said. "But I need a drink. That last one stuck in my throat."

Mark's amused smile made her cheeks warm, but he didn't say a word about her cooking. Or about the choking episode.

Dino rose and brushed off his jeans. "Okay if I go to the kitchen, Mark? You look after her a bit?"

Jessica stiffened. "I don't need anyone to look after me—"

Mark reached over and squeezed her hand. She swallowed and stopped talking. Even Dino looked surprised at the public gesture. But Mark was looking at her so sweetly, totally devoid of the frustration that had possessed him in the exercise room.

Mark nodded at Dino but kept his eyes on her. "Is Buddy ready to run?" he asked.

"Oh, yes." Anticipation made her smile, and she clenched her stomach, fighting her butterflies. "I have three bags of grass ready to celebrate after the race. He had a few bites now but not too much."

She waved goodbye to a grinning Dino and twisted around. Mark had sprawled out on the grass, and it was rather odd to see him so relaxed, chewing on a blade of grass, eyes closed as he absorbed the noon sun. "Is that why you're here?" she asked. "You were afraid I'd feed Buddy too much grass?"

"I'm here because I like to be with you, Jess. And my phone is off. It's quiet. No police, no child services, no stabber." He kept his eyes shut but was smiling.

279

Obviously he was no longer mad. She dropped to the grass beside him, hiding her happiness behind a little sniff. "I don't think you should be lying on the ground though. An owner might come by. It doesn't look very professional."

"Trainers can do what they want. Besides, my owners are already annoyed. Or about to be."

She studied him, resisting the urge to rest her head on his shoulder. He wouldn't like that, she knew, not at the track. It was monumental he'd held her hand for a brief moment. Besides, he seemed bothered by something. Not his owners though; it was no secret they all loved him. Mark even had a wait list. Dino said he had enough requests to fill another ten stalls.

"Tell me about your parents," he said abruptly.

She propped up on an elbow. She could see the contours of his chest as he breathed, could see his muscles ripple when he bent his arm to chew on the grass. But his eyes remained closed. Good. It was hard to talk when he leveled her with those penetrating blue eyes. Sometimes it seemed as though he could see right through her.

She plucked a tall piece of grass and tried chewing, but it wasn't as cool as he made it look so she tossed it aside.

"Dad died in a car accident when I was a kid. Cancer got Mom three years ago." She shrugged even though he couldn't see it. "Gramps was never happy with his only son's marriage. Mom tried, she tried hard, but nothing ever pleased Gramps. They were always arguing."

"She work for your grandfather's company?"

"Yes, as a personal assistant. She wanted to leave, but Gramps made it tough."

"Did he support your skiing?"

"No. They fought about it. Mom thought it best I go to school in Switzerland. Said it would help with my skiing." Jessica sighed. "I think she just wanted me out of the house."

"Or maybe it was to get you away from your grandfather," Mark said slowly, almost reluctantly. "Maybe he used you as a bargaining tool. You'll never know what really went on, so don't be too hard on your mom."

"You're just as hard on your dad."

"Check." His mouth curved in a smile. "And I am starting to empathize with him a bit, although I'll always wish he could have been content with one woman."

"Some men never are."

"I could be," he said softly.

"My God!" Jessica shielded her eyes from the sun, pretending to stare at the adjacent barn. "Is that Trish sunning herself topless again?"

Mark jerked up and stared, then grinned and dropped back on the grass. "Sneaky. But looking is different from availing."

"Availing?" She rolled the word around. "That's a good word. Like last night when you didn't avail yourself of me?"

"I wanted to. Had to settle a few things first."

"Is everything settled then?" she asked, scarcely daring to breathe.

"Yes."

"So you're going to hire me?" She twisted with delight. "Keep me on as a groom?"

He shook his head.

"A hotwalker then?" A groom would be better, but a hotwalker was okay too. She just wanted to stay at Mark's barn. Stay close to him.

"No, honey."

Her hopes crashed. She averted her head and ripped at the blossom of a dandelion.

"Maybe it's not time to hang up your skis," he added. "Why don't you get a second opinion? Maybe the doctor you're seeing is a little...off base."

A cloud rolled over the sun, cooling the air, and she shivered. "What exactly are you saying?"

"Your knee looks great," he said. "If you were a horse, I'd race you."

And that was the real problem. His focus was always horses. She was pleading to stay, and he didn't care enough to let her.

She wrapped her arms around her chest, trying to keep her heart from cracking. "Please don't make me leave, Mark." Her words caught on a convulsive choke. "I'll work for food and the little tack room. And I'll pay twenty percent interest on anything I owe you."

"God, Jess, it's not that." He sat up and squeezed her shoulder. "The horses can wait—I'll wait. But you need to do this other stuff. Without your grandfather's interference."

The guard shot them curious glances. Mark immediately dropped his arm, leaving her colder and more alone.

"Great." She scrambled to her feet. "That's what I'll do then. Just get Buddy settled then fly over to Europe and rejoin the ski team. Perfect." She snatched the empty cookie container, snapped on the lid and stalked off.

Mark was an idiot! Three doctors had said she was finished. Well, only one to her face. Her grandfather had been so attentive that first week, even flew her home in a private jet. She hadn't talked to the team doctor. Anton had been optimistic about her return, but it hadn't happened.

She grit her teeth, shoving away the memories. That was a lifetime ago, and she was a dedicated horse person now. Didn't imagine or want any other life. Buddy shoved his head over the stall door, watching her with his liquid eyes.

She slipped into the stall and pressed her head against his neck. When she scratched his jaw, he twisted his head, grunting with pleasure. He was so handsome, there'd be no problem finding him a home. His whiskers and ears were now neatly trimmed, and his dark coat gleamed. Technically he was a bay, but he looked black except for the jagged white striping his nose. So easy to spot in a race.

"Don't run too hard today," she whispered. "Just get around. I'll be waiting at the finish line."

He made an agreeable whooshing sound and stuck his nose against her pocket, always so gentle. She could probably learn to ride him if they had more time. A shame she'd never even sat on his back.

She edged forward and peered down the deserted aisle. Some horses were lying down, enjoying their morning nap. Buddy was in the eighth race, and Mark had another two horses in the third and fourth, so it would be a long wait. Mark had disappeared, probably gone to join Dino, and the two guards were looking outward, doing exactly what they were supposed to be doing.

She stepped back in the stall, knowing it might be her last chance to sit on Buddy. This was the perfect time. However, he was a tall horse, almost seventeen hands, and when she tried to swing up he skittered away in surprise.

She hurried to the tack room and returned with a plastic stool. When she plunked it down in the straw and stepped up, he resumed eating, as though having a white stool in the middle of his stall was a common occurrence.

She pushed the stool closer and leaned over his back. It was probably dangerous to have a stool next to a loose horse, but he'd have to learn about mounting blocks soon enough. Besides, this was Buddy and he was always very, very quiet.

She sucked in a breath. Swung her leg over his back and pulled herself on.

Oh, God. It was glorious. From her lofty position, she could see through his ears all the way down the aisle. Could see the lazy brown gelding that napped all day, the bay with the sore front leg, and Assets who jerked at his huge hay net like a rebellious teenager.

Wow! She leaned forward and stroked Buddy's silky neck. He felt so different from Ghost, slimmer and elegant, and his trusting personality filled her with confidence. He was the kind of horse who'd always look after his rider.

His braids were perfect too, all in a tight, straight line except for a clump of hair at the withers. Mark always yelled about leaving enough mane for the jockey to grab, and she drew her legs up and crouched like Emma Rae. Yes, he was right. There wasn't enough mane. Maybe she should take out a couple more braids. The tiny strand she'd left really didn't give Emma Rae much handhold. She'd never considered it from the jockey's perspective before.

She slipped her hand in her pocket and pulled out a peppermint, and Buddy stretched his head around and lipped it gently from her palm as though he'd done it a thousand times before. What a cool horse. She could probably ride him bareback to the kitchen, walk back with a coffee and not spill a drop.

I want to keep him. The admission rocked her. She leaned forward, wrapping her arms possessively around his neck, sucking in the smell of horse, hay and contentment, knowing now she couldn't give him away.

She looked up and froze. Mark stood two feet away, his hands clenched on the stall guard, his jaw tight. She straightened, trying to think of something to say. Getting on Buddy had been stupid and impulsive, and she knew it.

Buddy's head rose as her legs tightened, and he suddenly felt like a giraffe. She squeezed her legs tighter, trying to grip his slippery back, trying to get a handhold between the stupid braids and the mane, but Buddy felt her tension and skittered sideways. *Crack!* His left hoof landed in the middle of the plastic stool. He leaped in panic, but somehow Mark grabbed his halter.

"Whoa, boy. Slide off slowly, Jessica," Mark said, in the same soothing tone.

She quickly slid off. Mark grabbed Buddy's leg, freeing it from the jagged plastic. And then Buddy was free but snorting and shying at the straw as though wondering what had jumped up and bit him. Mark ran his hands over Buddy's leg, rose and scooped up the broken stool.

"Go to your room," he snapped.

He didn't look at her as she fled from the stall and stumbled to her room. She closed the door and hunched on her cot, waiting. Minutes ticked by. If he was trying to make her sweat, it was working. This was bad. If an owner had walked in, the professionalism of the entire barn would have been questioned. Worse, Buddy could have been hurt.

She dropped her head in her hands and groaned. Safety was the primary thing Mark stressed. Safety for horses, safety for people. She heard footsteps and lifted her head, but they shuffled past—and besides, the steps were different, tentative, and not at all like Mark's assertive walk.

She grabbed a *Blood-Horse* magazine and scanned the pictures of the vast farms, trying not to worry about his reaction. Tried to think of something positive. If she could talk her grandfather into buying a small acreage, she'd be able to keep Buddy. Pay back Mark and maybe give a few other Thoroughbreds a home. Gramps would probably agree if she promised to work for Boone the rest of her life.

Or she could just take the dog money and use it for horses, but that wasn't ethical and it certainly wasn't their agreement. Of course, that was assuming she could hang onto her job for another six days. She'd definitely given Mark enough grounds to fire her.

Someone knocked, too gently to be Mark. "Come in, Maria," Jessica said.

The knob turned, and Maria's excited face smiled in the doorway. "I just talked to the lawyer, and Pedro and I are getting a new apartment! It's only five blocks from the track, but the lawyer thinks it will help us get interim custody."

Jessica flipped the magazine shut. "When did this happen?"

"This morning. Mark's been so busy. He found a nice lady and gave her a list of questions, and Abdul answered them all. He doesn't have a home, and he wants to stay with me, and the lawyer said he'd be in danger if he returned to Pakistan, so..." Maria blew out a big breath and did a little dance step. "Jessica, I might be able to keep him!"

"You were right," she went on. "We should have told Mark at the beginning. He's been so helpful, and he gave me a reference, saying I'd make a good mother. And thanks for pretending it was your idea to hide Abdul. Mark's not blaming me at all."

Pain clawed Jessica's chest, but she forced a smile. "That's wonderful, Maria. I've sorted out the last of those tickets, and we have another sixty-seven dollars. You can use it toward the legal fees."

"No. Money won't be a problem. Not now. Belle is running in the Breeders' Cup undercard. Mark isn't saying she'll win but Carlos is, and I know she'll run a huge race. The bonus from that, well, you can keep all the stooping money. I'll be rich!"

Maria stepped forward and hugged her, radiating so much happiness it pushed away Jessica's regret. They both heard the rumble of Mark's voice and stepped apart.

"Boss still makes me nervous though," Maria whispered as she scooted from the room and darted to the left.

Two minutes later, Mark walked in, crossed his arms and glared.

"I'm really sorry," Jessica said. "Getting on Buddy was a stupid thing to do." She stared miserably at the toes of her boots. They'd been so stiff and spotless on her first day. Now they were worn and creased and comfortable. She peered up. Mark had lowered his arms and propped his hip against the door. Didn't look quite so pissed.

"We've all done it, I guess," he said reluctantly.

"Really? You did that?" She loved hearing stories about Mark.

"When I was four."

"Did you get in trouble?"

"Spanked."

"Oh." She edged toward the back wall, her hands automatically drifting to her rear.

"With a belt," he added as he turned and firmly closed the door. "So, your penance is twenty minutes."

She stared, fixated by his worn leather belt, the tough-looking buckle. She'd never been spanked before, but twenty minutes sounded like an unusually long time.

"Twenty minutes of guard duty." He stretched out on her cot and closed his eyes. "Don't let anyone find me, Jess."

His face relaxed within a minute. He wasn't snoring, not quite, but she could hear from his breathing that he was already asleep. She gave him a gentle kiss and covered him with her blanket. Someone argued in the aisle, and her sense of protectiveness welled. She hustled out to shut them up, quietly closing the door behind her.

"Jessica, have you seen Mark?" Dino called as he strode down the aisle, brandishing a clipboard. "The shipper screwed up. We got two horses out front and no stalls."

"A couple of horses left from the barn next door," Jessica said, edging further from her room, afraid they'd wake the sleeping man inside.

"That's right." Dino nodded. "I forgot Bobby sent a load to Gulfstream. Carlos, see if we can borrow two stalls for a couple days."

"What horses?" Jessica asked.

"The two Mark bought in Keeneland. A four-year-old and a two-year-old. Want to help?"

"I'd love to." She grabbed a lead rope and eagerly followed Dino to the trailer. She recognized the bay colt immediately, hip 665. She led him down the ramp and held him for Dino's detailed inspection.

"Damn. This feels like Christmas." Dino grinned like a kid as he circled the horse. "Look at the shoulder on this fellow, Jessica. Hope he can run like his dad. Lead him around the shedrow for twenty minutes. Let him stretch his legs."

"Wow, is that the Hard Spun colt?" Maria asked as Jessica led the colt down the aisle. "I wonder who Mark will get to rub him. He likes to see them when they arrive. Checks out their personality. Then he matches them with a groom."

"He does that? Maria, can you take this guy for a sec?" Jessica asked quickly. "I forgot something."

She shoved the shank in Maria's hand, checking her watch as she rushed to her room. Twenty five minutes. She slipped in and shook Mark's shoulder. His eyes whipped open.

"The two horses arrived," she whispered. "The ones from the sale."

"They're not supposed to come yet." His arm looped around her, and he tugged her onto his chest. "I can't remember. Did I give you a suitable reprimand before I fell asleep?"

"Oh, yes." She wiggled as his hand flattened over her rear. "I'm still sore."

"Good." He tilted her chin with his other hand. "You want to ride a horse, you do it right. So how did Buddy feel?" he added with a boyish grin.

"Wonderful, and I love it that you never stay mad." She reached up and impulsively planted a big kiss on his cheek.

He stiffened at the word *love*, so she scrambled up, determined to hide her feelings. "So, don't you want to see your new arrivals?"

"Of course."

But he didn't seem in too much of a hurry because he tracked her across the room, lingering to give her a thorough kiss before heading out to meet his horses.

CHAPTER THIRTY

Jessica removed Buddy's hay and water. He seemed to be dozing, as though aware he was going to race and determined to conserve every ounce of energy. She didn't want to bother him so slipped out of the stall to wait.

Time turned weird on race day. First it dragged as though the race would never arrive. Then it was suddenly time and you rushed to get your horse ready and your heart pounded in anticipation, and you barely had time to tape and bandage.

It was like that today.

"Time to head over, Jessica," Dino called with a grin. Mark already had two wins so far, and the entire shedrow buzzed.

She grabbed the bridle, cleaned and polished to a soft shine, and eased the bit in Buddy's mouth. Tongue tie, no blinkers today, rundown bandages, hoof pick and rag in her pocket. All set. She blew out a sigh and kissed his soft nose.

"Grass when you come back," she promised. *And then you're mine.* Mark had even said he'd give her a riding lesson on Buddy tomorrow. She was aware of her pounding heart, her sweaty palms. Knew she had to tone it down. Already Buddy arched his neck and jigged as she led him from the assembly barn.

"You're the man!" someone called. "Eat 'em up, old boy."

More shouts. "Good luck, Buddy!"

Dino fell in beside her. "Last runner today. I'm going over to cheer on the old fellow. Mark's on a roll. Bodes well for next weekend."

She nodded, barely hearing but glad of his company. Maria joined them on the walk over. Jessica gave her a grateful smile, realizing Maria had left Abdul with Pedro in order to watch Buddy run one last time.

Buddy pranced but just the right amount. Didn't waste a lot of energy, only enough to show he was ready. His ears pricked as they turned into the walking ring, and he bent his head to his chest and preened for the crowd.

"Mommy, look at that pretty horse with purple pigtails," a little girl said as she climbed on the rail. "He looks like Black Beauty. I like him the best."

Mark stood by slot four, arms folded, watching her lead Buddy past the confusion of faces. On their second circle, he waved her into the saddling enclosure. She glimpsed Sophie and Devin, but Mark and Buddy dominated her senses.

Buddy chomped at his bit and stared at the other horses. She jigged the reins to distract him while Mark placed the saddlecloth on his back and followed with Emma Rae's tiny saddle. He tightened the overgirth, picked out his feet, and stretched Buddy's front legs. Jessica pulled out her cloth and gave Buddy's nostrils one last swipe.

"Okay," Mark nodded. "Take him back out. Careful of the three horse."

Jessica circled Buddy around the walking ring, keeping well back from the three horse, a washy chestnut who kicked out, spraying dirt and delighting the crowd. Riders filed from the jockey room, and she saw Emma Rae's face. How could the jock possibly look so composed?

She adjusted her grip, feeling her palms stick to the leather line. "Twenty minutes, and you're mine," she whispered, stroking his warm neck.

Emma Rae shook hands with Mark, her head bobbing as she absorbed his directions. The paddock judge yelled, "Riders up!"

Jessica's heart slammed against her ribs. She swallowed, trying to ease the dryness as Mark legged Emma Rae into the saddle. She met Mark's gaze for a split second then led Buddy past the ivy-framed windows of the grandstand and into the darker tunnel.

"Mark told me to take care of him," Emma Rae said, looking down at her with a conspiratorial smile. "So don't worry, honey. I'll have your horse back in no time."

The pony rider met them on the track, leaned over and took the lead, and Buddy trotted off in a line of beautiful horses. Jessica watched him go, numb to the crowd. Someone tugged her sleeve, and Dino and Maria pulled her in by the rail, where she had a perfect view as the horses paraded past.

Buddy moved fluidly, purple mane gleaming in the sun, and Emma Rae's smile radiating confidence. Jessica pressed her hand against the envelope in her front pocket, checking that Sophie's money was safe. She glanced at Mark's box and saw Sophie nodding at something Mark said. She averted her gaze. She'd been invited to join them but didn't want to spoil Buddy's last race, not with Sophie's toxic presence.

Dino saw her tight face and gave a reassuring smile. "Two minutes to post, an eternity to wait. Jock's going to let Buddy coast, and if the old guy wants to run a little down the lane, that's okay. No one's going to beat him up, Jessica."

She nodded and leaned over the rail, straining to see the horses as they disappeared into the starting gate. A familiar arm slid around her waist.

"Buddy's in. Standing good," Mark said, giving her a hug.

"Not watching with your owners?" Dino asked.

"Not my owners much longer," Mark said, and they all laughed. The moment seemed perfect. "The three horse will be scratched," he added, frowning through his binoculars. Sure enough, thirty seconds later the announcer said, "Scratch the three horse."

Jessica watched on the infield screen as a horse was led away from the starting gate. Finally the gates snapped open, and the horses broke in a mass of churning color. She swung her head back and forth, watching the screen and the clump of horses on the far side of the track, undecided which gave the best view. Mark stood unperturbed behind her, glasses pressed to his eyes.

"He's fourth on the rail," Mark said. "Full of run."

Jessica bit her lip, mesmerized by the unfolding drama. Emma Rae tried to tuck Buddy behind a front runner but when they entered the turn, Buddy shot through a hole on the rail and his stride quickened.

Dino chuckled. "Looks like he wants to go out in style. Come on, Buddy!"

Jessica clenched her fists and leaped up and down, unable to contain her excitement. Buddy had jumped from twelve thousand claiming to eighteen. He wasn't supposed to be this good—*The Racing Form* had merely written 'overmatched'—but clearly Buddy didn't share that opinion.

And even though Emma Rae had a stranglehold on the reins, Buddy surged up to challenge the leader, a pricey bay with red blinkers and half his age. They swept by the eighth pole with the bay half a length in front and Buddy a gritty second. The bay faltered, seemed to be tiring. His jockey raised his stick, striking him on the right side.

And then everything switched to slow motion. The bay's head jerked up. He swerved to the left, bumping Buddy's shoulder and somersaulted. Buddy stumbled and went down, and Emma Rae disappeared beneath thundering hooves.

Jessica stopped breathing. There seemed to be no sound, just a hushed crowd and faces of wide-eyed riders standing in their stirrups, mouths open as they desperately tried to avoid the knot of fallen bodies. She saw Mark's back as he ran to Emma Rae and a downed horse, but the thrashing horse wore blinkers, and she had no idea what had happened to Buddy.

And then she saw him trotting back, looking at the crowd as though searching for her, and she leaped over the rail and ran to him. He put his nose against her chest, and it seemed like everything would be okay. But then she saw how he held his front leg and knew nothing would ever be the same again.

Dino appeared, unsaddled Buddy and gestured for a horse ambulance. But a man attached a red ribbon to Buddy's bridle and when she tried to follow Buddy into the ambulance, Dino grabbed her arm and pulled her back.

Her wooden legs didn't work, and she stared blankly at the fallen jockeys circled by somber attendants. Emma Rae lay on a stretcher but signaled a brave thumbs up to the crowd. Dino grabbed Jessica's arm and propelled her toward the barn while a sobbing Maria stumbled after them.

"Where's Buddy going?" Jessica asked but her voice was so weak it squeaked.

"He was claimed, Jessica. That's what the ribbon meant. Radcliff bought him."

"Claimed even though he was hurt?"

"Ownership changed once he left the gate."

"But—" She turned around. Two horse ambulances sped in one direction and another human ambulance in another, and she couldn't see Mark.

"You can't do anything for him now," Dino said gently. "Mark will stay and do what he can, and there will be an inquiry and let's just hope Emma Rae is all right."

"Yes, of course," Jessica said. "Poor Emma Rae. God." She tasted salt on her lips and realized she was crying.

They walked back to the office. Dino put his arm around her but didn't make a single joke, and she guessed he felt just as bad.

"Mark has rum for occasions like this." He pulled out a bottle and passed it to Jessica. She took a gulp and then Maria did and Dino took about five. And soon her eyes burned, and she didn't know if it was the rum or her tears.

Carlos came by with a pizza, and Dino found another bottle of rum. Jessica decided she worked with the nicest people in the world, and after a while both she and Maria sat on Dino's lap. She didn't know when Mark came but Dino picked her up and placed her in Mark's arms, and the men talked for a minute, and she decided she was having a really good time.

"Radcliff's a bastard," Dino was saying. "Surgery is an option, but he won't spend a dollar on a cheap horse like that."

She felt Mark look at her, and he passed her a glass of water and told her to drink.

"Jesus, Dino. Three bottles," Mark said, but he didn't sound mad.

"How's Emma Rae?" Jessica asked but no one seemed to hear, so she grabbed Mark's arm and tugged, and then he listened.

"Not too bad," he said. "Broken wrist, broken collarbone, broken ribs. She rolled under the rail."

Dino started talking again, and Maria interrupted to announce she was no longer afraid of Mark, and Carlos rolled his eyes and said he'd walk her home. Jessica tried to get up too, but the floor tilted. So she sat back on Mark's lap and wondered how she was ever going to make it to the bathroom.

After a while, she lurched up and tried again. Dino grinned and said he had to go too, but Mark said he'd take her.

Then they were all sitting around Kato's grave. Mark had his own bottle of rum, and he wouldn't share, but she didn't care.

She leaned against his chest, listening to it rumble while he and Dino spoke about horses and breakdowns and Barbaro.

"What's wrong with Buddy?" she asked, and both men turned silent.

"Broken leg," Mark finally said. "Condylar fracture." And he let her take a sip of rum.

She kept sipping as Dino talked about euthanasia and how Buddy wouldn't feel a thing, and later in her haze she heard Mark tell Dino they weren't going to Breeders' Cup after all, but that didn't make sense because Breeders' Cup was at Belmont that year and they were already there. Mark kept wiping her cheeks and murmuring about possible deals, and she fell asleep.

When she woke, Dino had Mark's rum, and the two men were arguing about where they were going to sleep. When she woke again, she was still dressed but in her bed, and Mark had all the blankets. She got up, shivering. Stumbled down the aisle and into Buddy's stall, but it was empty, and then she realized it wasn't a nightmare.

She dropped to the straw and wept.

"What's wrong?" The security guard touched her shoulder.

She stared into Terry's concerned face but her throat was too raw to talk. Mark arrived and guided her back to her room.

"Was it because I rode him?" she asked brokenly. "Was it the stool?"

Mark didn't answer, just gently stroked her hair and spoke in Spanish and she guessed he must be a little drunk too. He rose, took his clothes off, then hers, and she reminded him of his no-sex rule, but it was hard to talk and cry and kiss and besides, they weren't her rules.

CHAPTER THIRTY-ONE

Jessica stepped into the aisle and rubbed her aching head. Trudged out the back door so she didn't have to pass Buddy's empty stall and stood in the shower for a long, long time. She walked mechanically back toward the barn, feeling dull and dead and drained.

Strange that the shedrow looked the same. Everyone still followed the morning routine. She could see Mark leading a string to the track, Dino arguing with the hay man, and the nasty bay colt everyone avoided still bucked on the hot walker. Horses moved through the morning mist, and someone even laughed.

She circled back to Missy's stall, concentrating on putting one heavy foot in front of the other. After all, she still had one horse to look after.

"Missy's finished," Maria called. "Mark had her out first set, and Dino cleaned her stall. Want to come over to the apartment for breakfast? Abdul has drawn some really good pictures."

The thought of Abdul's shrieks made Jessica wince. "Don't you have a headache?" she asked, her voice hoarse.

"A bit," Maria said. "But life goes on."

It sure does, especially around here, Jessica thought bitterly, as she walked into her room. The pictures on her walls seemed silly now, like posters left after everyone in the dorm had packed up their dreams and moved on.

She ripped them down, crumpling them in her hands. Jammed them in the garbage bin. Dumped out Buddy's bags of grass. Dragged Lefty's bike outside and left it beside the dumpster. Well, she'd move on too. No sense to hang around and hope Mark would let her stay. The insides of her chest were already too shredded.

The last set returned, and five sweaty horses were led down the shedrow, happy, tired and anticipating their baths. The horse Emma Rae usually galloped had a different rider, another apprentice jockey fighting to break into Mark's lineup. Maybe the rider was happy Emma Rae was smashed up and stuck in the hospital.

Jessica bit her lip and stared, transfixed by the horses, each one acting the same as they did yesterday. The impatient bay still pawed. The nervous gray still chewed at his bit, and the pretty chestnut still flattened her ears when Assets called to her. The grooms still patted their horses. The exercise riders still twirled their whips.

Even though Buddy was gone.

She couldn't expect everyone to act differently. If Buddy were alive, he'd be eating hay too. He'd be dropping pieces of alfalfa over his stall guard and blowing his warm breath down the back of her neck. She was lucky to have known him, and she'd never ever forget him.

And she was going to walk into his empty stall and say thank you, and maybe find a piece of his tail to wrap in plastic and keep forever.

"Good morning, Jessica," Dino said as he walked past.

"Good morning, Dino." She paused. "Thanks for last night."

"We've all gone through it, honey," Dino said, his handsome face uncharacteristically solemn. "Believe me, it never gets any easier."

She forced a nod. *But it can't get any harder.* She saw Mark standing across from Buddy's stall and smiled at him because, even if he didn't want her, she couldn't stop loving him. He smiled back, a deep gentle smile that made her heart lurch, and she didn't feel quite so dead.

A bay horse with a star on his forehead stuck his head out of Buddy's stall, and her heart froze. Cathy Wright walked up to Mark, kissed his cheek and said how much she liked TV Trooper.

Jessica's legs turned clumsy, but she forced them to carry her past Mark and Cathy, past the new horse, Trooper, who'd settled so nicely into Buddy's stall. She heard them talking about Aqueduct and how much fun Trooper would be, and how they might go to Florida.

She shivered in the doorway and struggled to breathe.

"Cold?"

She knew it was Mark but didn't turn around. "Nothing matters to you, does it?" she whispered brokenly. And she wanted him to hug and comfort her but knew he wouldn't because he was at the track and everyone would see.

"Jesus, Jessica. Trust me a little bit." He left her and returned to Cathy, and her heart shriveled.

She circled to the back. There wasn't much to pack: Abdul's drawing, Kato's dish, Buddy's win picture. She threw away the old Mars Bar wrapper, tossed her bag over her shoulder and walked away.

CHAPTER THIRTY-TWO

"That's right, young lady." The doctor peered at Jessica over half-moon glasses and resumed writing. "No clinical signs of damage."

"You mean my knee is fine?" She gripped the edge of the examining table, stunned by his pronouncement.

"It's perfect. But you'll always have a little scar and some needle marks." He shook his head. "I don't understand the needling, but maybe you were looked after in a…primitive hospital?"

She stumbled to her feet and walked dully into the street. The track was eight blocks to her right, her grandfather's house a two-hour bus ride to the left. Neither was an option.

The concrete sidewalk stretched in front of her and she shuffled along in a trance, picturing her grandfather's smug expression when he'd said she couldn't ski any more, how he'd patted her hand and said it was for the best. Rage filled her.

Mark had been right.

She slumped against a wall bright with graffiti while people and traffic streamed past. The rush, the babble, the confusion were so foreign, her head pounded, and it seemed like her entire world had derailed.

A teenager talked on a corner payphone, gesturing with one hand and gripping the arm of a pig-tailed child in the other. When she hung up, the phone would be free. Jessica could confront her grandfather. If she had a quarter.

She patted her pockets and felt the bulge of an envelope. Oh God, Buddy's money. Unneeded now. Of course, she should return it. She should walk back to the track, pass it to Mark, and clean Trooper's stall. She'd only been gone five hours. He might not even know she'd left.

But he didn't want her sleeping in the barn. He'd feel responsible and take her home even though all he really wanted to do was prepare for the Breeders' Cup.

The teenager left the phone booth and jogged across the honking street, child in tow. Okay, so now the phone was free. She could call her grandfather and tell him he was a cruel, controlling snake.

She hesitated, staring at the phone and chewing on her lip until it throbbed. If her grandfather suspected Mark had pointed her to the truth, he might move Assets out of spite. Probably safer to wait six days before confronting him. At least give Mark his Breeders' Cup.

An orange and white ambulance screamed past, curling through a line of clogged cars, and she wondered if it headed to Dick's hospital. Maybe she'd visit him again. She had plenty of time now, and Dick was always happy to see her.

But not today. Today she needed a cheap place where she could hole up, a place where she didn't have to talk, a place where her battered heart had a chance to heal.

CHAPTER THIRTY-THREE

"Guess I'll rewrap him," Mark said as he bent over Assets' legs. "I like the bandage lower on his hind. Protects him when he kicks the wall." He couldn't look at Dino. Felt sick. Wanted to hide Assets, not gift-wrap him.

Dino scowled and tossed Mark another rolled bandage. "Don't know why you worry."

"I still want the colt to win on Saturday."

"You're more generous than me. Boone moving all three?"

"Yeah." Mark thought he managed to keep his voice level, but his hands fumbled, and he dropped the wrap in the straw and had to start again.

"They're here, boss," Carlos said as his glum face appeared over the stall guard.

Mark glanced up and saw Trish and two other grooms he recognized from Radcliff's barn. They shuffled in, slightly self-conscious, with lead ropes slung over their shoulders. He gave Assets a last pat and left his gloomy barn.

Radcliff sat on a golf cart in front of the shedrow, waiting for his new horses. Assets appeared first, prancing and tossing his head, excited about this change in his routine. His sleek muscles rippled beneath the sun.

Radcliff glanced at Mark. "Looks fit," he said grudgingly.

"He is," Mark said, just as grudgingly.

Next came the talented filly, Belle. She snorted as she stepped outside, as though surprised she'd been taken from her lunch, but trustingly followed her new groom down the road.

"Belle coliced two months ago. Doing well now though." Mark cleared his throat as the last one, hip 665, walked out. Maria called him Rocky, and he strutted after his stablemates, as though aware people watched and fully anticipated their admiration.

"That's the Hard Spun colt that I...Boone, bought at Keeneland," Mark said. "He's got a few hives. Allergic to alfalfa."

Radcliff nodded. "All right." He nodded, straightened in the cart and sped after his new horses.

"Did you tell him not to run Assets in blinkers?" Dino's voice tightened with resentment as he watched Radcliff's receding cart.

"Guess I forgot," Mark said, glancing at his employees who stood in a solid ring by the barn door. "Call a staff meeting. Gotta figure a way to get through this. Carlos and Maria might need a loan. They were depending on Breeders' Cup bonuses. So were some of the hots and riders."

"Don't know if we can swing it." Dino shook his head. "The account is damn low."

"We'll make it work. I'm going to set up a new schedule too, so everyone gets a day off."

He gripped his phone as he headed towards his office. Owners rarely switched trainers five days before a Grade 1 race and even more rarely before the Breeders' Cup. In a few hours the media would call, eager to hear the dirt. But he had a few hours of relative peace, and he needed to regroup.

He walked in, closed the door and stared at the gap on the wall above his desk. That hole wouldn't be filled this year, maybe never. A trainer could wait a long time for a horse like Assets. "God damn you, Boone!" He kicked his chair, watching as it flipped upside down and crashed against the desk.

"Fire her, or I'll take my horses," Boone had said. He hadn't been bluffing.

Mark dropped his head in his hands. He didn't think Jessica had anything to do with the horses moving, but she'd looked so bruised this morning, she probably wouldn't have tried to stop her grandfather. He knew she wouldn't have picked Radcliff as their trainer. That had been Mark's last-ditch negotiation.

He swore again.

How could she doubt how he felt? He'd shown her in every possible way, bent every single rule. He'd always feared she was attracted to him because he was the boss, and granted, that had made him a little edgy. Food and shelter ranked high on anybody's list, and Jessica was a pragmatic woman. But it was impossible to run around the barn holding her hand every minute.

And this morning she'd walked away, just like Boone's horses. No doubt winging her way to Europe or wherever it was they skied. At least she finally escaped her grandfather's sticky web.

He ripped out Boone's contact sheet, balled it up and tossed it into his wastebasket. Time to move on. The Boone family left a sour taste in his mouth, and he had a racing business to keep afloat.

He groaned as the phone buzzed insistently. Radcliff had probably called the media, delighted to spread the juicy news. But the display showed Kurt MacKinnon.

Mark slowly opened the phone.

"Your friend belongs to an Emirati group," Kurt said, "who believe the UAE rulers are apostates violating Islamic law. A small timer, name of Josef Haddad."

Mark blew out a sigh. "Why is he here?"

"No idea. Maybe he thinks your horse is owned by the sheikh," Kurt said. "Need some help? Want me fly up?"

"Not necessary."

"I have some people I can call." Kurt sounded concerned. "They'll keep anything safe."

"Thanks..." Mark cleared his throat. "But it's no longer my problem. Owner pulled all his horses half an hour ago."

"Jesus, what an asshole! Who got them?"

"Radcliff."

"Your horse run in blinkers?"

"No."

"Good. Radcliff sticks them on all his two-year-olds. Your ex-owner just lost the Breeders' Cup." Kurt's chuckle was deep and wicked, and Mark could picture him relaxed in his chair, feet propped on his desk, sucking on a coffee. "Tough to lose a horse like that," Kurt added. "But I saw the colt at the sale and didn't bother to bid. You spotted him, turned him into a racehorse. You can do it again."

"I need money though," Mark said wryly. "Is there a reward on this Haddad fellow?"

"Jesus, don't go near him." Kurt's voice hardened. "And in an hour some of our intel people will be calling you with a shitload of questions. Sorry, buddy, couldn't stop them. Not when they learned Haddad's name." He chuckled. "At least without a big horse, you now have some spare time."

"Always a bright side," Mark said.

CHAPTER THIRTY-FOUR

Dick adjusted the top of his hospital gown. His hand lingered over the angry purple line on his neck, and he made a rueful face.

"The scar's not so bad," Jessica said. "It gives you a rugged look."

"My dear, that is not a look I ascribe to."

No, that was more Mark's look, she thought. That dark stubble before he shaved, the way his jaw set when he was annoyed, how his muscles rippled when he was all sweaty—

Dick rolled his eyes. "You're thinking of him again."

"I am not." She filled Dick's water glass, eager for something to do. "Now that I've left the track, I hardly think of him at all." Except when she was awake. She turned away from Dick's knowing smile and stared out the window.

Saturday morning, Breeders' Cup day. Traffic was only moderate but probably jammed at the track. Tomorrow she'd call her grandfather and ask some tough questions. Then drop by the track and congratulate Mark. She had no doubt Assets would win. She'd also tell Mark he'd been right about her knee and thank him for everything. Pay back his money and apologize for leaving because he had put Cathy's horse in Buddy's stall.

Maybe they could keep seeing each other even though she was unemployed and homeless and impulsive, and he could pick from any number of successful women. Confident women like Cathy or Emma Rae. Or maybe he'd already decided she was simply too much trouble.

Her hand trembled, and she tugged the curtain back, hoping the sliver of sun would warm her thoughts.

She should be happy. She was healthy and could do anything she wanted. Didn't have to worry about pleasing her grandfather any more—or for that matter, Mark. Dick had it way worse. He was stuck in a hospital bed, and his well-wishers had trickled down to a grand total of one.

"It's a different world, isn't it?" She glanced over her shoulder at Dick. "The backside. It's tough and transient and everyone forgets you in a heartbeat. Why do people do it?"

"Some because that's all they can do," Dick said. "Others because they can't not do it."

"You must be in the second category?"

"You tell me. But every winter my boss moves his stable to Florida, and I stay in New York and fundraise. And every spring I end up at the track. The horses get in your blood until it's not even a choice. And my dear, if you can't be happy with a man who thrives on strange hours and stranger owners and is maybe thinking of a horse instead of you, then you better keep running."

"I'm not running. And it's only been five days." She wheeled from the window. "Besides, he wouldn't keep me on as a groom."

"Maybe he doesn't want you as a groom. Oh, don't glower so." Dick patted the bed. "Come sit down. The television is hooked up, and we have a perfect view of the Breeder's Cup. We can criticize the clothes, pick out the ugliest hat and you can point out all the rich folk so I can hit them up for a donation."

"Damn clean in here." Dino stepped into Mark's office, squeezing past a cardboard box bulging with tattered condition books, stained liniment bottles and two cracked helmets.

"Yeah," Mark said. "Found another bottle of rum in the filing cabinet too. Maybe Dutch will want to celebrate later."

"Don't know. Those California sprinters look tough."

"They are. But just having a horse running in the Cup…" He shrugged and poured Dino a coffee.

Dino settled back in his chair and flipped open *The Racing Form*. "You going over to watch?"

"Nope. Found the little TV when I cleaned up. I'll watch from here."

Dino nodded, sipping coffee and scanning *The Form*. "Assets is down to even money," he said. "Sheikh's horse is four to one. I'm thinking it's a good day to bet against the favorite. Oh, and here's another picture of you and Radcliff. Nice shot of you, but

Radcliff looks shifty." He grinned. "No wonder. This is written by that pretty little reporter who felt so sorry for you."

Mark drank his coffee while Dino poked fun at the articles, clearly trying to make him smile. Seven more hours and it would be over. Seven more excruciating hours.

"More 'no comments' from you," Dino said, his eyes hidden by his hat. "Oh, but this is a good quote from Boone. 'Trainer just wanted to fuck my granddaughter.'"

Mark half rose, then sank back while Dino chuckled. Mark scowled and propped his boots on the desk, not appreciating the joke. "You're loving this, aren't you?"

Dino grinned and tossed *The Form* aside. "Can't help it. You've always been so focused. I never dreamed you'd toss it all for a woman. That's my job." He sobered. "Any regrets? Now that the big dance is here, and Radcliff has your horse?"

"Nope."

"Think Assets will win?" Dino asked.

Mark shook his head, already aching for the cocky colt who was going to have his heart broken today. He didn't want to see it, wanted Assets to run well, but the colt was feeling too good, had drawn the inside post and was bound to go with the speed horse in the four hole.

"If Radcliff runs him in blinkers, they'll run that first quarter in just over twenty-two and burn out by the eighth pole. Radcliff is using that hotshot jockey from California, and the long stretch will kill them. Damn shame."

"Stop. You're making me cry." Dino snorted. "So that's two races the sheikh will win today. Looks like the Classic is his too, now that Spud's horse is out. Did they get the necropsy report back on that horse?"

"Haven't heard, but security is beefed up. It's tighter than a drum now."

Dino drained his coffee and stretched. "I'm off to lay some bets. See if I can make enough money to get me through the winter." He paused, fingering one of five cell phones strewn on Mark's desk. "This looks like my old phone."

"Nope, that one was Lefty's. But if you have a charger, plug it in. No one knows his next of kin. Maybe I can find someone to notify. And do something useful today."

Dick tied his Keeneland scarf with an elaborate flair and posed in front of the disapproving nurse. "How do I look?"

"Like you're well enough to go home." The nurse gave a disapproving sniff. "There's way too much of a party atmosphere in this room."

"I'm leaving your fine establishment tomorrow." Dick opened an oblong box and offered her a chocolate. "And the Breeders' Cup only comes once a year. It's sold out, but Jessica and I plan to enjoy it on television."

"What's the Breeders' Cup?" the nurse asked, biting into the chocolate. "Is that like the Kentucky Derby?"

"No, Breeder's Cup is two days in the fall when the best Thoroughbreds from all over the world meet in a lot of different races. Two-year-old races, turf races, dirt races, sprints. The Derby is one race on the first Saturday in May. It's only for three-year olds."

"Which race has the most money?" the nurse asked, eying the TV speculatively.

"Today's biggest race is four million, way more than the Derby. The owner gets most of it, but winning trainers and jockeys get ten percent. Of course, what it does for their reputation is priceless."

"Do you have a horse running?" She studied the chocolates before picking another one from the box.

"No, but Jessica touched a Breeders' Cup horse once. Let me tell you about that. It was a cloudy day in September—"

"Some other time." The nurse glanced toward the door, checking her escape route, grabbed a third chocolate and fled.

Dick gave a satisfied grin. "And that's how you get rid of the nurses, Jessica. Bore them to tears, and they won't be back for hours. It's safe now. Shut the door and crack the peach schnapps."

"Is this a traditional Breeders Cup drink?" Jessica asked, pulling out the smuggled bottles and mixing a generous measure of peach schnapps, orange juice and ice. "Glad it's not rum." Her stomach still lurched at the thought of rum, although this Fuzzy Navel drink smelled delicious. "Sorry I couldn't find a *Racing*

Form," she added. "I got off the bus twice to check some stores, but no one had any left."

"It's all right." Dick raised a sardonic eyebrow. "It's doubtful the hospital has off-track betting, and I already know I'm cheering for the Irish boys and their adorable accents. Except, of course, your man's horse. I do hope Ambling Assets wins the Juvenile."

My man. I wish. Jessica's skin pricked with anticipation. In an hour or so, she'd see Mark. Sure, it was only on TV, but she was going to see him. She couldn't imagine being in the shedrow now. Mark and Dino and Carlos and Squeaky must be out of their minds trying to hide their nervousness from the colt.

She wondered if Assets knew he was going to race. Buddy had always known. The change in routine, the tension of the handlers and, of course, once Assets left for the assembly barn the media would be all over him. Carlos and Mark would have to walk over, circled by cameras and microphones and questions.

"When is the Juvenile?" She rose and dragged out a more comfortable chair, not wanting to see the pretty face that now filled the small screen.

"Second race, right after the fillies," Dick said, his gaze on the TV. "Wow, look at the ESPN lady and her stylish outfit. Now that is fetching."

"Don't you think the color washes her out?" Jessica asked. "Especially with such bleached blond hair?"

"Meow," Dick said with a knowing smirk.

She slammed more ice in her glass, turning her head from Cathy Wright and her truly gorgeous appearance.

Coverage switched back to a retired jockey flanked by two solemn-sounding men, and Jessica sank back in her chair. "Who usually interviews the winners?" she asked. "I hope it's the jockey. He has more interesting stuff to say than Cathy."

"Yes, he's good at providing color. But Ms. Wright's job is to find the provocative questions." Dick openly leered. "My, she certainly is provocative."

Jessica tossed an ice cube at him. "I like the retired jockey best. He's much more interesting."

They watched the young fillies circle the paddock. A few looked calm, but most pranced and jittered and rolled their eyes at the surging crowd. "Poor babies," she said.

"They'll be okay once they get on the track," Dick said. "And if they run well today, they can look forward to a pampered life of freedom, grass and studly visits."

"Studly visits? How like a man." She shook her head but her thoughts skipped to Mark. Her breathing sped up, and she wiggled in her hard chair. If she found a job with afternoons off—and if he wasn't with Cathy—maybe she could still see him. He'd have to leave at four, of course, to return to the barn, and she'd have to leave and go back to her job. She wouldn't be able to groom horses any more though. And that was truly depressing.

And then it happened as it always did, when it seemed the race would never come, but there they were, loading the horses in the gate. Jessica felt proud as each young filly walked in and stood like a seasoned pro. Just babies really, but they knew their jobs. She prayed each one would break clean and bring their rider home safe. When Dick asked who she liked, she only shook her head blankly.

She did cheer one filly on though, a petite bay who shot from the four hole and grabbed the lead, leading the pack joyously around the track. But she strained down the long stretch, and it was clear she was exhausted. The filly wobbled, and the jockey pushed, but a long-legged chestnut appeared on the outside, strong and eager, looking like she just realized it was a race. The chestnut surged past everyone, running like a champ, but Jessica felt sorry for the little bay who had so bravely led the way.

Do they even know how long the race is, she wondered, realizing now why Mark liked his jockeys to work the horses and familiarize themselves with any quirks. She thought of Steve, Assets' jockey, who was probably pulling on his shiny leather boots, getting ready to meet Assets in the paddock. Soon Mark would leg him up and off they'd go. She desperately wished she were there.

She wiped her warm forehead, clinked more ice in her drink and looked at Dick who just winked and said, "Soon."

"Did you ever rub a big horse?"

"No," he said. "I've only worked for claiming barns. But even at the lowest level, I think the trainers worry as much, and the horses want to win as much, and the workers love them every bit as much."

"I think you're right," Jessica said, remembering Buddy and how proudly he pranced after his win, as though saying, "Wasn't I great!"

The lump that clogged her throat whenever she thought of Buddy remained, but it was a bit smaller, and she could smile when she pictured him. The commercial break ended, and it was time for the Juvenile. Even Dick plucked at his scarf as Cathy introduced the twelve two-year olds. Jessica saw Assets right away, and he looked good. Not scared of the crowd as he strutted with his typical cockiness. But it wasn't Carlos leading him—it wasn't anyone Jessica knew.

"Turn the volume up, Dick." She dragged her chair closer to the screen but already coverage switched. She jerked forward, staring at two familiar faces. Cathy's perfect eyebrow arched as she turned to the white-haired man beside her, and Gramps nodded and looked grave.

"Yes. We had a fundamental difference of opinion, so it was necessary to switch trainers," her grandfather said.

"Your original trainer, Mark Russell, selected this unheralded colt from hundreds of prospects and then developed him into a world-class racehorse. Prevailing opinion says it was spiteful to move Ambling Assets to another barn only days before the biggest race of his career. What's your comment on that, Mr. Boone?"

"Everyone has an opinion. I just want the horse to run his best today, and I feel he'll do that with Mr. Radcliff."

Cathy nodded but looked at the camera, frowning in a way that showed her skepticism. "You've also elected to change jockeys, despite the fact that Steve Murray has been the colt's regular rider—in fact, the colt's *only* rider. Won't that hamper your horse today, especially when he'll have to hold off the late-running charge of Desert Bloom?"

Jessica stopped breathing. She stared at the screen, watching her grandfather's lips clench. He was clearly annoyed, but Cathy nodded and acted so sweet, and Jessica knew he didn't want to walk away and prove he was a spiteful, manipulative man.

"The blinkers are also a new addition," Cathy added with a deadly smile. "Records show this horse has never raced or worked in blinkers, and it seems odd—"

"I have to go," Gramps muttered. He turned and walked away.

Cathy's disapproving face filled the screen. Her mouth moved, but the roaring in Jessica's ears was too loud. Gasping, she pressed her hands to her head and staggered to the bed.

Even Dick looked stunned.

Mark turned the sound up on his tiny TV, watching as Assets strutted around the paddock and nipped at his handler. Completely unfazed by the crowds, the cameras and the occasion.

What a horse. And he no longer cared about the circumstances or Boone or Radcliff. He just wanted Assets to win.

"Don't use a hood," he willed, but of course Radcliff thought he knew best. He stepped up to the colt and buckled on blue blinkers, color coordinated with Boone's checkered silks. And Mark could see Assets swell with resentment, could see his neck darken with sweat even though they were still in the paddock.

Then Mark couldn't see Assets because the sheikh's horse, Desert Bloom, filled the screen, a calm, cool colt with a floating walk, and Mark feared it would be Sheikh Khalif being whisked into the winner's circle today. The TV flashed an image of a forlorn Steve left in the jock's room, watching the monitor as a strange jockey was boosted onto Assets' back. Anger burned Mark. He couldn't stand to watch any more and snapped off the television.

He yanked Lefty's phone from Dino's charger, but his fingers were clumsy with emotion and he couldn't pull up the directory. Kept hitting the camera feature which was fucking useless. Just dark, blurred pictures of a long box and two men digging up the infield next to the great Ruffian's grave. Looked a bit like Haddad, except for the gardener's outfit.

The next picture showed Haddad staring with the same flat eyes Mark had seen in Dick's picture. Lefty's last image was a blur of bike spokes and ground.

Mark leaped from his chair so fast it smashed against the wall. "Jesus Christ!" He grabbed his phone and bolted from the office.

He pushed through the backstretch workers who crowded around the gap, applauding the line of horses as they approached the starting gate. Mark shielded his eyes from the sun and frantically scanned the infield. The lake glittered benignly. A flag fluttered close to Ruffian's grave. He couldn't see if anyone lingered by the floral horseshoe, only saw confusing masses of people as they swarmed the grandstand.

He pressed Dino's number and charged toward the clubhouse, grappling with his horrible suspicions and trying to picture the winner's circle. For Breeders' Cup, they used an elevated podium on the inner side of the track. Close enough to Ruffian's grave.

"Is there a clear path from the infield to the winner's circle?" Mark asked when Dino finally answered his phone.

"Going to charge in and grab the trophy?" Dino gave a nasty chuckle. "Good idea. I'll help."

"Lefty's phone had some pictures." Urgency sharpened Mark's voice. "This Middle East thing—the thefts, the poisonings—it could be all about getting the sheikh *into* the winner's circle so Haddad can take a clean shot. Now the sheikh has a good chance of winning both the Juvenile and the Classic." Mark waved his credentials, phone pressed to his ear as he rushed past a vigilant ticket lady. "The sheikh always watches from a safe location. So the only reason he'd brave the crowd would be if he won."

"But he'll have bodyguards," Dino said, "and nobody can get a gun onto the track."

"The bodyguards will face the crowd. But the winner's circle is against the infield. I think they already hid a weapon by Ruffian's grave, probably the night Lefty drowned—if the poor guy really did drown. We have to alert security."

The bell clanged and the crowd roared. Mark wheeled and stared at the big screen above the paddock, watching as Assets burst from the gate and charged to the lead. "Where are you, Dino?" he yelled into the phone.

"Just past the finish line."

"Go, boy," Mark murmured to Assets then rushed through the pods of people gathered around screens and monitors and doorways. He heard yells, cheers and the time of the suicidal first quarter. Could see Assets' blinkered head leading down the lane, saw the jockey flail with his whip, saw the horse's great courage as he fought to respond.

Mark groaned as the sheikh's horse edged up, challenging for the lead. The stretch was so fucking long. And then another horse appeared, and another, and Assets' blue head was lost in a wave of horses. Mark watched as the colt staggered across the finish line, exhausted, beaten, bewildered.

"You still there, Dino?"

"Yeah, broke my heart."

"Sheikh's horse get it?" Mark asked.

"Yeah. If the sheikh shows up for the presentation, they'll escort him out the side gate and up a small flight of stairs to the winner's circle."

Mark rushed up the grandstand steps, shrugging off the usher's prim request to see his wristband. He pressed his binoculars against his face and scanned the infield. Saw a wheelbarrow by the floral grave, but no Haddad.

"Looks like they've moved, Dino," he said into the phone. "They could be with the media people by the inner rail. See anyone with a blanket over their camera?"

"About twenty of them," Dino said, his voice edgy. "I've grabbed a security guard. He's with me now."

A microphone was stuck in Mark's face. "Mr. Russell, do you think the fast quarter had any bearing on Assets' meltdown?"

"Not now." He pushed past the reporter, his gaze on the returning horses. Assets trotted back sound, thank God, and there was the sheikh's horse being met by his triumphant trainer. Maybe the sheikh wasn't coming; maybe he knew he'd be vulnerable. Mark scanned the infield, forcing his breathing to steady.

But a huge black limo cruised to a stop in front of the winner's platform, and out surged a group of men and—oh, Christ, there was the sheikh.

Mark scrutinized the photographers on the inner rail, all bent over their cameras, all surrounded by a confusion of equipment. There was even gear loaded on a golf cart protected by a large sunshield.

His heart jerked as he spotted Haddad's face, shaven now, but recognizable. "Dino," he yelled, "Haddad's in the golf cart!"

He jammed his phone and Dino's voice into his pocket and leaped over the rail, knowing there wasn't time to explain. Whipped through the group of milling runners and up the steps to the winner's circle where Desert Bloom's connections jubilantly assembled.

A hard-eyed man blocked his way.

"Man with a gun!" Mark gestured, knowing time was running out, but the man grabbed his arm. Mark drove his elbow into his face and charged onto the platform. Saw the trophy, the proud smiles, Sheikh Khalif's outstretched hands.

"Get down!" He lunged toward the sheikh.

Shouts, curses. Something ripped his shoulder, slamming him into the carpet. He tried to rise, but his arms were stuck and a vise squeezed his neck. Impossible to breathe. He struggled, desperate. His lungs burned. Bodies pressed against him, screaming in a language he didn't understand. Then everything stopped hurting. His spotting vision faded, and he was sucked into a vortex of black.

Jessica watched the race numbly, trying to absorb the fact that Assets was now in another barn, racing for another trainer. Racing well, too. His distinctive blue blinkers led the charge. He looked like a knight's horse, only Radcliff and her grandfather certainly weren't chivalrous knights.

"Such a low blow. Hope Assets doesn't win," Dick said. "Where's my Irish horse?"

Bile filled Jessica's throat. To be so close and have your dream yanked away. Mark didn't deserve this. There was nothing he could have done to deserve this. She stared at the screen in a nauseous haze as a flood of horses surged to the wire, passing Assets who struggled gamely but finished sixth.

"Ha! No money there," Dick said. "Who is this Boone prick?"

"My grandfather." Her voice cracked. "And I need to call him if I can borrow your phone."

"It's in the Bible drawer, but please let me see this first. Good grief." Dick shook his head in disgust. "The sheikh can't walk across the track. Has to be driven to the winner's circle. Talk about paranoid."

313

She fumbled through Dick's drawer and pulled out his phone.

"Oh, dear," Dick said, and the regret in his voice pulled her gaze back to the television. She gripped the phone, watching in disbelief as Mark burst into the winner's circle and tried to steal the sheikh's trophy. Faces swarmed, and coverage abruptly switched to the retired jockey and his two cronies.

"Well," the first man said, staring blankly at his companions. "Well…"

The retired jockey waited a beat then smoothly filled the silence. "They say pace makes the race, and this was a clear example of Ambling Assets being used too early. The fast quarter set up for a closer, and Desert Bloom benefited from the scenario today." He glanced at his fellow commentators, but they remained silent, staring at something beyond the camera.

"There's a delay with the trophy presentation, so we'll return after the commercial break," the jockey added, obviously conditioned to think much more nimbly than his media cronies.

Dick gave Jessica a comforting hug. "Mark simply had too much pressure. And then to lose Assets. Any man would crack. But he'll recover."

She nodded, her voice splitting. "He really wanted to win the Breeder's Cup. Nothing was more important."

They sat in silence through the endless truck and airline and beer commercials. Finally Cathy Wright's strained face filled the screen.

"There was an attempt on Sheikh Khalif's life," she said, "bravely thwarted by Mark Russell, a Belmont trainer who's been removed in an ambulance. Emergency vehicles are behind the finish line where two more men are down. We'll keep you updated, but there was never any spectator danger. I repeat, there is no danger. Now it's back to the paddock to meet the horses for the third race."

Jessica staggered against the bed frame, struggling to absorb Cathy's words. Mark was hurt. *Oh, God. Please, please, please let him be all right. Please, just let him live. Please, God. Let him live.*

"Where will they take him?" she finally managed, her voice small and scared and shaky.

"Not sure. Maybe North Shore. The jockeys prefer that hospital."

"Is that where they took Emma Rae?" she asked. "The same place where we sent the flowers?"

"Yes." Dick pulled his chair closer, and they stared at the television. Horses were running and one was winning, but she had no idea who it was or even what race it was. She just wanted to see Cathy. She'd know from Cathy's expression if Mark were alive. She dropped her head in her hands and cried.

CHAPTER THIRTY-FIVE

"Front page news. Aren't you the hero." Dino grinned and tossed two newspapers onto the crisp white sheets of the hospital bed.

"How did Dutch do?" Mark winced as he reached for the sports page.

"Eighth, but he had a good time. We drank all your rum, by the way."

"Good. Who won the Classic?"

"The runner from Canada. Total surprise. Haddad picked the wrong horse to poison for that race."

"Did Assets come back okay?" Mark asked as he scanned the Breeders' Cup results.

"Heard he did. But we've been pretty busy. Had to put up a 'No Media' sign, or we wouldn't have been able to get anything done." Dino dragged a chair closer to the bed. His voice lowered as he glanced toward the door. "So I guess the sheikh is grateful. What did he say?"

"He said 'thanks.'"

"That's it? Come on. You saved his life. And there's a crazy-eyed man standing outside checking visitors. Either he thought I was another assassin, or the sheikh left a cash reward in your closet that he's guarding."

"Nope, he only left a guard." Mark grinned. "But he did promise to send me some horses."

"Really?" Dino's face brightened, and he pumped his fist. "This is almost worth it then. Wonder what he'll send."

"Probably two-year-olds."

"Hot damn." Dino bounced a circle around the room. "Cathy dubbed you the best two-year-old trainer in North America. People believe everything they hear on television."

"Make sure her name is on that visitors' list." Mark coughed, trying not to grimace at the pain radiating from his wound.

Dino leaned forward, his eyes concerned. "What happened to your voice? It's all hoarse."

Mark glanced warily at the door. "Either the anesthetic or that damn bodyguard when he was trying to choke me. Move slow around him, Dino. He's the one I got by, and he didn't like it. Almost killed me. Has hands like meat hooks."

"But why's he checking visitors?"

"Sheikh's orders. He asked me not to talk to the media." Mark shrugged. "Haddad is dead and the other guy's in custody, so I expect interest will disappear quick enough." He flipped the paper in frustration. "Did you get all the horses out today?"

"Yeah, but barely. The backside's swarming, and cops cordoned off the area around the lake. Now they think Haddad killed Lefty because he saw them bury the gun and snapped some pictures. Poor old Lefty. He was probably pumping that bike like crazy, trying to get away."

"Yeah, he stuck the phone under the seat. Jessica was lucky. Haddad thought she had Lefty's phone." Mark pretended a renewed interest in the paper but could make no sense of the words. He had told Jessica he'd wait—that day sitting on the grass—and maybe, just maybe, she was still around. "Did you see her with Boone yesterday?" he asked, careful to keep his voice neutral.

"Who? Jessica?"

"Well, of course, Jessica." He jerked his head up in time to spot Dino's knowing smile.

"No, she wasn't with Boone. But she told Maria she'd call her." Dino sobered. "Guess she flew the coop."

"Yeah, maybe she went to Europe. She's a skier, you know." Mark continued to stare blankly at the paper.

"Well, she wasn't with Boone," Dino repeated. "When you getting out?"

"Need another operation to tighten some ligaments. The bullet's out though. You okay running things?"

"Sure am. I'm loving it." Dino winked. "Tomorrow I'm going to make everyone call me 'boss.' Might have to start my own stable."

"Just make sure you put rundown bandages on that gray filly. She's hard on herself. And get some bar shoes on Trooper. And I'm a little worried about that knee..." Mark sucked in a breath and quit talking. Dino knew exactly what to do. Besides, his throat hurt, and he didn't want to think anymore about shoes and knees and Jessica.

"Just one more minute," Jessica said, staring at the computer screen.

"This is a women's shelter," the clerk snapped, "not your personal office."

Jessica ignored her, desperate to read the race news. *"In a bizarre twist, Mark Russell, who only days earlier saw his champion runner whisked to another stable, saved the life of a sheikh and is now hailed as a hero. Mark is recovering at North Shore University Hospital and is expected to be able to return to the track within weeks."*

He was going to be fine! *Thank you, God.* She glanced at her watch, shaky with relief. North Shore. A half-hour bus ride. She'd promised Dick she would help him move to his home upstate, but first she had to see Mark. She grabbed her bag, thanked the clerk for the week's accommodations and rushed out.

Forty minutes later Jessica was in the hospital lobby, surrounded by anxious eyes and strained faces. She weaved through the crowd, making her way to the reception desk. "Excuse me," she said. "Can you tell me the number of Mark Russell's room?"

The lady checked her records, then glanced up, shaking her head. "Sorry. His room is closed to visitors."

"But can you tell me how he's doing?" Jessica asked.

"No, I'm sorry. Check with his family."

"But I am family. I just flew in from Texas." She added a slight drawl, lifted her leather bag and rested it against the counter.

"Well," the receptionist said, her face softening in sympathy, "I can't give the room number, but you're welcome to report to the desk on the fifth floor."

"Thanks." Jessica eagerly wheeled around.

However, the nurse on the fifth floor was much tougher. "You'll have to show me some identification," she said, barely looking up from her mound of forms.

Jessica pulled out her driver's license. "I'm married, so of course my brother and I have different last names."

"I see. Well, I'll have the attending doctor speak to you when she arrives." The nurse slapped the documents on her desk. "That will be in three hours. And you'll have to show something that proves you're related."

"But I don't want to speak to the doctor. I just need to see my brother."

"Look," the nurse said, devoid of humor. "We're very busy, and these media stunts only make our job more difficult. You're the third person to claim they're Mr. Russell's sister. It didn't work yesterday, and it's not going to work today."

"I'm not actually media." Jessica's hands shook as she replaced her driver's license and fumbled for her track credentials. "Look, I'm really his groom. And we have a horse that is sick, and only Mark knows what to do, so please, just let me see him for a minute. I h-have to see him." She didn't plan to cry, even though it would have been a nice touch, but her voice cracked, and the tears pricking her eyes were utterly genuine.

"What's wrong with the horse?" the nurse asked, her voice slightly less chilly.

"I'm sorry. He w-was the best horse." Jessica rubbed her eyes, trying not to think of Buddy. "And Mark tried to look after him, tried to look after everyone, and now he's in the hospital. He had such a raw deal." She swiped at her cheeks, wishing she could stop crying.

The nurse leaned back in the chair, confusion lining her brow. "I can see you're upset," she finally said, "and I'm a horse lover too." Her voice lowered to a conspiratorial whisper. "Mr. Russell is in room five nineteen. Visitors are restricted, but you can check with the man at the door. He's very…strict."

"Thank you so much." Jessica picked up her bag and hurried down the rust-colored hall, past the patient room with the murmuring TV and into the smell of disinfectant, drugs and toast. She didn't know what to say, didn't know why she felt so weepy. She prayed a heartfelt apology would be enough. Her urgency increased until she was running.

A man with a thick neck unfolded from the wall, blocking her way. His chin was bruised, and a scar notched the right side of his cheek.

"Yes?" He spoke with a slight accent.

"I'm here to see Mark." She squared her shoulders and forced a tremulous smile. "Please," she added politely.

"Name?" He didn't smile back, just looked at his sheet.

"Jessica." She paused, reluctant to say Boone. But maybe this sullen man didn't follow horse racing. "Jessica Boone. I work for Mark."

"No."

"No, what?"

"You can't go in."

"Are you sure my name isn't there?" She stretched past him, trying to scan the short list.

"I've only been given one lady's name," he said. "And it's not yours."

"I can see that. But if you would just ask him, I'm sure, well I hope—"

"No."

"He's going to be released in a few weeks. Could you just ask him, please?" Her gaze flickered to the closed door. Five nineteen. Only a few feet, and she was fast. She could make a dash.

The man seemed to guess her thoughts; he grabbed the top of her arm with his huge hands and propelled her toward the elevator. "Go," he growled. "Don't come back."

He pushed her then, so abruptly she stumbled into the wall and smashed her elbow. She struggled to regain her balance, shocked by his aggressiveness. He stared at her with cold eyes, and she held his gaze for a moment—purely out of stubbornness—then turned away in defeat.

She'd never been treated so roughly, but the fact Mark didn't care enough to even put her name on his list scared her much more than any over-zealous guard.

"Do you want the clothes racks set up here or in the den?" Jessica rubbed her arms, unable to completely shake the memory of the aggressive guard, and glanced into the big room. Dick's winter home was spacious and creatively furnished, but the house had been vacant since spring, and the stale air only heightened its forlorn feel.

"Leave the racks for tomorrow." Dick waved a benevolent hand. "We moved enough today."

"We?"

"Mainly you," he said cheerfully, "but I did make some calls."

"There's no reason a neck injury should stop you from lifting. Tomorrow I'll do the phone work."

"You're in a bitchy mood, my dear. I may rethink you living here. Thought you'd be happier after Maria said Mark was recovering nicely."

Jessica sank into an overstuffed chair, centered the clipboard on her lap and blew out a sigh. "He didn't have my name on the visitors' list. Seven days, and he forgot me. Now it's all about Cathy."

"You're so quick to assume rejection. Maybe it wasn't a good time to see him."

"It's always a good time to see him." She clicked the end of her pen.

"So you can beg for a job? Offer yourself as his roomie?" The scorn in Dick's voice made her wince.

"What's wrong with living with him?" she muttered.

"Not a thing. And maybe he'd be happy with that. But you wouldn't. He's the hotshot trainer, getting hotter every day, and he makes me and countless others drool."

"And?"

"And he found the life that completes him. You need to find yours."

She forced a flippant smile, resenting the truth in Dick's words. "You just want me to stay and work for you."

"Yes, well, that too. Tomorrow I'll teach you how to work the phones." He opened the window, and a crisp autumn breeze freshened the room. "But you have to ask for clothes, not donations for horse retirement."

"I don't know anything about horse retirement."

"You know enough, and you're always talking about it. More importantly, you feel it. All you need is to set up a charitable foundation. Find some prominent directors. You already have the connections. Just do it."

She leaned back and let the wind cool her face. When she'd first walked into Dick's house, she'd felt foggy, unable to stop sneezing, but now her brain had cleared. She could picture clubhouse faces. People she knew, people with money who enjoyed watching their animals run and who might be grateful for a way to give back to the industry.

Some of them were on the *Forbes 500* list. Jessica knew one dynamic lady, Doris Rogers, whose style and opinions carried immeasurable weight. If she could convince Doris that helping racehorses was a worthy cause, her peers would rush to help. And the retired jockey who had covered the Breeders' Cup would be an excellent director. He was a good speaker with established connections. And she could invite a vet and other professionals to join.

She leaned forward, clicking her pen with growing enthusiasm. There would be much to learn. Much to do. But it seemed logical that if the horses were retrained, it would widen the adoption scope. Some people considered Thoroughbreds flighty, but Buddy had been much quieter than Mark's quarter horse, Ghost. And Thoroughbreds were certainly athletic.

There were probably many existing organizations happy to give advice, like The Thoroughbred Retirement Foundation. And she could talk to the Finger Lakes people and the Ferdinand group. One of Mark's magazines had detailed how Ferdinand, a Kentucky Derby winner, had ended his life in a Japanese meat factory. The sad story still left her sick.

She straightened her clipboard and began jotting names, ideas and plans and, for the first time in a week, stopped agonizing about Mark.

CHAPTER THIRTY-SIX

"The April auction raised over two hundred thousand, and Joe Wood is matching it, bless his heart." Doris sounded as gracious on the phone as she did in person. "Our next event is the celebrity dinner. Julie Krone has agreed to be the emcee. We also have the little Pony Club girl coming. Her horse never won a race, but oh my, he certainly can jump. This winter has been so much fun, dear," Doris added. "Thanks for letting me get involved. How are you making out in the country?"

"We have fourteen horses and twenty-four more stalls to be built. Five horses ready to be placed after two months of riding. The other ones need more work. Lots more work."

She said good-bye and closed her phone, shaking off her unease as she saw Jack, a tall bay with a crooked blaze, leap sideways and knock his handler to the ground. Jack looked like Buddy but had a personality like Assets. He wasn't fast enough to race so the owner had shipped him to Jessica, hoping she'd find him a more suitable career.

He might make a nice dressage horse with his brash attitude and big movement. He was a hard guy to work with though. Most of the staff were afraid of him, including her. Mark would have matched him with a groom who could appreciate the horse and simply focus his aggressiveness on winning. But she wasn't training horses to race, and most people wanted a more submissive personality. She simply didn't know how to handle the tough animals.

Another question for Maria, she thought, as she passed the ring and trudged back to the old farmhouse. Fourteen horses, and already she was swamped. She'd be in trouble with ten more, especially if they were challenging ones. Maybe she should concentrate on taking only the quiet horses, like Buddy. They were quicker to retrain and easier to place.

Best of all, the sensible ones could be turned out in the huge pasture. She paused to admire the mares as they gobbled the spring grass. On the other side of the fence, four geldings played like little boys. It was wonderful to watch them run free. If she had more time, she would have lingered for hours, enjoying their antics.

At least Doris handled the fundraising. Probably time to tell her to slow down. They'd already purchased the farm outright and after only six months of operation had so much money, the directors were nervous.

"This is a not-for-profit organization," they'd warned. "You need to build an indoor arena or pay the staff more. Whatever you do, spend it before year end."

Her phone chirped. She checked the display as she opened the porch door. Maria. She flipped open the phone, slamming the screen door in her haste to hear the latest in Abdul's legal wrangling. "What did the judge say?" she asked.

"Decision was postponed." Maria's voice quavered. "Even though our apartment is off track, she thinks our work hours are too irregular. Pedro wants to take Abdul and go back to Mexico before we lose him forever."

"Oh, no." Jessica squeezed her eyes shut and dropped into the closest chair, staggered by the news they might leave. Maria was still Jessica's closest friend. Jessica called her every afternoon, and it wasn't just to pepper her with horse questions. And Abdul! Jessica couldn't imagine not being able to see him. On her frequent trips to the city, she always stopped by their tiny apartment, despite how her heart pounded whenever she was within a two-mile radius of the track.

She swallowed and stared out the window, watching as Jack kicked the top rail, smashing it into two jagged splinters. "What a jerk," she said, in no mood to appreciate his spirit.

"Who?"

"Oh, nothing. It's just a horse here who needs an attitude adjustment. I wish you and Pedro could come and teach him some manners."

"If you could pay us, we'd come."

Hope jerked Jessica from the chair. "But of course I'd pay you. We need a stable manager. Someone who's used to bad actors. You and Pedro would be perfect. I just never dreamed you'd leave the track."

Or leave Mark. Jessica couldn't imagine anyone choosing to do that. A familiar excitement warmed her, just knowing she was going to hear his name. She tried to avoid asking many questions, but sometimes Maria passed on tidbits, and every night Jessica scanned her computer for race news.

After the Breeders' Cup, she'd written a check repaying Buddy's money. She'd also spent three days drafting a letter, but when Maria said Mark and Cathy seemed to be dating again, she'd ripped it up and immersed herself in establishing Buddy's Thoroughbred Retirement Center. At least she'd mailed the check. And if Mark wanted to talk, he'd find her. Last month there had been an article written about the Center, so he could find out where she lived. He simply hadn't cared enough to track her down.

He might care though if she stole one of his grooms. Might call and complain. Even pay a visit and yell. That thought sent a wicked thrill coursing through her body.

"I could come by your apartment and load everything in the horse trailer," Jessica said as she paced around the kitchen, excited now and talking fast. "Move you out in a few hours. But what would Mark think? You know, about you leaving? Leaving to work with me." She picked up an apple then dropped it back into the wooden bowl, unable to remain still.

"Oh, he wouldn't care," Maria said. "He'd replace me in an hour. People are always begging him for jobs. The sheikh is so happy with the way Mark developed Strike A Pose, he sent him more horses. Strike wasn't even a top two-year-old, but now has a shot at the Derby. Mark is so good with youngsters. Takes them slow. Willing to wait and let them mature."

The bottom of Jessica's stomach pitched, and she sank back in the chair. He wouldn't care. He wouldn't care if Maria walked, just like he hadn't cared about Jessica. She was barely able to concentrate as Maria continued talking about Mark's chances of winning the Kentucky Derby. No, it didn't sound like he'd chase after another errant groom—not when he had sheikhs calling with their fancy Derby horses.

She glumly reached for an apple again, unable to quiet her restless hands, unable to resist a little probing. "So how is everyone else doing?" she asked. "How's Trooper running for the ESPN people?"

"Pretty good. Emma Rae is healthy again and rode Trooper to a third. Strike won this weekend too, with Steve riding. That was Strike's last prep before the Derby."

Jessica palmed the apple, remaining silent, hoping for more. She already knew the race results, was glad Emma Rae was riding again, was glad Strike A Pose was a Derby favorite. But it was the barn gossip she wanted. She squeezed her eyes shut and finally asked, "So? Is Mark really seeing Cathy?"

"Hard to tell. He's reserved round the barn, but sometimes they leave together, and that's enough fuel for the *Tattler*. You should drop by. It's different now. We all get a day off and since the spring meet started, there're more people around. Everyone would love to see you."

"Really?" She walked down the hall and studied her face in the mirror. A strand of hair had escaped from her ponytail, and she tucked it behind her ear. She needed a haircut, maybe highlights. Cathy was always impeccably groomed.

She shook off her melancholy and grabbed a pen, jotting down numbers, trying to figure what salary would be generous enough but not too outrageously high for the accountants. A groom's pay was low, but the bonuses Mark handed out would be considerable. She didn't want Maria and Pedro to take a loss.

"What kind of salary would you need?" she asked.

"The judge wants to see a more traditional environment." Maria blew out a sigh. "We don't need a lot of money." She tentatively suggested a figure that was so low, Jessica tossed the pen aside, buoyed with fresh optimism.

"But we can at least double that." She gave a little skip as she crossed the kitchen, realizing this just might work. "And they built a new school here. The bus stops across the road and picks up a boy who looks about Abdul's age. His name's Timmy and he loves horses."

CHAPTER THIRTY-SEVEN

Jessica watched in delight as Pedro moved Jack around the pen. The horse was much improved, loved to work and merely needed a firm hand. She'd note on the website, 'Needs experienced rider, but lots of attitude and potential.'

"Let's include a video, Maria," she said as Jack moved into his beautiful floating trot. "He has lovely suspension. Eventers might love him."

Maria nodded. "And the gray gelding is doing well too. Pedro will build more jumps this afternoon once the school bus comes. Abdul and Timmy love to hammer." Her eyes were slightly misty as she looked at Jessica. "I'm so glad we moved here."

"So am I." Jessica gave Maria a fervent hug. It had been a good move for all. They'd only been here five weeks, and she didn't understand how she'd managed without them. Abdul was flourishing, and so was the facility.

"You didn't tell me you had more horses coming," Maria said, watching a gleaming white trailer crunch up the driveway.

"Didn't expect any." Jessica walked out to meet the rig.

A ruddy-faced man with blue suspenders stepped down from the truck, clipboard in hand. "Jessica Boone?" he asked.

At her nod, he stepped forward and offered his pen. "Need your signature. The horses' papers are in the envelope along with the Coggins test and vet records."

Frowning, she ripped open the manila envelope. She didn't want to turn horses away, but she only had a few stalls left and had already promised a Belmont trainer she'd take his 'good old boy.' She flipped through the papers, her frown turning to a gasp as she looked up and saw a heavily muscled bay strut down the ramp.

Such a distinctive walk. The horse inspected his surroundings with an imperious gaze, like a king surveying his domain. The mares crowded the fence, recognizing attitude, and he strutted for them with masculine arrogance.

"Oh my! A colt. Looks a lot like Assets," Maria said. "Acts like him too," she added as he nipped at his handler.

"It *is* Assets." Jessica's voice thickened with emotion. "And the other two are Belle and Rocky."

"Belle and Rocky!" Maria squealed. "I never thought I'd see them again. But stakes horses in their prime? They're worth millions. What are they doing at a retirement center?"

"He's giving them to me," Jessica said as she reread her grandfather's note.

Jessica, I hope some day you'll forgive me. Despite what you think, I only wanted what was best, although it appears you've found that on your own. I asked Mark Russell to train these animals, but he refused to take them back. I expect he'll give you a different answer. Doris told me of your accomplishments. I'm very proud. Love always, Gramps.

She pressed the note against her chest, her emotions swirling. *He was proud.* Her throat was so thick, she was glad Maria was too stunned to ask any questions.

Pedro rushed up, his face alight with reverence. "I've always wanted to lead a stakes horse, boss. With your permission, I'll put these fine animals in corner stalls."

Jessica gulped and nodded, still unable to speak. Something pricked her eyes, and it took several clumsy attempts before she could slip the note back into the envelope. She'd called her grandfather the day after Breeders' Cup, but he'd never admitted he had sabotaged her ski career. He'd also refused to say why he had moved his horses, only that they needed a different trainer and Mark had suggested Radcliff.

She'd known then her grandfather was lying. Mark would never recommend Radcliff. It would have ripped him apart to see Assets in the barn of a man he despised. She folded her arms, aware of Maria standing beside her. Still motionless. Still gaping.

"I'm not sending them back," Jessica said softly. "But yes, this makes me an owner. Sometimes we just have to accept things."

"*Dios mio*. Only a fool would send them back." Maria shook her head. "But you? An owner? Of stakes horses? It just takes some getting used to, that's all." She allayed Jessica's fears with a beautiful smile that seemed to wrap her entire face. "You've come a long way, kid."

Jessica's stomach churned as she paced the kitchen, willing the clock to move faster. Finally. Late morning. Eleven o'clock. The perfect time to call Mark. She hadn't called earlier when he'd be training, didn't want to call in the afternoon when he might be with Cathy and definitely not in the evening when he could be busy with owners.

She knew his number by heart. So many times she'd wanted to call, especially after a few glasses of wine, and now she had the perfect reason. Everyone knew he was the best trainer for Assets. Since the Breeders' Cup last fall, the colt had run two more times for Radcliff. Each race he'd flashed his blazing speed but faded in the stretch.

Mark could bring Assets back to winning form. And he could train Rocky and Belle as well. He might have lots of business, but no trainer could afford to turn down three stakes horses. And Assets had always been his favorite.

With her horses in his barn, she'd have an excuse to visit. She drove to the city for meetings with Doris anyway and this time around, she wouldn't be begging for a job. She'd be cool and professional and prove she wasn't a liability. In actuality, she'd be hiring him.

She used her unlisted phone, afraid if he saw the Boone name he might not answer, and pressed his number before her courage fizzled. Two rings and a recording. Mark's abrupt voice made her stomach flip. Shit! Her cheeks flamed, and she broke the connection. If she left a message and he didn't return her call, she'd be stuck in limbo again.

She pressed her hands over her hot cheeks. Just the sound of his voice made her heart race. But why did he have his phone off this time of day? Maybe he was looking at a horse's leg or talking to the farrier or feed man…which meant he was in the barn. She pressed the barn number before she lost her nerve.

A strange voice answered. She asked for Mark.

"One moment," the voice said.

So far, so good. She steadied her ragged breathing. Listened and waited.

A horse nickered, and someone laughed. A bucket clanged. Then she heard Mark's deeper voice, his real live voice, and her heart rammed against her ribs. Oh, my God. Such an intense wave of longing filled her, she couldn't breathe.

But minutes passed, and he didn't come. She sucked in some air. Clamped the phone tighter against her ear, straining to listen, feeling like an eavesdropper. She recognized Dino's voice, Doc Walker too. Someone muttered, and she was certain she heard Mark curse.

He must be in a bad mood. Maybe a horse was hurt. Oh, God, this was such a bad time to call. She should hang up. But she clung to the phone like a lifeline.

"He's busy. Can I take a message?" the voice returned, so gruff her stiff fingers almost dropped the phone.

"I need a trainer for three horses," she managed. "Stakes horses."

"Just a sec."

The man was back in an instant. "Mark's full but says to try Kurt MacKinnon. Barn sixty-eight."

"Thanks." She spit the word out and snapped the phone shut. Dammit. Mark hadn't even asked the horses' names.

How important did he think he was? Just because a sheikh thought he was wonderful, and maybe Strike A Pose *had* won the Derby last month. Still, they hadn't won the Preakness, and Assets was just as good as anything the sheikh owned. And she and Mark had picked out Rocky together at Keeneland, and Belle was a brave, beautiful filly who'd battled and beaten colic.

Misery balled her throat, and she called Dick.

"Darling, I could do with your help here," he said. "The mice have taken over the apartment, and I'm afraid they've chewed some clothes."

"Oh, Dick," she wailed. "You're so lucky to be at the track."

"Yes, Belmont is wonderful," he said smugly. "All my favorite horses made it back from Florida, and Mary's my downstairs neighbor again. Do come and visit."

"I asked Mark to train my horses and he w-wouldn't." Her words caught on the painful brick in her throat.

"Well, he's a Derby winner now. And rumor is Sheikh Khalif wants him to go private, but he refused. There's another rumor too, darling." Dick's voice bubbled with barely contained glee. "I just came from the track kitchen and heard Mark no longer trains the ESPN horse. Apparently Cathy shipped Trooper to Dubai…when she got married."

"Married!" Jessica's smile was so big, her lips caught on her teeth. Obviously the *Tattler* had greatly exaggerated Mark and Cathy's relationship.

"Thought that would cheer you up." He laughed. "And since I've put you in such a good mood, would you share a few names from your Four Hundred list? Doris said you raised eighty percent of your money there."

"You can have anything you want, Dick," Jessica said. "Anything at all."

CHAPTER THIRTY-EIGHT

Jessica drove through the main gates of Belmont Park driving the Center's diesel truck and hauling a shiny aluminum four-horse trailer. The security guard gave a polite smile, called barn seventy-two to confirm, yes, she was indeed picking up a horse then waved her through.

"This is Harry. He's a good old boy," the trainer said, leading an inquisitive bay from the barn. "Six years old, thirty-two starts and still sound. Glad you'll find him a home. He isn't the fastest, but he's definitely the barn favorite. The owner wants to do the right thing for him." He scratched the horse affectionately on the shoulder. "Good luck, old man."

He spoke with such affection, Jessica's throat convulsed. She hadn't been able to save Buddy, hadn't even been able to say goodbye, but she was helping this fellow. Sometimes raw emotion bushwhacked her.

"I can send updates." She averted her head and gave her eye a swipe. "Let you know where he goes. What his new career is."

"I'd appreciate that. We all would." The trainer gestured at a solemn-faced group clustered around the shedrow and a groom limped over, clearing his throat as he fed Harry one last peppermint.

"I learned to gallop on him," a pert-nosed exercise rider said while she straightened Harry's mane. "He made sure I never fell off. You know how it is? When you get on a horse and just know he'll look after you?"

Jessica nodded, unable to speak.

"Well, that's Harry," she said. "He'd be a real good kid's horse. He'd be a real good anybody's horse." She patted him one more time, turned and walked away.

The trainer shook Jessica's hand then passed her the lead line and an envelope thick with papers. "Thank you, Ms. Boone." He left with hunched shoulders.

Harry's hooves echoed as he trustingly followed Jessica up the ramp and onto the trailer.

She drove off with Harry neighing behind her, a mournful sound that followed her down the familiar road and drummed up that stubborn, homesick feeling. *The track sure gets under your skin.*

And just why wouldn't Mark hire her? Her knuckles whitened around the wheel. She'd established Buddy's Thoroughbred Retirement Center, owned three fine racehorses and was pulling a trailer with good old Harry neighing in the back. Yet she couldn't get a job walking hots for Mark.

She yanked the mirror down, checked her sleek shirt, her newly highlighted hair, her glossy lips. At least she looked better than she had last fall when she'd sported a tired ponytail, dirty jeans and battered face. It was clear if she waited for Mark to call, she'd wait forever. There'd be no grand gestures. He wasn't the type to put himself out for a woman. Wasn't the type to show his feelings. She accepted that now.

But just maybe he'd be glad to see her.

She turned along the main drive, past the track kitchen, past a young man balancing three cups of coffee on a rickety bike. She twisted, certain it was Lefty's old bike. Nostalgia slammed her. But she drove on. Only three more barns. She eased into a wide gravel area, pried her clammy fingers from the leather wheel and forced herself to step out.

She checked on Harry, already calm and happily munching. He looked at her with inquiring eyes, hay protruding from his mouth, as though wondering why they'd stopped.

"You really are a good boy," she said, leaving the side door open so he could catch the spring breeze.

She wiped her damp hands on her jeans and walked along the gravel, along the route where Assets had dragged her. And now he was her horse. She raised her head a notch and walked a little prouder.

But her feet jerked to a stop when she spotted the shedrow. Damn. She'd waited too long. Loud purple now replaced Mark's drab stable colors, and geraniums bloomed in a profusion of hanging pots. This couldn't be his barn. Mark must have moved his operation. Maybe accepted the sheikh's offer or even followed Cathy to the Emirates.

Her gaze shot to Kato's grave, and she blew out a breath of relief. At least that was okay. Whoever had moved into Mark's barn was tending her beloved cat's grave, with a bright flowerbed marking his resting spot and a cozy picnic table anchored alongside.

She edged closer to the barn door and was immediately challenged.

A man with a gold earring that matched the color of his curly hair stepped from the shedrow. "Sorry. Mark isn't hiring." His watchful gaze absorbed her appearance, and he relaxed a notch. "Guess you're not looking for a job. You came to see the Derby winner?"

Her mouth turned dry. Mark hadn't left. "Yes, please," she managed and followed him into the shedrow, heart jerking into overdrive.

A bay horse with a white star stuck his head over the stall guard and nuzzled at the man's chest. So this was Strike A Pose. A Derby winner. My God, Mark was a genius. The horse didn't look special, just an average animal with a kind disposition. Not at all like Assets, who'd whipped every horse into submission just by glaring at them.

"He has a beautiful coat," she said, searching for something nice to say. "I guess a big horse like this gets lots of grooming."

The man shrugged and gestured down the aisle. "That's the boss's big horse. Arrived from rehab only ten days ago. Gets more attention than any of the others."

Three stalls down, a black head with a jagged stripe poked over the stall door, eyes hopeful, ears pricked. He nickered, such a soft familiar sound, and her ribs seemed to crush her heart.

"Oh, my God!" She gulped, unable to grab air. "Buddy?"

The horse nickered again, stretching his neck further over the stall guard. And then she was standing beside him and could feel his breath on her face, his soft muzzle as he sniffed her pockets. "Oh, Buddy." Her voice, her entire chest convulsed, the words coming out in a ragged gasp. "B-Buddy."

"Careful. He's headshy."

The groom stopped talking when Buddy pressed his head against her chest, remained silent as tears streamed down

Jessica's cheeks. "I can't believe he's alive." She choked the words out.

"He broke his leg last fall and was supposed to be euthanized, but Dino said the boss made a deal with Buddy's new owner. Sent him to a fancy hospital. There's a screw in his ankle, but he's okay now. Even trots sound."

"May I go in?" She slipped into the stall before the man could refuse. Touched Buddy everywhere. But when she spotted three purple braids at the top of his gleaming mane, her hands tangled in disbelief.

"Boss puts those braids in," the groom said with a shrug. "I don't dare ask why. He should be finished in the office soon, so you better get out of the stall."

Mark was in the office.

She sprinted down the aisle, ignoring the man's shouted protest, raced across the tow ring, up the two steps and flung open the office door.

A concrete arm slammed her against the wall. Her stunned eyes found Mark's even as a vise tightened around her throat.

"She's okay!" Mark yelled, his face ashen as he leaped halfway across his desk.

A man with a gray beard and watchful black eyes, wearing white robes and a headpiece, spoke softly from a corner chair.

The hand lifted from her throat. Oh God, she could breathe again. Her feet kicked when she hit the floor and she stumbled, would have fallen if the bodyguard hadn't twisted her arm.

Mark poised over his desk, tendons corded in his neck, as he glared at someone behind her. The man in the chair spoke again, and she was released.

"Sorry," she sputtered, clasping her burning throat as she stared at Mark. "Guess I shouldn't have rushed in like that."

His expression turned enigmatic, and he sank back in his chair. "Wait for me, Jess."

"Oh, I will," she said. "Long as you want. I'll be in the barn. With Buddy."

She was so happy she nodded at the man who'd almost strangled her. The same guy who had manhandled her in the hospital. "Nice seeing you again," she said, still nodding, still deliriously happy.

She backed out. Skipped across the dirt to the shedrow and bounced down the aisle and into Buddy's stall. He was still there. Still chewing hay. Still alive.

"Oh, my God." She wrapped her arms around his neck and let his satiny hair absorb her tears.

Moments later she sensed Mark's presence. She turned to face him, suddenly shy. "Hi," she said. He just stood there, looking at her, his blue eyes unreadable. "This is one of the happiest days of my life," she added, keeping a hand on Buddy's shoulder.

"Heard you started an adoption facility," he said. "Thought you might have a stall for him."

"Yes, thanks. I sure do." Her voice sounded strange. "And congratulations to you on the Derby. And the sheikh. How's your shoulder by the way?"

"Better." His face was impassive. "Were you here that day?"

She shook her head, wishing her tongue didn't feel so awkward. "I watched on TV. Came by the hospital, but your visitors were restricted."

"That was seven months ago. I assumed you were off skiing and didn't know. Wrong assumption."

The bleakness in his voice chilled her and she stiffened, stunned with the knowledge that she'd hurt him. She stared at his chest, stalling, gathering her courage. But he'd never said he loved her, professed to only want a casual relationship and if she admitted her true feelings, he might shut her down. Once you said those words they were out there, hanging like a weapon, and they could never, ever be pulled back. If he could just make this a little easier…

But already he'd withdrawn. Crossed his arms and turned toward the blond man gawking in the aisle. "Rake the other end, Jim," he said.

She watched as Jim rushed away. "Your new man," she sucked in a fortifying breath, "he said you made a deal to get Buddy. So that was with Radcliff? I can't imagine what you offered."

A muscle ticked in Mark's jaw, and it was then she guessed. "No!" she groaned. "Not Assets!"

"Your grandfather had already decided to move his horses." Mark shrugged. "I just made sure Radcliff was their trainer.

Look, I have an important meeting, but drop by again. Dino and Carlos would like to see you."

He backed up a step, preparing to leave. Words jammed in her throat, but she couldn't talk, didn't know what to say. Even her legs trembled.

As though sensing her desperation, Buddy nudged her, exposing the neat braids at the top of his neck. She sucked in a big breath. Mark hated braids. They had to mean something. She grabbed Buddy's mane, borrowing his courage but felt she was leaping into unknown depths.

"Mark, I love you." Her hands and voice trembled. She lifted her head, no longer trying to hide her feelings. His face blurred, but she forged on. "It hurt s-so much that you didn't want me. I needed to go away and accomplish something, to feel worthy—"

She didn't hear the stall guard open, but somehow his arms wrapped around her. "Not want you? Jesus. I said I'd wait. I'm wearing your colors." His voice rose. "Hell, I went purple."

"All that's nice. The braids too." His touch was intoxicating, but she resisted the urge to bury her face against his soft shirt. "Still, you wouldn't hire me when I needed a job." She couldn't quite keep the hurt from her voice.

"I didn't want a slumming heiress. Someone who only wanted food and a Jacuzzi. I wanted you to have options. Oh, sweetheart." He cradled her face between his big hands, staring with such tenderness her heart thumped.

"So you don't mind," she gulped, "that I love you?"

"Mind?" His eyes blazed and he kissed her then, so thoroughly, so convincingly, her legs turned boneless.

Minutes later, he lifted his mouth. "I knew I wanted you when your grandfather told me to fire you," he said, his voice gruff. "I couldn't do it. And it's been no fun without you. Even that damn Derby horse was boring."

"Gramps told you to fire me? And you didn't? That's why he moved Assets?" She stiffened in horror, shocked by the enormity of his sacrifice. "I'm s-sorry." Her voice broke. "You should have done what he wanted. You worked so hard for that colt."

"It wasn't even a tough choice." He stroked her cheek, letting her see the emotion glittering in his eyes. "I love you, Jessica Boone."

My God. He loved her, and he could say it. In his barn too, quite loudly. Definitely loud enough to reach Jim, who ostensibly swept the end of the spotless aisle but now craned his neck trying to see. "Good," was all she could manage.

"If that's all you needed to know," he said, "I'd have taken out an ad in *The Racing Form*. Please don't run away again."

"Never." Her voice bubbled and she gripped his shoulders, so lightheaded she thought she might float into the aisle. "And you won't have to choose again either. My devious grandfather gave me Assets. Belle and Rocky too."

"Really? No tricks?" His eyes narrowed. "You got their papers? It's all legal?"

"Definitely legal. I own them." She smiled. "But that only means you'll have to be extra nice to me."

"Promise." His smile turned rueful. "But first I have to finish my meeting with my second favorite owner. Then we'll go to my place, and tomorrow I want to see your famous horse farm. Maria too, who you lured away with such an outrageous salary." However, his eyes twinkled with approval. "The lawyer says Abdul's adoption won't be a problem now. You really are something—" He dipped his head, muffling his words with a deep kiss, a hungry kiss, taut with longing and love.

"The sheikh saw you," he murmured, lifting his mouth, his breathing ragged. "So he'll understand why I have to rush the meeting. But I can't make him wait any longer. It's just not done."

"Hurry then, so we can go home." She trembled with wanting, unable to resist pressing into his warm chest, then stepped back, groaning. Somehow his mouth, his hands, his sheer presence pushed away coherent thought. "Oh, no. I can't stay tonight. Harry's with me."

"Harry?" He raised an eyebrow.

"Harry from barn seventy-two. Recently retired."

"No problem." He grinned and tugged her closer, tenderly dragging his mouth over her forehead. "Old Harry can have a sleepover in my barn. Tomorrow we'll take Buddy and Harry to your place. Then bring Assets back. Work out some kind of commute." He sobered, cupping her head in his hands. "I know you're busy, but I do need to see Assets' owner. Every day if possible. Is that okay?"

Every day. Her heart thumped with joy. It would be easy to rearrange her schedule, but she couldn't stop smiling because already he was thinking of Assets. No mention of Belle or Rocky.

Still, once in a while something came along that simply captured your soul. And maybe in a month or two, when she wasn't so annoyed with her grandfather, she'd thank Gramps for finding her this wonderful man.

"It's all absolutely perfect," she said, snuggling into his chest, home at last.

And behind her, Buddy lifted his muzzle from the hay and blew warm breath lovingly down the back of her neck.

***

Read Chapter One of BEV PETTERSEN's next novel

FILLIES AND FEMALES

Becky pushed the empty wheelchair around the beautiful people preening in the owner's box and wished, once again, she were invisible.

"Over here. Hurry!" Martha Conrad called, her voice slightly querulous. Becky ducked her head, aware everyone watched. Accompanying her employer to the track wasn't her usual duty, but the weekend nurse was sick and Martha would have been devastated if she hadn't been able to attend the long-anticipated horse race. Not that there was anything wrong with horses—Becky liked them—but the type of people who thronged these glamorous affairs simply made her edgy.

All the usual society types attended. Few would refuse an invitation to watch the Lone Star Derby from a swanky skybox, stocked with an array of food and liquor as well as Martha's illustrious friends. But some of them weren't so nice. Becky's knuckles whitened as a lady with sculpted cheekbones and an equally sculpted dress turned her back, closing off her passage and forcing the chair's wheels to scrape the wall.

"Here you go," Becky said, once she finally maneuvered the wheelchair to Martha's side. "Do you want to switch chairs?"

"No. I just need you to check the side pocket for my binoculars. You did pack them, didn't you?"

Becky gave a reassuring nod.

"This is so exciting," Martha added, nervously fingered a striking string of pearls. "I just wish Malcolm were here."

Her thin chest flailed and Becky edged closer, watching with concern. Martha had been devoted to her husband and reluctant to sell the race stable after his sudden death. However, maintaining the horses was stressful, even with excellent staff, and doctors had warned the excitement was dangerous for her weakened heart.

"There's our colt now." Martha's voice steadied as she gestured at the horses parading in front of the grandstand. Her words even carried a trace of sarcasm. "Ted, do pay attention." She spoke with saccharine sweetness. "Hunter's the horse with number one on the saddle cloth."

Martha's nephew glanced at the row of horses with such indifference, Becky wondered why he'd bothered to come. Maybe, like her, Ted wasn't comfortable with crowds although in his case it seemed based on apathy rather than insecurity. He peered down his nose at the track even as enthusiastic guests murmured their admiration.

Martha's horse, Code Hunter, seemed to know he was being scrutinized. He arched his neck and strutted like a rock star. Becky edged closer to the balcony, fascinated by the horse's confidence, his bearing, his legitimate blue blood. Malcolm Conrad had spent twenty years developing Thoroughbreds with both speed and stamina, and Hunter was the result of his breeding program. In six starts, the colt was unbeaten and if race odds were any indication, Hunter would win again today.

"An impressive animal." Ted glanced down at Martha. "But he should be, considering the money Uncle Malcolm wasted."

A sneer edged his voice and Becky jerked her head away, pretending absorption with the post parade. Disagreements always made her heart pound but if she stayed silent, head down, people generally ignored her. It was much safer to avoid attention.

Silence also made it easier to observe others and, minutes later, she peeked back at Ted and saw that his apathy had been replaced with taut eagerness—rather surprising as boredom was his usual expression.

Ted shifted and she jerked her head away. He'd been visiting Martha more frequently since Malcolm's death and his pale blue eyes, so devoid of emotion, always made her uncomfortable. Sometimes he resembled a detached businessman rather than Martha's sole heir.

A lady giggled, and Becky's thoughts scattered as new energy zapped the skybox. *He was here.*

"Oh, gracious. My trainer has arrived. Over here, Dino!" Martha waved, suddenly the picture of health, and her seventy-four-year-old voice bubbled with girlish excitement.

The crowd parted as Dino Anders, hair dark and windswept, sauntered through the middle of the room, nodding greetings to the fawning guests. A white shirt emphasized his tanned throat and a sports jacket was slung over his shoulder. Becky gulped, struggling to breathe. He was movie star gorgeous, and in a moment he'd be beside her.

She studied her thick-soled shoes, hoping this time she could control her blush, control her squeak. Hoped his friendly attempts at conversation wouldn't make her stutter. But it wasn't just her. Even worldly Martha wasn't immune to the Dino effect.

"How's my lipstick, dear?" Martha whispered.

"Good." Becky grabbed a tissue and blotted a corner of Martha's lined mouth. "Now it's even better."

Martha gave Becky a naughty wink, cupping her mouth so Ted wouldn't hear. "I may be old but I'm not dead."

A moment later, Dino's deep voice sounded beside them. "Hello, Martha. You're looking very elegant today."

Martha giggled as he leaned down and kissed her rouged cheek. "I assume there will be a win picture with Hunter," she said. "Can you promise me that, young man?"

Dino straightened, his gorgeous brown eyes drifting to the horses warming up on the track. "No promises. But Hunter's training great and should run well. Very well."

"Of course, if he doesn't," Ted said, edging closer, "it's only logical the stables should be sold." He reached down and gave Martha's shoulder a solicitous pat. "Racing was Uncle Malcolm's passion, not yours. It's ridiculous to chase his dream at the expense of your health."

Becky's hands fisted with dismay. It was no secret Ted wanted Martha to sell, but this was the first time he'd stated his opinion in public, and it was thoughtless to be so blunt. She sensed Dino's similar disapproval, could feel his pulsating resentment, even though he stood several feet away. However his chuckle revealed only amusement.

"Then let's hope Hunter wins," he said, still smiling, "so nothing needs to be sold. You're nervous, Betty. Have you made a big bet?"

It took several seconds before she realized Dino was talking to her. She jerked her head up and stared into his teasing eyes—caramel, they reminded her of warm caramel with gold flecks. And the way he smiled. He never remembered her name yet always smiled at her with such intimacy, it made her knees wobble. No wonder the other nurses all clamored to escort Martha to the races.

She swallowed, trying to moisten her mouth so it wouldn't squeak. "My name's Becky," she finally mumbled, "and I don't bet." She forced herself to hold his gaze, to hold her head up like Martha advised, but it no longer mattered. A brunette with bold eyes and bright lipstick had swooped in from the other side and grabbed his arm.

"Yeah, Martha's horse drew the rail," Dino said, dipping his head toward the lady on his left and politely answering her questions. "Our jockey will try to take Hunter out quick, grab the lead and hopefully hold off the closers. With any luck, we'll all meet in the winner's circle."

He sounded relaxed, seemingly unconcerned that a horse he trained was running in the biggest three-year old race in Texas. He didn't seem to notice he was the center of attention, especially with the women, although even the men eyed him with expressions ranging from admiration to envy.

Were all trainers like Dino? He'd easily shrugged off Ted's rude comment and Becky sensed nothing now but the fascinating whiff of leather, soap and potent male. God, she wished she were half as confident.

She stared through the glass panel, fingernails pressing into the palms of her hands as the horses circled the gate. Dino was too close for her to really relax, but she had no more worries. His greetings were always unfailingly polite, but she could never think fast enough to reply. He wouldn't speak to her again, not with the lipstick lady murmuring in his ear. At least she could retreat into silence and enjoy the race. No one except Dino ever acknowledged her.

Chatter muted as the horses disappeared behind the starting gate. Guests stepped closer to the balcony, their attention shifting from drinks to the race. Hunter's jockey wore the bright silks of Conrad Racing Stable, a vivid yellow with a black diamond, and horse and rider were easy to spot. Becky tensed as an assistant starter led them into their slot and shot a worried glance at Martha.

"He's in the gate," Dino said, his big body motionless. Martha reached up and grabbed Becky's hand. Ted gestured at a waiter.

Two horses left to load. Anticipation pricked the air, and even the raucous crowd below stilled. Becky bent closer to Martha but kept her gaze fixed on the one hole, praying Hunter would break clean. Gate to wire, please. If the race were too close, it would be stressful for Martha. Even now, Becky could feel the trembling of her hand, the tissue-thin skin of her fingers.

Becky bent down, pretending to adjust the pillow behind Martha's shoulders, but she couldn't hide her concern. "Deep breaths," she whispered. "Hunter will do fine."

The nine horse balked, and two gate attendants rushed forward and pushed the reluctant colt into his slot.

"The horses are in," the announcer blared.

Crack! The gates snapped and ten horses burst out. Five strides and Hunter grabbed the lead. A bay horse joined him at the hip. However, Hunter was clearly in control, and Becky blew out a grateful breath. Hunter's jockey kept a tight hold, carefully rationing the colt's speed as the two horses pounded into the first turn, followed two lengths back by the rest of the pack.

Becky shuffled, wanting to jump up and down, but Martha had a death grip on her hand so she forced her feet to remain still. But, oh no. It looked like the bay was catching Hunter. "Go, Hunter!" she yelled, surprising herself with the outburst and clamping her mouth shut before she drew attention.

"Our horse is looking good, Betty," Dino said. "Jock's just rating him. The first quarter was almost twenty-four seconds, so he shouldn't be too tired to hang on."

Oh, God. Dino was talking to her again, even though a gorgeous lady clung to his other arm. And he called Hunter 'our horse.' Warmth spilled through her chest and she smiled, even though it was rather irritating he never remembered her name.

They'd met on nine previous occasions, three times at the races and six times at Martha's house, although of course she hadn't been counting.

She yanked her head back to the throng of galloping horses. Hunter had opened up a four-length lead and gaily led the group around the far turn and into the stretch. The colorful jockey crouched over Hunter's bobbing neck, urging him toward the wire. Someone yelled in Becky's ear, and Martha's fingers tightened their grip. Oh, wow. He was going to win easy.

And then inexplicably, Hunter quit. She watched in shock as the bay horse surged past, then another horse in red blinkers, then seven more. Oh God, this was awful.

Martha's horse had finished last.

Everyone silenced. Ice rattled in the tomblike room as the bartender mixed a drink. Becky was afraid to look at Martha, knew she'd intended this party as a coronation, not a humiliating defeat. And the trainer! She felt Dino's raw disbelief and fought the urge to reach over and give his arm a consoling squeeze.

No one moved except a silent waiter who delivered Ted an icy martini.

"Well, that's racing," someone said with a forced laugh.

"Your horse tried hard, Martha," another voice said, much too hearty to be genuine.

Dino leaned over Martha's shoulder, so close Becky caught the subtle hint of his aftershave. "So sorry, Martha," he said. "Not the result I expected or the one you deserve. I'll check on Hunter then ship him back to your stable. Obviously he needs time off."

He kissed her cheek and walked away.

Betting stubs fluttered to the floor as disappointed guests drifted from the railing and rushed to refill their drinks. Everyone had expected a trek to the winner's circle followed by indulgence in the ritual champagne. Even Martha's water glass was empty except for one lonely cube of melting ice. Only Ted had the luck to replenish his drink.

Becky's gaze settled on his full martini. She remembered him signaling the waiter almost as if he'd known Hunter would lose, which was impossible—the man was a hospital administrator, not a psychic. She raised her head then stilled, stunned by the expression on his face as he stared at Martha.

He turned and she quickly averted her gaze. But goose bumps rose in a shivering trail down her back because she was an expert at reading emotion and what she'd spotted in his face had been absolute malice.

ABOUT THE AUTHOR

Bev Pettersen is a two-time nominee in the National Readers Choice Award as well as a two-time finalist in the Romance Writers of America's Golden Heart® Contest. She competed for five years on the Alberta Thoroughbred race circuit and is an Equine Canada certified coach. She lives in Nova Scotia with her family and when she's not writing novels, she's riding. Visit her at www.bevpettersen.com.

Made in the USA
Middletown, DE
29 August 2021

47137228R00210